Iran, Iraq, and the Legacies of War

IRAN, IRAQ, AND THE LEGACIES OF WAR

EDITED BY

LAWRENCE G. POTTER AND GARY G. SICK

IRAN, IRAQ, AND THE LEGACIES OF WAR

First published 2004 by
PALGRAVE MACMILLAN™
175 Fifth Avenue, New York, N.Y. 10010 and
Houndmills, Basingstoke, Hampshire, England RG21 6XS
Companies and representatives throughout the world.

PALGRAVE MACMILLAN is the global academic imprint of
the Palgrave Macmillan division of St. Martin's Press, LLC and of
Palgrave Macmillan Ltd. Macmillan® is a registered trademark
in the United States, United Kingdom and other countries.
Palgrave is a registered trademark in the European Union
and other countries.

ISBN 1–4039–6450–5 hardback

Library of Congress Cataloging-in-Publication Data
Iran, Iraq, and the legacies of war / edited by Lawrence G. Potter and Gary G.Sick.
    p. cm.
    Includes bibliographical references and index.
    ISBN 1–4039–6450–5
    1. Iran-Iraq War, 1980–1988—Influence—Congresses. 2. Iran-Iraq War,
1980–1988—Atrocities—Congresses. 3. Middle East—Relations—United
States—Congresses. 4. United States—Relations —Middle East—Congresses.
    I. Potter, Lawrence G. II. Sick, Gary, 1935–

DS318.85.I635 2004
955.05′42—dc22   2004040009

A catalogue record for this book is available from the British Library.

Design by Newgen Imaging Systems (P) Ltd., Chennai, India.

First edition: November, 2004.
10 9 8 7 6 5 4 3 2 1

Printed in the United States of America.

Contents

Introduction

Lawrence G. Potter and Gary G. Sick

The Persian Gulf states, and indeed the entire Middle East, were profoundly affected by the Iran–Iraq War that raged from 1980 to 1988 and its sequels, the Gulf War of 1990–91 and the war against Iraq in 2003.[1] The first war was immensely destructive in terms of lives and infrastructure. It set back the development of both Iran and Iraq for perhaps a generation, inflamed ethnic and religious tensions, and raised the level of distrust in the region to new levels. The wars together focused international attention on the Gulf and led the United States to an unprecedented level of involvement there, beginning with the reflagging of Kuwaiti tankers in 1987, continuing in the dispatch of over half a million American troops to oust the Iraqi army from Kuwait in 1991, and culminating in the campaign against Iraq.

The Gulf/2000 project has, over the past decade, brought together citizens of the Persian Gulf states to explore their mutual concerns and to seek ways to improve personal contact and understanding.[2] In this case, Iranians and Iraqis were invited—for the first time, we believe—to join a few "outsiders" for a discussion of how the Iran–Iraq War affected the personal lives and politics of their respective countries and the region. This book is based on papers presented at that meeting—the ninth international conference organized by the project—from October 22 to October 26, 2001, in Bellagio, Italy.[3] These papers, now revised and updated, help clarify the evolution of relations between Iran and Iraq—how they developed historically, how they rapidly deteriorated when war broke out in 1980, and the issues that must be addressed in the context of future rapprochement. Those issues are likely to be amplified and given greater urgency by the fall of the Saddam Hussein government in the spring of 2003. The conference also examined the role of the United States in the region and its effect on the two states, a subject that has also been cast in sharper relief by subsequent events.

The idea for the meeting was to begin to work out a road map for reconciliation between the two states, in light of the "cold peace" that had prevailed since the end of hostilities in 1988. Over the past century, and particularly over the past 25 years, Iranians and Iraqis were much more likely to meet on the battlefield or in rancorous negotiations than they were to join in a setting that permitted, let alone encouraged, a reasoned discussion of their mutual suspicions and interests. We were therefore pleased to discover that there was a genuine interest on the part of scholars and officials from both countries to meet their counterparts and begin a dialogue that could help to shape future relations. The unresolved tension between Iran and Iraq is one of the most serious potential flashpoints in the future, and the healthy coexistence (or hostility) of these two states is certain to have a profound influence on the stability and well-being of the Persian Gulf region and the entire Middle East.

The discussions left no doubt that both Iran and Iraq had suffered greatly because of the war and its aftermath, and that numerous issues arising from this conflict, both internal and external, urgently needed to be addressed. People in both states felt a profound sense of victimization, by the international community no less than their adversary. War in the Middle East has the capacity to transform states and societies, and the Iran–Iraq War was a dramatic case in point.[4] As a new Middle East takes shape in the wake of the latest war, harmonious relations between Iran and Iraq will be critical to regional stability.

This groundbreaking conference demonstrated that enough time has passed since the Iran–Iraq War so that reconciliation can be envisioned, as happened between the United States and Vietnam or with the Soviet Union. A public debate about these issues has just begun in Iran, and may soon get underway in the new Iraq. After so much deceit, confidence-building measures are essential so people can begin to learn to trust. The path to peace and reconciliation has been hindered in Iraq by the suppression of Iraqi society by the Saddam Hussein government, and in Iran by the continuing domestic struggle between the reformers who first elected Mohammad Khatami as president in 1997 and the conservatives ranged in opposition.

A War Without Winners

As noted in Chapter 1 by historian Shaul Bakhash, the war between Iran and Iraq was not a continuation of previous disputes but a new kind of total warfare with a strong ideological component. The Iran–Iraq War was one of the longest and costliest conventional wars of the twentieth century. Iraq, responding to Iranian provocations and hoping to enlarge its role in the Gulf, had started what it thought would be a short, victorious war against its neighbor, which was in the throes of revolution. It soon became apparent that this was a mistake of historic proportions. Iranians rallied behind their leader, Ayatollah Ruhollah Khomeini, and repelled the Iraqi invaders in 1982. The war then settled into a bloody stalemate between the smaller but heavily armed Iraq and Iran, which was ostracized by the world but sustained by ideological fervor. From the beginning, the war was overshadowed by intense personal hostility between Khomeini and Saddam Hussein, the Iraqi president.

When the war ended, neither side had achieved its war aims and each felt that outside powers had cheated it out of victory. Iraq did not bring down the revolutionary government in Iran, and Iran did not foment revolution in Iraq. The leaders of both countries were still in power and their troops, with minor exceptions, were within their own borders. The number of casualties is still in dispute, with an estimated 400,000 killed and perhaps 700,000 wounded on both sides.[5] *The Economist* commented that "This was a war that should never have been fought . . . neither side gained a thing, except the saving of its own regime. And neither regime was worth the sacrifice."[6]

The Iran–Iraq War was an anomaly for the Middle East because it was the first time the superpowers were on the same side. This partly resulted from Soviet preoccupation with their own internal problems. Although the United States and the Soviet Union professed neutrality, both in fact aided Iraq—the Soviet Union with arms, and the United States with economic, diplomatic, and intelligence support. The main reason for Western involvement in the war was to protect oil exports. Paradoxically, although there were short-term fluctuations, the price of oil did not go up but remained depressed, despite the war on shipping in the Gulf. The superpowers' cooperation paved the war for greater unity during the Gulf War, and for a similarly important UN role in ending it.[7]

Legacy of War

In both Iran and Iraq, but especially in the latter, the conflict and the demonization of the opponent led to a stronger sense of national identity. Iran's calculation that the Shi'i majority in southern Iraq would rally to its cause and Iraq's conviction that the Arab citizens in Khuzistan would welcome the Iraqi army as their liberators were both wrong. The war helped the revolutionary government in Tehran consolidate power and distracted attention from pressing social and economic problems. Indeed, it was only when the leadership feared the revolution was in danger that Khomeini decided to "drink poison" by accepting the UN ceasefire proposal that had been on the table for a year. In Iraq, as noted elsewhere by Isam al-Khafaji, war and war preparation became normal as a social condition and a system of government, and was used to legitimate the regime and redefine Iraqi national identity.[8]

It was clear from the Bellagio conference, some of whose participants played wartime roles, that the conflict left a legacy of bitterness and suspicion on both sides that will be difficult to overcome. Just as the United States had a "Vietnam generation," which has taken decades to come to terms with that conflict, so Iran and Iraq both have a war generation that has not seriously been able to assess their experience, nor have they successfully transmitted knowledge of it to the younger generation. The role of this generation in each country is addressed in path-breaking evaluations (chapters 4 and 5) by Iranian political scientist Farideh Farhi and by Iraqi sociologist Faleh A. Jabar.

As recounted in chapter 4 by Dr. Farhi, Iran is in the early stages of a debate about the war. [9] The ruling elite today is made up to a large degree of war veterans, some of whom have sought to keep its memory alive to justify present political actions. Indeed, many are unhappy that the government has appropriated the war's legacy to solidify its own power. The roots of the distinctions between "reformers" and "conservatives," in fact, go back to the war. An examination of issues such as why the government continued fighting after liberating occupied territory in 1982 could be very divisive and harm the reputations of wartime leaders still politically prominent, such as Mr. Rafsanjani.[10]

In Iraq, by contrast, there was no consensus as to why Iraqis were fighting until the need for self-defense became predominant. There is still little debate about the war, although bitterness exists that Saddam Hussein rapidly acquiesced to Iran's territorial demands in the Shatt al-Arab—a major rationale for the war—on the eve of the second Gulf conflict. The tortured history of this boundary dispute is admirably illuminated here by geographer Richard Schofield (chapter 2). In Iraq, the crisis of the "war generation" runs much deeper since there was no time in between the first two wars to recover. The conclusion of all three wars has been profoundly painful and disconcerting for Iraqis.

Clash of Cultures

One reason for the persistence of bilateral tensions is that the clash of cultures and poisonous rhetoric that was fired up by the Iran–Iraq War has not subsided.[11] Aside from the military encounter, the countries waged a fierce struggle on the ideological and propaganda fronts. They invoked several broad themes: Arab against Persian, Sunni against Shi'i, and pan-Arabism against pan-Islam. The region has lived with the tensions arising from these differences for more than a millennium. They did not cause the war, but served to reinforce mutual hostility.

Iraq is a country mainly populated by Arabs who speak Arabic, a Semitic language. Iran has an Aryan heritage, and its official language, Persian, is an Indo-European tongue. Persians have often regarded their cultural legacy as richer than that of the Arabs, although their religion, Islam, was founded by Arabs and their holy book, the Qur'an, was revealed in Arabic. During the war, Iraq emphasized its Arab identity and characterized the Persian enemy as "racist" and resentful.[12] Saddam's government promoted the idea that the Arabs were the rightful leaders of Islam, whereas Khomeini and his government were imposters, apostates, even Zoroastrians.[13] Iraq consistently invoked the Arab geographical lexicon—such as in references to the "Arabian" not "Persian" Gulf, and to "Arabistan," the former name of the southwest Iranian province of Khuzistan.

The pan-Arabism of the Iraqi government was opposed to the pan-Islamic vision of the Iranian revolutionary leadership. Iraq, governed by a Sunni Arab minority, stressed its ties with other Arab countries in hopes of support against internal and external threats. Iraq emphasized that it represented and was defending the whole family of Arab nations in the war with Iran. Khomeini, on the other hand, believed that Islamic solidarity was more important than nationalism, and that Islamic unity should take precedence over present-day political frontiers.[14] Iran believed it had a special responsibility to liberate Muslims, especially in Iraq, from their insufficiently "Islamic" governments.

The terminology of the war is instructive for the perceptions and attitudes it reveals. The conflict is known in the west as the Iran–Iraq War or the Gulf War—terms that focus on the strategic importance of the region. The combatants themselves, however, used terminology rich in religious symbolism and colored by suspicions of conspiracy. In a bid to attract Arab support, Iraq called the conflict "Saddam's Qadisiyya," a reference to the Arab defeat of the Persians in the seventh century A.D. Iran refers to it as the "imposed war," based on the belief that the United States, humiliated by the hostage affair, encouraged Iraq to attack.[15]

Issues for the Future

While tensions resulting from mutual misperceptions and ethnic and religious differences will be slow to dissipate, a number of specific issues arising from the war need to be resolved for a true rapprochement to take place. These include settling the common boundary along the Shatt al-Arab waterway, the return of all prisoners of war,[16] and non-interference in each other's affairs as agreed to by both parties in the 1975 Algiers Accord. With the sudden liberation of Iraq's Shiʿis, a reinvigoration of the holy cities of Najaf and Karbala seemed likely, offering competition to the Iranian *hawza* at Qom. The increased involvement of Iranian and Iraqi Shiʿis in each other's affairs seems a distinct possibility. The current state of Shiʿi politics is surveyed here by Laith Kubba (chapter 6). A delicate question is how both states treat the opposition each sheltered in exile. The major Iran-based opposition force, the Supreme Council for the Islamic Revolution in Iraq (SCIRI), was accorded a place in the first interim government in Iraq. The Mojahedin-e Khalq (MKO), which was harbored by the Iraqi government and sporadically attacked targets in Iranian cities, surrendered to U.S. troops in April 2003. At the time of this writing, their future was unclear. Other issues include Iran's return of planes sent by Iraq for safekeeping during the Gulf War,[17] the necessity of continuing mine-clearing opera-tions along the border,[18] and environmental concerns. In addition, Iraq summarily expelled large numbers of Shiʿi citizens deemed to be of Persian origin who have ended up, much to the unhappiness of the Tehran government, as refugees in Iran.[19] Many of them may eventually return to Iraq. Today there are many Iraqis with ties to Iran, and some high-level Iranian officials are of Iraqi origin.

The future of the Kurds is another persistent issue that affects both Iraq (where they constitute about 21 percent of the population) and Iran (about 11 percent), as well as neighboring Turkey and Syria. This issue is addressed in chapter 3 by M. R. Izady. The Kurds comprise the largest ethnic group in the Middle East after the Arabs, Persians, and Turks, and are one of the largest nations today with no state of their own. Only in Iraq have they posed a continuing threat to the rule of the central government. During the Iran–Iraq War, Kurdish rebels took control of large parts of northern Iraq. As the war wound down, Iraqi forces used chemical weapons against them and the international community stood silent, as revealed in the compelling chapter by Joost Hiltermann (chapter 7). This episode, and the possibility of further Iraqi use of weapons of mass destruction (WMD), was repeatedly invoked by the Bush administration as a rationale for the recent "preventive" war. The Kurdish situ-ation will surely continue to complicate relations between the two states.

The future regional role for Iran and Iraq must also be considered. Iran resented the fact that some of the Gulf monarchies—notably Saudi Arabia, Kuwait, and the United Arab Emirates—supported Iraq financially throughout the war, and soon after its outbreak banded together against it in the Gulf Cooperation Council (GCC). However, in the Khatami era relations with the Arab Gulf states improved considerably, and Iran reached security accords with Saudi Arabia in 2001 and Kuwait in 2002. Gerd Nonneman in chapter 8 discerns the long-term patterns in relations among Iran, Iraq, and the GCC states.

Particularly since the rise of the Baath Party in 1968 and the increased importance of oil exports to the Iraqi economy, Iraq has aspired to a larger role in the Gulf.[20] Indeed, one of the stated aims of the Iraqi attack on Iran was to regain possession for the Arabs of three small islands in the Gulf, Abu Musa and the two Tunbs, occupied by Iran a decade earlier.[21] This brings it into conflict with Iran, which under both the shah and the Islamic government has regarded itself as the Gulf's rightful protector. Before the recent war, the rapprochement between Iran and Saudi Arabia had heightened Iraq's sense of insecurity. Iran, for its part, now perceives itself as vulnerable and surrounded on all sides by pro-American states.

The role of the United States and the international community in allowing Iran and Iraq to play a role in Gulf security in the future is unclear. To some degree détente in the Gulf depends on U.S. reconciliation with Iran, which could leave Iraq isolated once again. As outlined in chapter 9 by Rosemary Hollis, the United States has never sought to improve relations between Iran and Iraq. Rather, it tended to play off one against the other, as during the time of the shah. Treating the two states in a similar fashion, as at the time of the Baghdad Pact (when they were "good") or under Dual Containment or as members of an "Axis of Evil" (both "bad"), also has not enhanced regional stability. Today, a U.S.-backed Iraq may clash with an Iranian government trying to safeguard its revolution.

Regional states need to contribute to the rebuilding of Iraq. As it stands at present, the government that succeeds that of Saddam Hussein will be saddled with huge debts and reparations that will seriously hinder the development of the country. Iraq needs reassurance that it will be helped to restore its infrastructure and economy and not continue to be punished. Likewise, some way needs to be found to accommodate the Iraqi desire to be seen as a legitimate player in the Gulf, and to assure the security of its southern ports.

The issue of great power influence has important ramifications for both states. The Iran–Iraq War dragged in regional and external powers, whose intervention first aggravated and then eventually helped end the conflict but did not resolve the issues. Because of its overwhelming military and political dominance in the region, the United States is often blamed for meddling in internal affairs and indeed often determining the course of events, even when evidence is to the contrary. Since Iran and Iraq have both been affected directly and continuously by U.S. policies and actions for more than a decade, a new generation may hold the United States accountable for their misery for a long time to come.

Conclusion

The Iran–Iraq War was truly a war without winners that caused incalculable damage—human, material, and environmental—to the Gulf region. The war left a profound residue of distrust among the generation that now holds power and its legacy will continue to burden both countries into the twenty-first century. The beginning and the ending of the war were contested, and while a ceasefire has been in effect since August 20, 1988, no peace treaty has been signed. Unlike Iran, where reconstruction began under the Rafsanjani administration in 1989, Iraq had to face two even more destructive conflicts and still awaits a reckoning and rebuilding. The different pace of political development in Iran and Iraq will be a major factor in future relations. Iran has now experienced years of rule by a reformist president, and even if his agenda has often been stymied by hardliners, a serious dialogue is taking place in Iranian society on how to reconcile Islam and democracy that bears no resemblance either to the stalled society that was Iraq under Saddam Hussein or to the U.S. occupation and its aftermath that followed. However, the future course of events in both countries is unpredictable.

During the conflict both states, abetted by the media, drew on the lexicon of mutual recrimination that revived all the old stereotypes and misperceptions. This legacy of hostility will be one of the hardest and longest to overcome. Yet the geography of the region will not change, and as Iranian Foreign Minister Kamal Kharrazi acknowledged about Iraq, "we are condemned to be neighbors." Historically, there has been constant intermixture among the peoples of Iran and Iraq, a majority of whom are Shi'i by faith, and Iranians will always strive to visit the Shi'i holy places located in Iraq. All the regional fault lines—race, religion, language—converge in the Gulf region. While conflict may characterize recent decades, historically the states managed to coexist, and, in light of their many common interests, this should also be possible in the future. It was very clear from the Bellagio conference that the time for reconciliation has begun.

Notes

1. Sources on the Iran–Iraq War include Shahram Chubin and Charles Tripp, *Iran and Iraq at War* (Boulder, Colo.: Westview, 1991); Dilip Hiro, *The Longest War: The Iran-Iraq Military Conflict* (New York: Routledge, 1991); Efraim Karsh, "The Iran-Iraq War: Impacts and Implications," *Adelphi Papers* No. 20 (London: IISS, 1997); Efraim Karsh, *The Iran-Iraq War 1980–1988*, Essential Histories series (Botley, Oxford, UK: Osprey Publishing, 2002); Shirin Tahir-Kheli and Shaheen Ayubi, eds., *The Iran-Iraq War: Old Conflicts, New Weapons* (New York: Praeger, 1983); Farhang Rajaee, ed., *The Iran-Iraq War: Politics of Aggression* (Gainesville: University Press of Florida, 1993); Gary Sick, "Trial by Error: Reflections on the Iran-Iraq War," in *The Middle East Journal*, vol. 43 no. 2 (Spring 1989), pp. 230–44; and W. Thom Workman, *The Social Origins of the Iran-Iraq War* (Boulder, Colo.: Lynne Rienner, 1994). See also the web site of The Federation of American Scientists: <http://www.fas.org/man/dod-101/ops/war/iran-iraq.htm>. For a survey of events in Iran and Iraq in the decade following the war, see Dilip Hiro, *Neighbors, Not Friends: Iran and Iraq After the Gulf Wars* (London: Routledge, 2001).
2. Gulf/2000 is a research and documentation project on the Persian Gulf states based at Columbia University in New York. Created in 1993 as a membership organization, it is supported by The Ford Foundation, the John D. and Catherine T. MacArthur Foundation, the Carnegie Corporation, and the Open Society Institute of the Soros Foundation. Initially created with the generous support of the W. Alton Jones Foundation, it has also received support from the Rockefeller Foundation. Gulf/2000 was inspired by the imaginative efforts undertaken at the height of the Cold War, such as the Dartmouth and Pugwash programs, to develop personal contacts and dialogue across the political and military fault lines.
3. The group met at the Villa Serbelloni, the study and conference center operated by the Rockefeller Foundation, to which Gulf/2000 expresses its gratitude. Additional chapters by Faleh A. Jabar, Gerd Nonneman, and Richard Schofield were commissioned for this volume.
4. See the excellent chapter, "War, Institutions, and Social Change in the Middle East," by Steven Heydemann, in *War, Institutions, and Social Change in the Middle East*, ed. Steven Heydemann (Berkeley: University of California Press, 2000), pp. 1–30.

5. The true number of casualties is unknown. Iraq has not published figures on losses, but a figure of 180,000 killed was offered by Wafic al-Samarrai, former head of Iraqi Military Intelligence, in an interview for PBS Frontline in 2002 (See transcript in http://www.pbs.org/wgbh/pages/frontline/gulf/oral/samarrai/5.html). Amatzia Baram, a specialist on Iraq at Haifa University, previously estimated that 150,000 Iraqis had been killed (*The Jerusalem Quarterly*, no. 49 (Winter 1989)), pp. 85–86. Iranian figures have been more or less consistent over the years. General Rahim Safavi, the commander of Iran's Revolutionary Guards Corps, stated that the number of Iranian deaths was 213,000, with 320,000 disabled and 40,000 POWs (Comments at Friday prayers at Mashhad, February 2, 2001). The number of wounded was not specified. Hadi Qalamnevis, the director general of the Statistics and Information Department at the Islamic Revolution Martyrs Foundation said that 204,795 Iranians (including civilians) had been killed in the conflict (Tehran, IRNA, September 23, 2000, online). Mohsen Rafiqdust, the former head of the Islamic Revolutionary Guards Corps, told Robert Fisk of *The Independent* (June 25, 1995) that 220,000 Iranians were killed (this may include MIAs) and 400,000 wounded during the war.
6. Cited in Lawrence Potter, "The Persian Gulf: Reassessing the U.S. Role," in *Great Decisions* (New York: Foreign Policy Association, 1989), p. 25.
7. On the role of the United Nations, see Cameron R. Hume, *The United Nations, Iran, and Iraq: How Peacemaking Changed* (Bloomington: Indiana University Press, 1994). There are a number of issues concerning the end of the war that remain to be elucidated, according to former Iranian Ambassador to the United Nations Mohammad Jafar Mahallati (personal communication, April 19, 2003). These cannot be resolved until many of the principal players are ready to speak for the record.
8. Isam al-Khafaji, "War as a Vehicle for the Rise and Demise of a State-Controlled Society: The Case of Ba'thist Iraq," in Heydemann, *War, Institutions, and Social Change in the Middle East,* pp. 258–91.
9. See for example the special issue of *Goftogu* (Dialogue), no. 23 (spring 1999) on the Iran–Iraq War, published in Persian. Also see the outstanding chapter exploring the feelings of Iran's embittered war veterans, "Martyrs Never Die," in Elaine Sciolino, *Persian Mirrors: The Elusive Face of Iran* (New York: The Free Press, 2000), pp. 172–89.
10. In February 2003, when over a third of the Iranian *Majlis* called for the impeachment of the foreign minister, Kamal Kharrazi, the main reasons given were his handling of relations with Iraq, including his failure to obtain an apology or obtain compensation for the war, and a failure to resolve the POW issue. (See *Iran Times* (Washington, D.C.), February 21, 2003, p. 2.)
11. For an exploration of the mutual perceptions and stereotypes Arabs and Iranians hold about each other, see two complementary chapters, one by Abdullah K. Alshayji, "Mutual Realities, Perceptions, and Impediments Between the GCC States and Iran" and Bijan Khajehpour-Khoei, "Mutual Perceptions in the Persian Gulf Region: An Iranian Perspective," in Lawrence G. Potter and Gary G. Sick, eds., *Security in the Persian Gulf: Origins, Obstacles, and the Search for Consensus* (New York: Palgrave, 2002).
12. See for example Adeed Dawisha, " 'Identity' and Political Survival in Saddam's Iraq," in *The Middle East Journal,* vol. 53, no. 4 (Autumn 1999), pp. 557–62.
13. Amatzia Baram, "Re-Inventing Nationalism in Ba'thi Iraq, 1968–1994: Supra-Territorial and Territorial Identities and What Lies Below," in *Princeton Papers* 5 (Fall 1996), p. 38.
14. This is brought out in Hadi Khosroshahi, "Mutual Awareness Between Arabs and Iranians," in *Arab-Iranian Relations,* ed. Khair el-Din Haseeb (Beirut: Centre for Arab Unity Studies, 1998), p. 115.
15. In an interview with PBS Frontline on the history of the Gulf War, Wafic al-Samarrai, former head of Iraqi Military Intelligence, says he does not believe that the United States

gave Iraq a green light to go ahead with the invasion, although on the other hand it did not strongly deter Saddam Hussein from doing so. (See http://www.pbs.org/wgbh/pages/frontline/gulf/oral/samarrai/1.html.)

16. In May 2003, Iran returned to Baghdad what it maintained (for the third time) were the last Iraqi POWs it has held since the end of the Iran–Iraq War. Iraq claimed to have released all the Iranian POWs it held five years earlier, and Iranian Foreign Minister Kamal Kharrazi acknowledged in September 2003 that there were no more Iranian prisoners detained in Iraq (*Iran Times*, September 12, 2003, p. 3). After the U.S. occupation of Iraq, so far no Iranian POWs have been found, although on April 5, 2003, British forces found boxes containing human remains, some believed to be Iranian, in a warehouse near Zubayr. (See *Iran Times*, May 9, 2003, p. 2 and Radio Free Europe/Radio Liberty *Iran Report*, vol. 6 no. 16 (April 14, 2003).)

17. In late January 1991, Iraq sent 115 military aircraft and 33 passenger planes to refuge in Iran, supposedly without prior approval from Tehran. Iran, which acknowledged receiving only 22 planes, maintained that it would impound them as long as the fighting lasted. (For details on the numbers see Baghdad, INA in Arabic, April 12, 1991, in *FBIS-NES-91–072*, April 15, 1991, p. 26 and Tehran IRNA in English, April 14, 1991, in *FBIS-NES-91–073*, April 16, 1991, p. 49.) These planes have still not been returned and they may be retained as a bargaining chip with Iraq or as compensation for damages sustained during the Iran–Iraq War. In an interview with PBS Frontline for a series on the history of the Gulf War, Iraqi Foreign Minister Tariq Aziz acknowledged that Iraq had made a deal with Iran to accept the transport planes but not military jets. (http://www.pbs.org/wgbh/pages/frontline/gulf/oral/aziz/3.html)

18. It was reported in the spring of 2002 that only 12% of the 16 million mines the UN estimates were laid on the Iran-Iraq border had been cleared. Since the end of the war, 52 Iranian army mine-clearers had been killed up to that point trying to disarm them (*Iran Times*, April 19, 2002, p. 2).

19. On this see Ali Babakhan, "The Deportation of Shi'is During the Iran-Iraq War: Causes and Consequences," in *Ayatollahs, Sufis and Ideologues: State, Religion and Social Movements in Iraq*, ed. Faleh Abdul-Jabar (London: Saqi Books, 2002), pp. 183–210. Also, Neil MacFarquhar, "Iraqis in Iran: Unwanted in Both Countries," in *The New York Times*, June 12, 2003, p. A19.

20. Iraqi sociologist Isam Al-Khafaji makes the point that Iraq's real interests lie in the nations to its north and west, i.e., Turkey, Syria and the Levant, and not Iran and the Gulf (see "The Myth of Iraqi Exceptionalism," in *Middle East Policy*, vol. 7, no. 4 (October 2000), p. 64). On the increased centrality of the Gulf to Iraqi foreign policy, see Raad Alkadiri, "Iraq and the Gulf Since 1991: The Search for Deliverance," in Potter and Sick, *Security in the Persian Gulf*, pp. 254–55.

21. On the issue of the Gulf islands, see three linked articles in Potter and Sick, *Security in the Persian Gulf*, pp. 135–87: "On the Persian Gulf Islands: An Iranian Perspective" by Jalil Roshandel, "The Islands Question: An Arabian Perspective" by Hassan Al-Alkim, and "Anything but Black and White: A Commentary on the Lower Gulf Islands Dispute" by Richard Schofield.

Chapter 1

The Troubled Relationship: Iran and Iraq, 1930–80

Shaul Bakhash

The relationship between Iran and Iraq, since Iraq achieved independence in 1932, has been marked by periods of alliance and cooperation and also periods of rivalry, friction, and devastating war. Cooperation was largely the product of the common regional security needs of the two countries and brought Iran and Iraq together in the Saadabad Pact in 1937 and the Baghdad Pact in 1955. Friction resulted from border disputes, particularly over the Shatt al-Arab, competing regional ambitions, the differing domestic and foreign policy orientations of regimes, and, at various times, the alliances Tehran and Baghdad forged with competing world powers. The presence of large, often rebellious, Kurdish communities in both Iran and Iraq provided each country with the means to cause difficulties for the other—although the Kurdish problem proved far more acute for Iraq than for Iran. Iraq's large Shi'i community (a portion of whose members were of Iranian origin), the affinities members of this community felt with fellow Shi'is in Iran, and the fact that Shi'ism's holiest shrines were located in Iraq, created a potential instrument (though not always the reality) for Iranian influence in Iraq and aroused Baghdad's suspicions.

Except for common oil policies pursued under the umbrella of the Organization of Petroleum Exporting Countries (OPEC), which remained largely unaffected by Iran–Iraq relations on other issues, the two countries rarely displayed an inclination or ability to isolate and treat separately these different sources of tension. Rather, in each period of conflict, all these different elements were brought into play.[1] For example, when Iran raised the issue of sovereignty over the Shatt al-Arab in 1960–61, Baghdad responded by making territorial claims against Iran and harassing and expelling Iraqis of Iranian origin from the country. In the mid-1960s and 1970s, the shah pursued Iran's claims in the Shatt by aiding Iraq's rebellious Kurds.

Until the Iraqi revolution of 1958, regimes in Iran and in independent Iraq shared features in common that tended to contain the intensity of potential conflict. Both countries were monarchies. The foreign policy of both tended to a pro-Western orientation. Each country had interests, but neither displayed overweening ambitions, in the Persian Gulf. The revolution of 1958 in Iraq, however, added an ideological dimension to the conflict: it brought to power in Baghdad a regime whose rhetoric, self-perception, regional role and foreign policy orientation were at odds with the character and primary domestic and foreign policy orientations of the Tehran government. The element of regime difference, and the competing regional ambitions, foreign policy orientations, and great power affiliations to which it gave rise, was heightened by the Baath seizure of power in Iraq in 1968, and then again by the Iranian revolution of 1979. In each instance, regime change intensified and rendered more intractable the differences between the two countries.

Britain's intention to withdraw its military forces from the Persian Gulf, announced in 1968 and fulfilled in 1971, also contributed to the Iran–Iraq rivalry. It created the perception and reality of a power vacuum in the Gulf which the shah of Iran and Iraq's Baath rulers were eager to fill. British withdrawal, moreover, occurred at a time when particularly Iran but also Iraq had greater means to pursue larger ambitions in the Gulf region—including consolidation at home, rapidly rising oil revenues, stronger military forces, and the patronage of a superpower. A perception of opportunity and newfound strength led the shah in 1975 to push his dispute with Iraq over the Shatt al-Arab to a conclusion greatly favoring Iran; a similar perception of opportunity and strength led Saddam Hussein to declare war and invade Iran in 1980.

The Iraqi invasion of Iran represented a sharp break with the relative restraint Baghdad and Tehran had displayed for over four decades in pursing their differences. The hostilities, involving near-total mobilization for war and massive destruction of life and property, pursued by Iran and Iraq in the name of both of national interest and ideology, and aiming at the very annihilation of the other regime, also signified a dramatic change in the nature of Iran–Iraq relations.

History

The Fertile Crescent was a region often contested between whatever power held sway in Iran and whatever power governed or coveted the Tigris-Euphrates region. The Achaemenid Empire (550–331 B.C.) and the Sasanid Empire (226–651 C.E.) each included present-day Iraq in its domains. The Sasanid capital, at Ctesiphon (which formed part of what was later known in Arabic as Mada'in, "the cities"), lay in present-day Iraq. The Arab conquests in the seventh century made Iran part of the Islamic Empire; and during the early Abbasid Empire, in the eighth century, Iran was governed from the Abbasid capital at Baghdad. This older history is worth mentioning only because, in the 1980s, it provided fodder for the constructs of intellectuals, government propagandists, and the popular imagination—the idea that territorial and political control and perceptions of cultural superiority in the distant past served as a rationale and justification for the territorial claims and assertions of cultural and moral superiority in the present.

In more recent times the region of present-day Iraq (as well as the Caucasus frontier) was contested territory between the Ottoman and Safavid Empires in the sixteenth and seventeenth centuries, when frontier and sectarian differences resulted in major if low-level intermittent wars. The Perso–Ottoman "Treaty of Peace and Frontiers" of 1639 brought an end to the fighting, but defined the frontier only in general terms.[2] New Ottoman incursions into Iranian territory during the disorders following the collapse of the Safavid dynasty in 1722 resulted in considerable Iranian territorial losses in both the north and the west. Iranian attempts to recover these territories led to a new round of fighting in the 1730s and 1740s, terminated by a treaty in 1746, which basically reaffirmed the imprecise frontiers agreed to in the treaty of 1639.

Differences over the frontier and over the regulation of the movement of border tribes continued into the nineteenth century, when the Qajar dynasty ruled in Persia. The two states fought a brief war (1821–23), and signed a new treaty in 1823 that confirmed the frontiers as defined in earlier treaties.[3] Skirmishes and border fighting resumed in the 1830s, causing Great Britain, with interests in both Persia and the Ottoman Empire, to secure Russian cooperation for an effort to resolve the sources of dispute between the two states. The Perso-Ottoman frontier was subsequently demarcated with greater precision with the assistance of Britain and Russia. The protracted work (1843–47) of the frontier commission, composed of the representatives of Persia, the Ottoman Empire, Russia, and Britain, was incorporated in the Treaty of Erzurum of 1847;[4] it was not, however, until 1869 that the commission produced a map of the frontier zone within which the boundary lay. A remaining dispute over the town and district of Qotur was addressed in clause 60 of the Treaty of Berlin of 1878 (which ended a war between the Ottoman Empire and European powers, and in which Iran was not involved), when the Ottomans recognized Persian sovereignty over Qotur.

The Treaty of Erzurum also defined the frontier between Iran and the Ottoman Empire in the Shatt al-Arab. Instead of following the *thalweg* (or deep water) line, as is the usual international practice for dividing frontier rivers, the treaty fixed the boundary from Basra to the head of the Persian Gulf at the low water mark on the Iranian side of the Shatt, thus leaving the navigational channel and the bulk of the waterway in Ottoman hands.[5] The rationale (later repeatedly invoked by the government of Iraq) was that, while Iran benefitted from a long frontier and deep harbor possibilities on the Persian Gulf, Basra's only access to the Gulf and the open sea was through the Shatt al-Arab. The 1847 Shatt boundary was confirmed by the International Boundary Commission in 1914.[6] Already in the 1930s, Iran began to protest what it regarded as the inequity of these arrangements. A boundary agreement signed in 1937 confirmed the land frontier as defined by earlier treaties, but modestly modified the frontier in the Shatt al-Arab in Iran's favor. A triangular area, three miles long, lying opposite the Persian oil port at Abadan was awarded to Iran. This meant that ships loading or unloading at Abadan would do so in Iranian waters. The waterway was to be open on an equal basis to the ships of all states, but to the warships of the two countries only. The countries undertook to conclude a second agreement within a year for joint administration of the Shatt, including maintenance and improvement of the navigable channel and matters affecting piloting, dredging, and dues collection. Dues were to be used exclusively for maintenance of the shipping channel and facilities of the Shatt. Until such time as this second agreement was concluded (i.e., for a one-year period or longer if mutually agreed), Iraq was to be responsible, through the Basra Port Authority, for administration and dues collection in the waterway.

However, the second agreement was never signed. In subsequent years Iran blamed Iraq for the failure of the two countries to conclude such an agreement, and complained that Iraq failed to consult with Iran on administration of the Shatt and to report annually on the operations of the Basra Port Authority, as required under the 1937 agreement. It also charged that Iraq was diverting fees collected on the Shatt to purposes other than those designated in the treaty. Subsequently, Iran began to call not only for the full implementation of the 1937 agreement but for its thorough modification, arguing that, in keeping with international practice, the *thalweg*, rather than the low water mark, should define the river frontier between the two countries.

The Saadabad and Baghdad Pacts

The conclusion of the 1937 frontier agreement paved the way for the Saadabad Pact, a treaty of friendship and nonaggression between Iran, Iraq, Turkey, and Afghanistan.[7] The signatories agreed to adhere to the principles of nonaggression, noninterference, nonviolation of frontiers, peaceful resolution of conflicts and consultation in international disputes affecting their common interests. Each signatory also undertook to prevent activity on its territory by "armed bands, associations or organizations" hostile to another pact member. The pact established a council to meet once a year for consultation. Except for pressing for rotational membership of the signatory states in the League of Nations Council, the Saadabad Pact did not involve the signatories in any common undertaking. It remained no more than an expression of friendly intentions, and while never formally abrogated, it simply faded away.

More substantial considerations underpinned the Baghdad Pact, initially signed by Iraq and Turkey in February 1955, and joined by Britain in April, Pakistan in September, and Iran in October of the same year. The Baghdad Pact stemmed in part from Britain's postwar attempt to organize the Arab states of the Middle East in a British-sponsored military alliance, and in part from the Eisenhower administration's desire to assemble a defensive alliance (along the lines of NATO and SEATO) of the "northern tier" countries along the USSR's southern border. Both the shah in Iran and the Iraqi prime minister, Nuri al-Sa'id, promoted the treaty as a means of reinforcing their relations with powerful Western patrons (for Nuri al-Sa'id this meant England, for the shah, the United States), buying protection against Soviet expansionism or communist subversion, acquiring weaponry, and shoring up their regimes against internal opponents. For Iraq, the Baghdad Pact was also a factor in inter-Arab politics, a means of strengthening Iraq's hand against Egypt (Iraq's principal rival for leadership of the Arab world), and for setting the direction of the postwar foreign policy of the Arab states. The shah was not involved in inter-Arab politics. For him, the threat from the Soviet Union, with whom Iran shared a 1,200 kilometer border, loomed large. But the growing popularity of Gamal Abdel Nasser, his advocacy of socialism at home and a non-aligned foreign policy abroad, and the challenge he seemed to pose to the status quo and to the conservative monarchies of the Middle East, was worrisome to the shah as well.

Nasser, who became president of Egypt in 1956, opposed the Baghdad Pact. He regarded the pact as a bid by Iraq to dominate inter-Arab defense arrangements under British tutelage, while he favored a purely Arab defense pact dominated by Egypt. He had just secured British withdrawal from the Suez Canal Zone and saw the Baghdad Pact as an attempt by Britain to reenter Egypt and other Middle East countries through the back door. The Baghdad Pact thus proved controversial, deepened divisions in the Arab world, and strained relations between Iran and Egypt. It was probably as unpopular with politicized Iranians still resentful of the shah, Britain and the United States over the 1953 overthrow of Prime Minister Mohammad Mosaddeq, as it was unpopular among the Iraqi elites.

Iraq's membership in the Baghdad Pact did not survive the Iraqi revolution of 1958. During the brief three years when Iraq was a member, some consultation took place between member states and some preparatory planning was made for military contingencies. But more extensive planning, the implementation of a number of road and communications projects, and the maturing of mechanisms for consultation were chiefly the product of later years, subsequent to Iraqi withdrawal, when the treaty was renamed the Central Treaty Organization (CENTO). The period of Iran–Iraq cooperation in a common defense treaty was thus of short duration, and it was followed by a period of greatly heightened tension.

The Repercussions of the Iraqi Revolution of 1958

The Iraqi revolution of 1958 caused considerable concern in Tehran and introduced major strains in Iran–Iraq relations. The monarchy had been overthrown. The new regime was "revolutionary" and was engaging in disturbingly radical rhetoric. Its initial, seemingly pro-Nasserite, orientation proved short-lived, as did the role of communists in 'Abd al-Karim Qasim's government. But Iraq's deepening relations with the Soviet Union, the general air of revolution and turmoil on Iran's borders, and the fear of spreading republican sentiment, was unsettling to the shah.

Besides, Qasim adopted a more assertive policy regarding "Arab" interests in the Persian Gulf and a posture on Iran–Iraq issues that Tehran was bound to view as intransigient and truculent. Iran had reopened the question of joint administration of the Shatt al-Arab under the old regime, submitting a note and a draft convention to the Iraqi government in April 1949. Iraq did not reply to the Iranian note for 15 months, and then only to reject the appeal for joint administration. Iraq allowed the Iranian initiative to die by ignoring it.

Iran submitted another note to the Iraqi government in September 1957, outlining its position and suggesting the appointment of a Swedish arbitrator to help resolve differences on Shatt administration, navigation, and frontiers. Reopened negotiations were still inconclusive when the monarchy was overthrown in July 1958. When the shah reopened the question of the Shatt in a public statement in November 1959, charging Iraq with violating the terms of previous agreements and with pursuing an "imperialistic policy," Qasim responded by claiming the entire

Shatt, including the three-mile area around Abadan, as Iraqi territory and in effect nullifying the agreement. He expelled thousands of Iranian nationals from Iraq and placed work restrictions on others. Both countries placed their military forces on alert, some small incidents occurred on the river, and radio broadcasts grew strident. But both governments acted cautiously, and by April 1960, the two countries had agreed to settle their differences through negotiations. Affairs returned to the status quo prevailing before the outbreak of the mini-crisis. The Basra Port Authority remained under Iraqi control and continued to collect dues, and Iran remained in control of the three-mile strip opposite Abadan.

On the other hand, Iranian grievances remained unsatisfied. Iran had begun to press for recognition of the *thalweg* as the line defining the frontier in the Shatt al-Arab. Moreover, Qasim had raised the stakes by claiming the Iranian province of Khuzistan—the center of Iran's oil industry—which he called "Arabistan." The Iraqi cabinet adopted a resolution designating the official title of the Persian Gulf as the "Arabian" Gulf. It was the first Arab government to do so, adding strains to the relationship. Qasim was given to precipitate action, as indicated by the claim he made to Kuwait in June 1961, five days after Kuwait achieved its independence from Britain. However, Qasim's claim to "Arabistan"—a direct threat to Iran's territorial integrity—injected a new feature into the Iraq–Iran relationship. The tendency to escalate the terms of the conflict, to pose the issues in a manner that seemed to threaten the integrity of states or regimes, became more common under republican Iraq and was a tactic adopted by both sides in the 1980s, during the Iran–Iraq War.

After the failure of further discussions with the Qasim government, Iran issued a ruling on February 16, 1961 that ships entering Iranian waters on their way to and from Iranian ports must be piloted by Iranian pilots rather than pilots provided by the Basra Port Authority. The Basra Port Authority responded by refusing to handle any ships, along the whole forty-mile course of the waterway, headed to and from Iranian ports. Ships piled up in the Shatt. The export of refined oil from Abadan in March 1961 fell by 60 percent compared to March of the previous year. Storage tanks at the Abadan refinery filled up, production plummeted, and Iran incurred $30 million in losses in unexported refined products. Iraq, holding the cards, could afford to wait. In April, Iran agreed to return to the status quo, pending negotiations.[8]

Iraq's resistance to any change in the status quo in the Shatt al-Arab arose from various considerations, including national security. Basra was Iraq's only deep water port and the Shatt was Basra's sole access to the sea. National pride and the fear of adverse domestic opinion were also factors. Iraq, a champion of pan-Arabism, could not be seen ceding "Arab" territory to Iran. Besides, a policy of procrastination, of discussing but not seriously addressing Iranian demands, seemed to have worked. Occasional crises had not spun out of control. Until the mid-1970s, then, Iraq saw no pressing need to address Iranian desiderata in the Shatt al-Arab.[9]

The Shatt issue also got in the way of resolving other conflicts. In 1963, for example, Iran and Iraq, with little difficulty, reached agreement on continued joint exploitation of an oil field that straddled the Iran–Iraq border, at Khaneqin on the Iraqi side and at Naft-e Shah/Khaneh on the Iranian side. But negotiations on division of territorial waters at the mouth of the Shatt in the Persian Gulf stalled. Iran concluded an agreement with Saudi Arabia in 1968, delimiting the continental shelf between the two countries in the Persian Gulf, and a similar agreement with Qatar in 1969. But a continental shelf agreement with Iraq could not be concluded, and a continental shelf agreement with Kuwait was thwarted, not because of Kuwaiti objections, but because of Iraq's claim to Kuwait's Bubiyan island. The Shatt issue continued to prove intractable despite several high-level visits and negotiations between the two countries in the later 1960s. These included the visit to Baghdad by Iran's foreign minister, Abbas Aram, in December 1966; a state visit to Iran by Iraqi President 'Abd al-Rahman Arif in March 1967 (when Arif was warmly hosted by the shah); and the visit of Prime Minister Tahir Yahya to Iran in June 1968.

Iran and the Baath Regime, 1968–78

The Baath seizure of power in Iraq in 1968 greatly exacerbated relations between the two countries. The Baath regime, having taken power in a bloody coup, facing internal enemies, and intent to solidify its position, could not appear weak in foreign policy. The Baath leadership was eager to assert both its Iraqi nationalist and its pan-Arab credentials. Several other features of the regime were disturbing to Tehran. It adopted socialism at home, a stridently anti-Western posture in foreign policy, and a revolutionary rhetoric directed at conservative Persian Gulf and Arab regimes. It developed a close military and economic relationship with the USSR—the Iraqi–Soviet Treaty of Friendship was signed in April 1972—which was an issue of particular concern to the shah.

The Baath supported an amorphous front for the liberation of Khuzistan. It also supported the insurgency in Dhofar, Oman, the left-leaning revolutionaries in Yemen, and the Popular Front for the Liberation of the Occupied Arabian Gulf. These activities placed Iraq and Iran (along with a number of Arab states in the Gulf) on opposite sides in a series of local conflicts and insurgencies. In January 1970, the Baath regime executed 37 men and women on charges of attempting to overthrow the government, allegedly with Iranian assistance. It then expelled the Iranian ambassador, closed down Iranian consulates in three cities, and expelled thousands of Iranians. The impending British withdrawal from the Persian Gulf was bound to set off a scramble for advantage among the three principal Persian Gulf states, Iraq, Iran, and Saudi Arabia.

Rising oil revenues in the early 1970s provided both Iran and Iraq with the means to engage in patronage, an arms buildup, and rapid economic expansion. In Iraq, the huge imports required for an ambitious economic development program enhanced the importance of the ports of Basra and Umm Qasr and of unfettered control over the Shatt al-Arab. Iran in the 1960s began to exploit its offshore oil resources in the Persian Gulf and constructed major oil loading facilities on Kharg Island. Iran reduced its reliance on Abadan for the export of oil products by investing in pipelines to carry refined oil from the Abadan refinery to export terminals in the lower Persian Gulf. But this only underlined Iran's concern that Iraq could yet interfere with Iranian shipping in the Shatt. Iran's main port at Khorramshahr, adjacent to Abadan, became the lifeline for the import of millions of tons of goods annually. In addition, state and private sector investment in petrochemicals, steel, pipe and rolling mills and ancillary industries was transforming Khuzistan into a major industrial center. For both countries the strategic importance of the Shatt and the Persian Gulf greatly increased. In 1973, for example, Baghdad attempted to persuade Kuwait to transfer or lease to Iraq the Kuwaiti islands of Bubiyan and Warba. These two islands dominated the inlet leading to Iraq's Gulf port of Umm Qasr and their possession would have allowed Iraq to expand Umm Qasr and develop a deep water port on the Gulf. When Kuwait refused, Iraq attempted to seize the islands by force.

The shah, moreover, had begun to pursue a more ambitious policy in the Persian Gulf, a reflection of Iran's increasing weight in regional affairs. His relations with the United States were excellent. In 1972, President Richard Nixon had agreed to allow Iran to purchase all but the most advanced American weaponry, generally in quantities of the shah's own choosing. The United States looked to Iran and Saudi Arabia to serve as the "twin pillars" to maintain Gulf security, following the British withdrawal. The shah was building up Iran's naval forces. His relations with the Soviet Union were stable. Although a degree of rivalry was built into the Iran–Saudi relationship, and the smaller Persian Gulf states remained suspicious of Iranian ambitions, the shah had assiduously and successfully courted both the Saudis and the emirate shaikhs. In a significant policy speech in 1972, the shah envisaged a naval role for Iran extending beyond the Persian Gulf into the Indian Ocean. Across a whole gamut of issues, Iran and the new Baath regime appeared set on a collision course.

The first crisis erupted in April 1969, when Baghdad informed Tehran that, since the Shatt was Iraqi territory, ships flying the Iranian flag must lower their flags, and Iranian naval personnel on board must disembark, when passing through the waterway. This time Iran reacted forcefully. The Iranian Senate formally abrogated the 1937 treaty. Iran placed its naval and air forces on alert and the Iraqi government was advised against interfering with Iranian shipping. All ships bound for Iranian ports were provided with military escorts and Iranian ships with Iranian pilots. In the 1961 confrontation with General Qasim, Iran had been forced to back down from its demand that Iranian pilots guide ships in Iranian waters and ports, because it lacked the means to enforce its demands. But in 1969, it was Iraq's turn to back down. Iran's naval forces in the Gulf were considerably stronger than Iraq's and the Baath regime was embroiled in internal difficulties, including renewed fighting with the Kurds. In 1961, the confrontation produced no change in the status quo. In 1969, the prerogatives Iran asserted were not reversed. Iran continued to pilot its own ships in the Shatt, under the Iranian flag, and to pay no dues to the Basra Port Authority. Both incidents underlined the truism that superior force, and the ability not so much to use it as to threaten to use it, was a factor in the relationship.[10]

A second crisis occurred over Iran's claim to three Persian Gulf islands, the two Tunbs and Abu Musa, that were also claimed, respectively, by Ras al-Khaimah and Sharjah. Iran, considering the islands critical for securing the Strait of Hormuz, through which all shipping to Iran's main commercial and oil ports had to pass, began to press its claims to the islands more energetically in 1968, after the British announced their intention to withdraw their military forces from the Persian Gulf. The shah had two important cards to play in pressing his claim on the British, whose posture would weigh heavily in determining the eventual disposition of the three islands. Iran had a longstanding claim to Bahrain, and British withdrawal from the Gulf and grant of independence to Bahrain could not go smoothly if Iran's claim to Bahrain remained unresolved. Iran also refused to recognize the federation of Arab emirates (the later United Arab Emirates), of which Bahrain was to be a member and that the British were hoping to put together before leaving the Gulf, unless its claims to Bahrain and the other islands were satisfied.[11]

The shah played his cards uncommonly well. He pressed Iranian claims to Bahrain vigorously, but his eye was on the three islands. He appears to have reached a tacit understanding with the British that he would give up Bahrain in exchange for a free hand on the two Tunbs and Abu Musa. In January 1969, the shah said he would not insist on Bahrain's union with Iran if the people of Bahrain preferred independence. In April 1970 the UN Security Council endorsed the report of a UN fact-finding mission that found an overwhelming majority of the people desired independence. The Iranian Parliament endorsed a resolution along these same lines in May 1970. The shah's reasonable policy on Bahrain was welcomed by the Arab states.

The shah now felt free to pursue Iran's claims to the three small islands. He reached an agreement with the Shaikh of Sharjah over Abu Musa, but the Shaikh of Ras al-Khaimah refused to accommodate Iran over Greater and Lesser Tunb. On November 30, 1971, one day before the British military withdrawal from the Gulf was completed, Iranian troops seized the islands by force. The Iranian takeover of the Tunbs was opposed by all the Arab states, but most vehemently by Iraq. The Baath regime broke diplomatic relations with both Iran and England, unsuccessfully tried to push a resolution through the Arab League for all members to rupture relations with Iran, began to expel thousands of Iraqis of Iranian origin from the country (eventually, over 30,000 persons were dumped on the Iranian side of the border) and revived the claim to Khuzistan. Border clashes broke out in the spring of 1972, though they did not escalate into wider fighting. Iraq allowed Teymur Bakhtiar, the former Iranian security chief, who was plotting against the shah, and other Islamic and radical Left opponents of the shah to operate from Iraqi soil. In February 1973, Pakistani police raided the Iraqi embassy in Islamabad and seized machine guns and ammunition, smuggled in as diplomatic baggage and apparently intended for a separatist movement in Iranian Baluchistan.[12] Iraq charged Iran with supplying heavy weapons to the Kurds in Iraq.

The Kurds in the Iran–Iraq Equation

The Kurds, and their demand for far-reaching autonomy, proved a perennial problem for Iraqi governments following the 1958 revolution. Serious fighting erupted between the Kurds and the government in 1961, during the presidency of Qasim, and continued until a ceasefire was negotiated in early 1964. Fighting resumed in 1965. At one stage, the Kurdish leader, Mustafa Barzani, was master of a large swath of territory in the Kurdish countryside, covering some 35,000 square kilometers and one million inhabitants. He had set up his own administration in the north and controlled the borders with Iran and Turkey. The government suffered serious setbacks in heavy fighting in the spring of 1966, forcing the new president, 'Abd al-Rahman Arif, and the moderate prime minister, 'Abd al-Rahman al-Bazzaz, to negotiate an agreement that went far in meeting Kurdish demands for autonomy, language rights, representation in an Iraqi legislature, and a share in government and civil service posts.

However, the agreement was never implemented. Fighting resumed in 1968–69, after the Baath takeover of power. The Kurds caused damage to oil installations in Kirkuk, the source of most of the government's revenue and, in what had become a full-scale war, the government eventually sent four divisions north and used its air force to bomb Kurdish territory. Unable to prevail, the government negotiated another agreement with Barzani in March 1970, going even further than the Arif regime had under the 1966 agreement. However, serious fighting resumed in 1974 when it became clear that the government had no intention of honoring the agreement.

For obvious reasons, Iran took advantage of Iraq's inability to resolve its problems with the Kurds. Fighting in the north was financially costly, sapped resources, occupied Iraq's military forces, contributed to Iraq's instability, and absorbed the attention of Iraq's leaders. By aiding Iraq's Kurds the shah could both exacerbate Baghdad's problems and acquire leverage against it. Regime difference also weighed heavily with the shah; the character, indeed the whole tenor, of post-revolution Iraqi regimes, and particularly the Baath government, appeared at odds with the regional state system with which the shah felt comfortable. Moreover, by the mid-1960s the shah felt confident of his own Kurdish population. He felt he could assist Iraq's rebellious Kurds without risking a similar autonomy movement in Iran. The concern Iraq's Kurds expressed over Iraqi–Egyptian unity negotiations in 1965 was shared by Iran.

The shah renewed links with Barzani in the mid-1960s, began to supply heavy arms to the Kurds, and assisted Barzani's forces in other ways. When fighting resumed under the Baath in 1969, and again after the breakdown of the 1970 autonomy agreement, the shah provided the Kurds with extensive financial and military assistance, including antitank missiles and artillery. Iranian forces may have directly assisted the Kurds. Iran's support was augmented by Israeli and American help. In May 1970, President Nixon directed the CIA to advance $16 million to Barzani.

Both in 1966 and in 1970, Iranian support for the Kurds had created sufficient military difficulties for Baghdad to settle with them, largely on Kurdish terms. In 1975, the Iraqi government once again concluded that the Kurdish war, and Iranian involvement, posed a serious threat to the regime, which could not be handled militarily. This time, Baghdad dealt with its Kurdish problem by settling with the shah. Negotiations led to an agreement, signed by the shah and the Iraqi strongman, Saddam Hussein, in Algiers in March 1975.[13] The agreement gave Iran what it had long sought in the Shatt al-Arab. The existing land frontier was confirmed, with minor modifications. But in the Shatt, the frontier was delimited along the *thalweg*. In return, the shah tacitly agreed to end Iranian support for the Kurdish insurgency. Iran began to withdraw its military equipment from Iraq within hours of the signing of the agreement, and the Kurdish revolt rapidly collapsed. Barzani and some 30,000 Kurds crossed over into Iran; the majority of the Kurdish insurgents gave themselves up to the Iraqi authorities.[14] The Algiers Agreement appeared to usher in a period of calm in Iran–Iraq relations—a calm that was quickly fractured under the impact of the Iranian revolution.

The Islamic Revolution and the Iran–Iraq War

In the same way that the Iraqi revolution of 1958 caused consternation in Tehran, the Islamic revolution of 1979 was profoundly disturbing to Baghdad. The revolution seemed threatening to all the regimes in the Persian Gulf, but the threat looked particularly menacing from the perspective of Baghdad. Iran and Iraq shared a long border, and the "spill-over" effect of the revolution was most acute in case of Iraq. Iran's message of a new, revolutionary Islam resonated with peoples across the Gulf region, and challenged Iraq's brand of secular Arab nationalism. Especially disturbing to Iraq was the possible appeal of the revolution to Iraq's large Shi'i community. Iran's revolutionary leader, Ayatollah Khomeini, had taught, and mobilized opinion against the shah, from his exile at the shrine city of Najaf in Iraq in the period before the revolution. He had a considerable following among Iraq's Shi'is in Najaf and other shrine cities. After the revolution, a number of Iranian clerical propagandists appeared in the Persian Gulf emirates, denouncing Gulf rulers and preaching Iran's brand of Islamic revolution.

Shi'i grievances against the Iraqi government, unrelated to Iran, had led to serious disturbances and riots in Najaf and Karbala in 1977 and to further disturbances after the Iranian revolution, in June 1979. A clandestine Shi'i party, al-Da'wa, was suspected of complicity in the attempt to assassinate Tariq Aziz, a high-ranking member of the Revolutionary Command Council (RCC), on April 1, 1980, and the minister of culture and information later that month. The Iraqi authorities responded by arresting suspect Shi'is and expelling 35,000 Iranians.[15] The arrest and execution by the Iraqi authorities of a senior and politically minded Shi'i cleric, Ayatollah Baqir al-Sadr, who was linked to al-Da'wa, generated much bad feeling in Iran. The disturbed state of affairs in Iran and the activities of Kurdish insurgents in both countries encouraged border incidents, which escalated in September 1980.

The revolution also stopped the work of an Iran–Iraq frontier commission that was mapping the border between the two countries, as required under the 1975 Algiers Agreement. The work of the commission was almost completed but stopped before a small rectification could be made in Iraq's favor around Qasr-e Shirin. The new Iranian government, embroiled in internal problems, seemed little inclined to complete the work.

By 1980, Saddam Hussein also saw the Iranian revolution as an opportunity. Iran was in turmoil. Its army had been ravaged by executions, purges, and wholesale dismissals. Available military units were embroiled in a low-level insurrection in Iranian Kurdistan. A failed plot involving members of the officer corps, centered on the Nozheh military base in western Iran, and supported by Iraq, resulted in a purge and crippling of the air force. (The Islamic Republic had to release Iranian pilots from prison after the Iraqi invasion and use them to fly bombing missions.) The regime appeared wracked by factional struggles. It was also internationally isolated; the seizure of the American embassy and its diplomats in November 1979 had earned Iran America's hostility. Prominent Iranian exiles, in contact with Iraq, were predicting the collapse of the regime, if only a sufficient push were provided.

In sending his army into Iran in September 1980, Saddam Hussein believed he could accomplish three aims: severely undermine, perhaps even overthrow, the revolutionary government in Iran and replace it with a government beholden or at least friendly to Iraq; enhance his standing, in the Persian Gulf and the Middle East, as a defender and champion of the Arab cause; and restore full Iraqi control over the Shatt al-Arab. In October 1979, Iraq had formally denounced the 1975 Algiers Agreement and called for Iran's withdrawal from the Tunbs and Abu Musa. One of Saddam's last public acts before the invasion was to appear on Iraqi television and tear up the Algiers Agreement. In addition, if the reiteration of Iraqi claims to Khuzistan following the invasion had a serious intent, the Iraqi president may have had his eye on Iran's rich oil resources. While Iranian actions in the weeks and months leading up to the war could be considered provocative, they did not constitute acts of war. The conflict was Saddam's war of choice; and given his war aims, he no doubt sought to provoke it.

The Iran–Iraq War was not merely a continuation of earlier conflicts, albeit on a more expanded scale. It was profoundly different in intensity, in character and in its implications. Border incidents had occurred in 1960–61 and there were subsequent confrontations, but both sides had been careful not to allow events to escalate into a wider conflict. The threat of force was implicit in the shah's successful grab for additional rights in the Shatt in 1969 but both Iran and Iraq saw to it that force did not have to be used. In the 1970s, the shah supported armed insurrection by the Kurds in Iraq and used Iranian forces to support the insurrection. But both sides understood that his aims were limited, and once the shah secured a satisfactory settlement of the Shatt issue, he abandoned the Kurds. In 1980, Saddam Hussein broke with this tradition of carefully managed crises, and for the first time in three centuries launched the two countries into all-out war.

There was also no precedent, in the previous several decades of conflict and friction between Iran and Iraq, of employing national armies not simply for territorial gain or leverage but for the purpose of overthrowing or fundamentally changing regimes. Yet Saddam went to war in 1980 partly to overthrow the Islamic Republic. Once the hostilities began, toppling Saddam Hussein, and possibly replacing him with a Shi'i dominated regime, became an Iranian war aim as well. The conflict took on the many characteristics of "unlimited war."[16]

The Iran–Iraq War was also exceptional, in the recent history of the two countries, for the role of ideology and the nature and intensity of war propaganda. In periods of tension between Iran and Iraq since 1932, real and imagined past history, and traditional Iran–Arab and Shi'i–Sunni animosities, had been invoked and had been a feature of the disputation. But the war pitted a highly ideological Baath regime, with a strong propensity for national myth-making,[17] against a revolutionary Iranian regime driven by a potent, ideological vision of Islam.[18] As a result, on the Iraqi side the conflict became a war of Arab against Persian, Muslim against infidel, the Prophet's armies against Zoroastrian fire-worshippers.

These themes were repeatedly sounded by Saddam Hussein, Iraq's deputy foreign minister, Tariq Aziz, and other Iraqi officials. Iran threatened not only Iraq, but the whole Arab nation, which Iraq was defending. Iran was an ally of the Zionists, whose domination of the Arab world it was facilitating. Iran wished to impose "Persian racial dominance" over the Arabs.[19] Even in early speeches on the war, in the full flush of Iraq's initial military victories, Saddam Hussein and Tariq Aziz issued vague but menacing threats against Iran's territorial integrity. Tariq Aziz demanded autonomy and recognition for the "national characteristics" of the Arab inhabitants of the Iranian province of "Arabistan" (Khuzistan) and spoke of Iran itself as a country composed of various ethnic groups, each of whom deserved autonomy.[20] Saddam Hussein emphasized Iraq's responsibility to recover, in Iran, not only Iraqi territory, but also "usurped Arab land." He refused to say whether he intended to withdraw from captured Khuzistan, to secure its autonomy, annex it, or the make it an independent state.[21] He added:

> When the war started, it was not among our decisions to divide Iran. Yet when Iran persists in its enmity to Iraq and the Arabs . . . certainly these considerations must occur to the Iraqi or Arab planner.[22]

In the later phases of the war, when Iraq again had the upper hand, Iraqi officials suggested that the disintegration of Iran into its constituent ethnic components was not entirely undesirable.

On the Iranian side, Khomeini and the Iranian leadership described the war as one for the defense not only of Iran, but of Islam and the very spirit of the revolution. Since the Iranian revolution belonged to the whole world, Prime Minister Mir-Hosein Musavi said, "if Iran were defeated, all the revolutionary forces would be defeated."[23] Just as Iraq defined the war in terms of the battles the early Muslims/Arabs in seventh-century Arabia fought against the "fire-worshipping Iranians," so Khomeini identified Iran's struggle with the battles the Prophet fought against the enemies of the early Islamic community. This was a war against blasphemy. Iran was fighting for its religion, not for territory. Compromise with Iraq "would be tantamount to annihilation." In the view of God and the prophets, "to compromise with oppressors is to oppress." As Khomeini told Iranians:

> You are fighting to protect Islam and he is fighting to destroy Islam . . . There is absolutely no question of peace or compromise and we shall never have any discussions with them; because they are corrupt and perpetrators of corruption.[24]

Not since the first Safavid–Ottoman war in the sixteenth century, and the Shi'i–Sunni character of that war, has ideology and propaganda played so major a role in a conflict between Iran and a neighboring power. And the Safavids and the Ottomans lacked the destructive weapons of modern warfare or modern technology for the propagation of the ideology of war. This ideological dimension of the Iran–Iraq War contributed to its intensity and its prolongation, to its destructive force and to its terrible cost in human life. The war left a legacy of mistrust that would prove difficult to overcome and of contentious issues that would prove difficult to resolve. On sovereignty over the Shatt al-Arab, the two countries remained far apart. For many years, there were difficulties in repatriating prisoners of war. Iranian reparation claims against Iraq remained unsatisfied. Before the U.S.-led war against Iraq in 2003, Iraq hosted, funded, and armed an Iranian opposition group and Iran an Iraqi one. Almost two decades after the end of hostilities, the two countries still had not signed a peace treaty or settled the war's residual issues.

The Iran–Iraq War was also significant for its impact on regional military and strategic alignments and military involvement in the region by the United States. The other Persian Gulf states carefully avoided entanglement in earlier instances of tension and confrontation between Iran and Iraq. Their instinct, and preference, was to sit out the Iran–Iraq War as well. But even before the outbreak of hostilities, Iran had engaged in irresponsible rhetoric and in actions that appeared to threaten the stability and to bring into question the legitimacy of the Arab regimes of the Gulf. Once the tide of war turned in Iran's favor in 1982, the Gulf states were alarmed by the implications for themselves of an Iranian victory. At the height of Iran's military successes, Khomeini gave an indication of his future vision of the region. He predicted that after Saddam's defeat, the Iraqi people "will set up their own government according to their wishes—an Islamic one. If Iran and Iraq merge and be amalgamated, all the smaller nations of the region will join them."[25] The prospect of a merger of Iran and Iraq, with the small states of the Gulf being drawn into the union was hardly a reassuring one.

Saddam played skillfully on the fears of the Gulf states, on what he described as the requirements of Arab solidarity, and on his claim that Iraq was the "shield" protecting all Persian Gulf states from Iran's hegemonic ambitions. However reluctantly, the Arab states of the Gulf collectively ended up providing Iraq with financial assistance estimated at $35 to $50 billion, selling oil on Iraq's behalf, and providing port and overland facilities for goods bound for Iraq. Iraq's capacity to export oil was considerably enlarged by a major new pipeline through Saudi Arabia.[26] The Gulf states, particularly Saudi Arabia and Kuwait, became, in effect, supporters and financiers of Iraq's war effort. When Iraq expanded attacks on Iranian offshore oil facilities and on Iranian oil shipping in 1987, Iran retaliated by attacks on Kuwaiti and, to a lesser extent, Saudi shipping. It hoped to persuade them to desist from their assistance to Iraq's war effort.

These attacks, in turn, led Kuwait to ask Moscow and Washington to allow Kuwait's ships to sail under the Soviet and American flags. The United States, concerned about the consequences for its allies and regional stability of an Iranian victory, had already begun quietly to assist the Iraqi war effort with credits, supplies of military and other goods, and intelligence on planned Iranian offensives and the positioning of Iranian troops. It responded to the Kuwaiti reflagging request with alacrity. The reflagging proved to be the beginning of a process (greatly accelerated by the Iraqi invasion of Kuwait in 1990) by which the American military presence in the Persian Gulf region dramatically increased.

Conclusion

Relations between Tehran and Baghdad since Iraq achieved independence have displayed certain consistent features. The period of meaningful security cooperation during the Baghdad Pact proved short-lived. It derived from the conjunction of similar monarchic regimes, a common perception of threat from the Soviet Union and internal opponents, and a shared dependence on the West for military support and security. That cooperation ended with the Iraqi revolution of 1958, which changed the nature of the Iraqi regime and its foreign policy orientation, exacerbating differences between the two countries. The period of cautious peaceful coexistence launched by the Algiers Agreement of 1975 ended abruptly with the Iranian revolution four years later.

Sources of friction have been more persistent. The border dispute over the Shatt al-Arab has proven stubbornly resistant to settlement, fed by national pride, Iran's demand for equal sovereignty over the waterway, and Iraq's perennial sense of vulnerability due to its narrow access to the Persian Gulf. The 1975 Algiers Agreement appeared at the time a pragmatic solution for both sides of this decades-old dispute. But in retrospect it is clear that Saddam Hussein, the Iraqi signatory to the treaty, was merely waiting for an opportunity to undo it. Iraq has tended to view its large and often discontented Shi'i community, traditionally under-represented in government, business and the professions, as a security issue that Iran has sought to exploit. Support by Iran for Iraq's rebellious Kurds has been another persistent feature of the relationship. (Iran's "Kurdish problem" was far less severe than Iraq's, providing Iraq with fewer opportunities to retaliate.)

A number of factors, as we have seen, have made more difficult the management of the differences between the two countries. Regime difference, resulting from the 1958 revolution and the 1968 Baath seizure of power in Iraq, and from the Islamic revolution in Iran, tended to exacerbate relations because, in addition to more aggressive policies that characterized new, revolutionary regimes, the very nature of one regime was seen to be a threat to the other. Rising oil revenues, prospering economies and more stable governments in both Iran and Iraq in the late 1960s and 1970s created stronger governments. But they also provided resources—larger and better-equipped military forces, money for international largesse, firmer commitments from great power allies—for more ambitious regional goals. The shah on the whole managed his newfound military and economic clout in the Gulf with caution and a degree of success. But caution was not the hallmark of Saddam Hussein, once he rose to the top of the Iraqi heap in 1978, or of the shah's successors in Iran. The period of Saddam's ascendancy in Iraq and the early years of the Islamic Republic provide a reminder that ideology, the personality of leaders, and overweening regional ambitions in either Iran or Iraq can dangerously heighten tensions and lead to open hostilities. Full-fledged war, as noted, can in turn easily draw in other regional states, force them to take sides and make them, in effect, parties to the conflict. The financial and other resources that the Arab states of the Gulf put at Iraq's disposal helped sustain Iraq's war effort and, along with American assistance, made the difference that tilted the war in Iraq's favor.

Finally, the role the United States came to play in the Iran–Iraq conflict reflects the potential of such a conflict to draw in outside powers. The injection of significant and more permanent American forces in the Persian Gulf was subsequently made possible by the Iraqi invasion of Kuwait. But, ironically, Iran and Iraq, the two countries among the Gulf states that believed themselves best equipped to benefit from the British military withdrawal and desired most strongly to exclude American military forces from the region, played the largest role in facilitating America's military presence there. Whether, given its large military presence, the United States will replicate the role Britain once played in the Persian Gulf or manage its growing security responsibilities in a different way will become clear only with the passage of time. But it seems certain that the American presence will alter the regional balance of power and significantly affect the role of both Iraq and Iran.

Notes

1. This point is also made in Shahram Chubin and Sepehr Zabih, *The Foreign Relations of Iran* (Berkeley: University of California Press, 1974), p. 174.
2. For the text see "Treaty of Peace and Frontiers: The Ottoman Empire and Persia, 17 May 1639," document 11 in *The Middle East and North Africa in World Politics: A Documentary Record,* vol. 1, *European Expansion, 1535–1914,* 2nd ed., ed. J.C. Hurewitz (New Haven: Yale University Press, 1975), pp. 25–28.
3. For the text see "Treaty of Peace (Erzurum): The Ottoman Empire and Persia, 28 July 1823," document 61 in Ibid., pp. 219–21.
4. For the text in Persian, see Feridun Adamiyyat, *Amir Kabir va Iran,* 4th ed. (Tehran: Khwarazmi Publications, 1354/1975–76), pp. 135–38.
5. These arrangements are well described in John Marlowe, *The Persian Gulf in the Twentieth Century* (London: Cresset Press, 1962), p. 205.
6. The 1847 Iran–Iraq boundary was also confirmed by the Tehran Protocol of 1911 and the Constantinople Protocol of 1913. See R.K. Ramazani, *The Foreign Policy of Iran, 1500–1941* (Charlottesville: University Press of Virginia, 1966), p. 263.
7. For the text see "Treaty of Nonaggression (Sa'dabad Pact): Afghanistan, Iran, Iraq, and Turkey, 8 July 1937," document 118 in *The Middle East and North Africa in World Politics: A Documentary Record,* vol. 2, *British-French Supremacy, 1914–1945,* 2nd ed., ed. J.C. Hurewitz (New Haven: Yale University Press, 1979), pp. 509–10.
8. For an account of these various disputes, see Chubin and Zabih, *The Foreign Relations of Iran,* pp. 172–76; Phebe Marr, *The Modern History of Iraq,* 2nd. ed. (Boulder, Colo.: Westview Press, 2004), p. 109; and R.K. Ramazani, *Iran's Foreign Policy, 1941–1973* (Charlottesville: University Press of Virginia, 1975), pp. 401–03.
9. See also the analysis in Chubin and Zabih, *The Foreign Relations of Iran,* pp. 176–78.
10. On the 1969 dispute, see Ibid., pp. 185–87.
11. The handling of the dispute over Bahrain and the three islands is described in Ramazani, *Iran's Foreign Policy,* pp. 408–18. See also Richard Schofield, "Anything but Black and White: A Commentary on the Lower Gulf Islands Dispute," in *Security in the Persian Gulf: Origins, Obstacles, and the Search for Consensus,* ed. Lawrence G. Potter and Gary G. Sick (New York: Palgrave, 2002), pp. 171–87.
12. Ramazani, *Iran's Foreign Policy,* p. 356.
13. The details of the agreement reached in principle by the shah and Saddam Hussein at Algiers were spelled out three months later in the "Iran-Iraq Treaty on International Borders and Good Neighbourly Relations," signed by the Iranian and Iraqi foreign ministers at Baghdad on June 13, 1975. The treaty and its three protocols lay out mutual undertakings to ensure border security, define the land frontier between the two countries, define the *thalweg* as the median line in the Shatt al-Arab and outline agreed principles governing shipping in the Gulf. The text of the treaty is reproduced in Majid Khadduri, *Socialist Iraq* (Washington, D.C.: Middle East Institute, 1978), pp. 245–60.
14. On Iraq's Kurdish problem and Iran, see Marr, *The Modern History of Iraq,* pp. 104–07, 152–57; also Chubin and Zabih, *The Foreign Relations of Iran,* pp. 178–83.

15. Marr, *The Modern History of Iraq,* pp. 172–76, 182.
16. Shahram Chubin and Charles Tripp, *Iran and Iraq at War* (Boulder, Colo.: Westview, 1980), p. 3. The authors paraphrase Clausewitz to note that in unlimited wars "where the issues are not territorial and subject to negotiation, but rather the 'overthrow of the enemy,' only a complete military victory suffices to achieve the goal." Chubin and Tripp characterize Iran, much more than Iraq, as fighting a war not just for territorial gain or for limited aims, but for broad, ideologically defined concepts (such as "the defense of Islam") where nothing but total victory will suffice. They argue that Saddam Hussein went to war with more limited territorial aims that he imagined would be achieved, as had been the case in previous Iran–Iraq confrontations, once (Iraqi) military superiority was demonstrated, but that he misunderstood that he was facing a regime very different from the shah's. (Ibid., pp. 27–30). However, even if he began the war with limited aims, and reverted to them when Iraq was on the defensive, the rhetoric he and Iraqi officials and propaganda organs utilized often mirrored Iran's in describing the war as one for the very soul of Islam, Arabism and Iraqi survival, and a war between antagonistic regimes, ideologies, religious orientations, even races.
17. On Iraq and Baath nationalist myth-making, see especially the writings of Amatzia Baram, including "Mesopotamian Identity in Ba'thi Iraq," *Middle Eastern Studies*, vol. 19, no. 4 (1983); and "Culture in the Service of Wataniyya," *Asian and African Studies*, no. 17 (1983), pp. 265–313.
18. The best account of the ideological dimensions of the Iran-Iraq war, and the extensive mobilization of whole societies that it involved on both sides, is in Chubin and Tripp, *Iran and Iraq at War.*
19. See, e.g., Tariq Aziz, speech on Iran-Iraq relations, May 1980, published in *Al-Thawrah*, and reprinted in Tareq Y. Ismael, *Iraq and Iran: Roots of Conflict* (Syracuse: Syracuse University Press, 1982), pp. 89–100; and "President Hussein's Press Conference on War with Iran," November 1980 (Baghdad: Dar al-Ma'mun for Translation and Publishing, 1981).
20. Tariq Aziz, as cited in Ismael, *Iraq and Iran,* p. 91.
21. "President Hussein's Press Conference," pp. 31–32 and 46–47.
22. Ibid., p. 30.
23. Quoted in Chubin and Tripp, *Iran and Iraq at War,* p. 39.
24. All quotations from Khomeini cited in Ibid., pp. 38–39.
25. Quoted in Ibid., p. 164.
26. Ibid., p. 154.

Chapter 2

Position, Function, and Symbol:
The Shatt al-Arab Dispute in Perspective

Richard Schofield

Introduction

Even in those cases in which the existence of boundary disputes has contributed to the outbreak of conflict, there is no guarantee that unsatisfactory territorial definition will be addressed in its immediate aftermath. Iraq's turbulent recent history is a good example. No one would doubt the diligence of the UN Iraq–Kuwait Boundary Demarcation Commission (UNIKBDC), which ultimately settled the boundary question in May 1993. Yet treatment of the Iraq–Kuwait boundary in United Nations Security Council Resolution (UNSCR) 687 of April 3, 1991—which effectively set down the basis for the UNIKBDC operation—was hardly notable for its detail, far-sightedness, or sophistication. As more pressing issues of diffusing an international crisis understandably took priority, treatment of the boundary question was both obvious and minimal. Arguably, had a little more attention been devoted to the boundary in March 1991 in drafting UNSCR 687, the UN demarcation team might have been afforded more flexibility of operation, while the dynamics of regional relations in the northern Persian Gulf (hereafter abbreviated to the Gulf) might have been addressed more sensitively.

By the middle of 2004, it seemed clear that affairs will have to return to the regional arena before the status of Iraq's historically troublesome boundaries at the head of the Gulf could be considered. Many international questions arising from the U.S.-led invasion of Iraq will have to be finalized before the "new Iraq" can be reconciled to its region. Neither of Iraq's boundaries with Iran and Kuwait should present insuperable barriers to regional reconciliation, for the status and location of both lines have recently been finalized in international law.

Yet minor and not-so-minor issues remain, potentially at least. The Iraqi government had reluctantly assented to UNIKBDC's operations in the spring of 1991 and, by extension, had accepted in advance any decision they would reach on the boundary.

The blessing demanded of Iraq for the UNIKBDC ruling—not strictly necessary legally but certainly welcome symbolically—was not given until November 1994 but would at least be unequivocal when it arrived. Ironically, however, many of the exiled opposition groups opposed the border ruling vociferously. For there was a widespread, if mistaken, perception that UNIKBDC had reallocated Iraqi territory to Kuwait.

The Iran–Iraq boundary supposedly remains regulated by the elaborate package of agreements concluded between the two states in 1975. The June 1975 "Protocol concerning the delimitation of the river frontier between Iran and Iraq" remains the most sophisticated river boundary agreement signed to date in international law. Yet despite containing every conceivable safeguard against future dispute over the course and status of the boundary, the 1975 package obviously failed to forestall conflict in 1980. Having attempted to unilaterally abrogate the river boundary agreement as a prelude to prosecuting war in September 1980, the Iraqi government would suggest it was ready once again to be bound by its terms a decade later when seeking to neutralize Iran in the early days of its occupation of Kuwait. There has, however, been no formal follow-up to the Hussein–Rafsanjani correspondence in the period since.

Furthermore, the current allied occupation of Iraq has highlighted some minor ambiguities and inconsistencies in the supposedly unimpeachable 1975 boundary settlement. First, the English and French texts of the December 1975 "Protocol concerning the redemarcation of the land frontier between Iran and Iraq" that were registered with the UN secretariat in New York differ in specifying the location of seven fixed land boundary points. Second, almost thirty years have now passed since Iran and Iraq agreed to a *thalweg* boundary delimitation along the lower reaches of the Shatt al-Arab. One complication of adopting a river as a natural boundary is that, as natural fluvial features, they are subject to change. Even a cursory examination of satellite imagery will confirm that if a boat today were to navigate the *thalweg* as defined by the 1975 river boundary agreement, it would end up beached on a sand bar. Presuming therefore that Iran and Iraq formalize adherence to the 1975 boundary agreement package at some point in the next few years, one or minor two adjustments will have to be made.

Just as a change in the regional order or regional power dynamics can activate disputes, it can also provide opportunities for cooperation. While there is no denying that the northern Gulf has long been characterized by territorial instability, historically the regional states have managed to conclude a succession of boundary agreements. Much more elusive has been any real progress toward the integrated economic development of the mudflats, islands, and waterways that comprise the coastline in these parts. In fact, not since the British-controlled Basra Port Authority oversaw most aspects of economic life along the Shatt in the 1920–30s has there been any real prospect of coordinated regional development. Yet, even then, Britain could not get the signatures of Baghdad and Tehran on a succession of draft conservancy conventions. Ironically, by the early summer of 1990—just weeks before Kuwait was invaded—Iran and Iraq had made considerable progress toward clearing the Shatt al-Arab of the rusting wreckage that had blocked the river since the first days of the war in September 1980.

Regime change—whatever one thinks of the means by which it has been effected—does at least represent possibilities for more integrated regional economic development in the northern Gulf. One consequence of the UNIKBDC ruling is that the approach channels to Umm Qasr along the Khor Abdullah waterway lie in Kuwaiti territorial sea. As such, Iraq cannot maintain and dredge the navigation channels that it began to develop in the 1960s. This is a problem since virtually all channels in this region are subject to heavy siltation and sediment accumulation. There is substantial potential now for a meaningful thaw in Iraqi–Kuwaiti relations. It would not be surprising to see future cooperation actively manifest itself where Iraq most needs it—addressing the age-old question of easing access to its second dry-cargo port of Umm Qasr. What would be the price of the development of a symbolic joint Iraqi–Kuwaiti port facility at Umm Qasr and the borderlands to its immediate south?

Established Themes

Perhaps no divided international river other than the Rhine (and the associated Alsace dispute) has received so much attention in the academic literature as the Shatt al-Arab. This is no coincidence. The relatively small number of boundary rivers worldwide attests to their general inappropriateness, while the Iran–Iraq boundary has a longer treaty history than any other, with the Perso-Ottoman "Treaty of peace and demarcation of frontiers," signed at Zohab, dating back to pre-Westphalian times in 1639. To be fair, consideration of the Shatt al-Arab as a boundary did not begin in earnest until the 1840s, as Britain and Russia sought greater stability in the borderlands and the Ottoman/Persian territorial divide began to crystallize in the delta region, impinging increasingly upon the effective autonomy of the regional power-broker, the shaikh of Muhammara.

The slow transition over a 130-year period from a river boundary delimitation along the eastern bank of the Shatt to the mid-channel *thalweg* line, as well as the long history of Persian positional demands for the latter, has been the subject of several outstanding legal studies over the years. The works of Lauterpacht (1960) and Kaikobad (1988) are notable in this regard.[1]

The historically vexed process of whittling down a millennia-old political frontier zone to a single line and then of marking that limit on the ground is the subject of several historical studies; perhaps the most readable are those written by Hubbard and Ryder, two of the individuals charged with the responsibility of undertaking such a task in 1913–14.[2] Adjusting to the very presence of a fixed international boundary has been problematic for many sections of the borderland population, historically and contemporaneously.

Naturally enough, political dispute and, more recently, actual conflict between Iran and Iraq have provoked examinations by historians, political geographers, and political scientists of the role played in them by the Shatt dispute.[3] Many subscribe to the view that dispute over the river has been symbolic of established national and regional rivalries, rather than aimed at any intrinsic dissatisfaction with the river boundary itself.[4] Moreover, in launching the 1980–88 Iran–Iraq War, President Saddam Hussein certainly invoked territorial symbols as a strategy for mobilizing support domestically.[5]

One cannot, of course, view the Shatt al-Arab boundary in isolation from Iraq's land boundary with Kuwait, lying a short distance to the southwest. For there is a triangular relationship evident in the conduct of Iraq's boundary disputes in the northern Gulf whereby the status of one affects the other. Historically, whenever Iran has held the upper hand in the Shatt dispute, Iraq has looked southward toward Kuwait to improve its access to Gulf waters. This pattern was certainly discernible in the late 1930s and late 1960s and was possibly a factor in 1990 also.[6]

Very much connected to the linkage issue is the degree to which the economic development of the Shatt al-Arab historically was affected by the dispute over the river's status.[7] There seems to be some grounds for suggesting that the dispute did not seriously hinder development. Arguments were forwarded by Iraq and, more specifically, the Basra Port Authority, in the late 1930s that since the Shatt al-Arab's river traffic levels were already approaching the saturation point, alternative facilities ought to be developed on leased land along the shoreline of Kuwait Bay or at Umm Qasr further north. Yet they had clearly been exaggerated. Port facilities and functions would ultimately move out of the river to a large degree during the 1960s to locations further south in the Gulf, although this had less to do with the existence of the Shatt dispute than the substantial increase in size and draught of vessels navigating the waterway. The Iranian navy vacated Khorramshahr but more significant still was the relocation of oil export facilities from Abadan to Kharg island in Gulf waters proper.

Finally, a number of articles have examined how treaties propose to deal with the prospect of physical change in international boundary rivers, adopting the Shatt al-Arab as their centerpiece.[8]

Many of these issues and themes are reflected upon at greater length in the following summary of the Shatt dispute. The chief purpose of this chronological review is to characterize precisely the changing territorial definition of the river boundary over time.

"A Phenomenon of Procrastination"

The chronicler of the four-party demarcation of the Perso-Ottoman boundary in 1913–14 characterized attempts to settle this territorial dispute during the previous seven decades as "a phenomenon of procrastination unparalleled even in the chronicles of Oriental diplomacy."[9] Certainly it had been a confused and confusing episode.

The second Treaty of Erzurum, signed on May 31, 1847 by the Persian and Ottoman governments (as well as the mediating powers of Britain and Russia), had first specified the Shatt as a boundary river. Or had it? For the treaty made no mention of control of the river itself, merely control of the land to its immediate east. The second of the treaty's nine articles dealt with territorial definition in the Shatt region as follows:

> And the State of Turkey also firmly undertakes that the town and seaport of Mohammerah, and the island El Khizr, and the anchorage place, and also the lands of the eastern bank, i.e., of the left side of the Shatt-el-Arab, which are in the possession

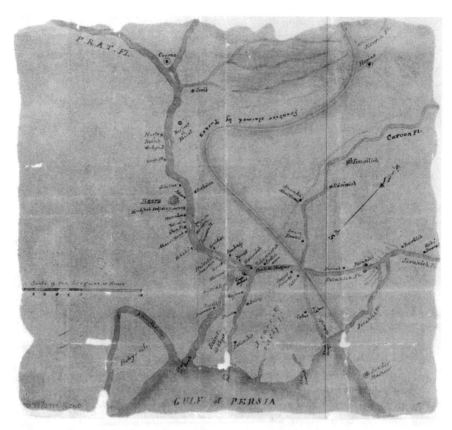

Map 2.1 Original sketch of deltaic borderlands claimed in 1846 by the Ottoman Empire in the area between Qurnah, Hawizeh, Bandar Mashur, and Bubiyan island. Enclosed within Mr. Wellesley's despatch of November 3, 1846 (originally included in FO *78/2715*, National Archives, Kew).

Reprinted from *The Iran–Iraq Border, 1840–1958*, Richard Schofield, ed. [1989] Archive Editions, Farnham Common, Volume 10, map M160.04.

of tribes acknowledgedly attached (subjected) to Persia, shall be in possession of the State of Persia, in full sovereignty. And besides this, Persian ships shall have the right to navigate the said river in full liberty, from the place where it flows into the sea, as far as the point of junction of the frontiers of the two parties.[10]

Even arriving at such a vague territorial definition had been troublesome. The Ottomans had only agreed to the above insofar as it would not "affect the Porte's right of property to the river, the course of which was still to belong wholly and exclusively to the Porte, which only granted freedom of passage to Persian vessels."[11] That the text of the Erzurum treaty would not be signed until mid-1847 was due to Ottoman nervousness about what they might be giving away (see map 2.1). Doubts would only be formally assuaged by the issue of a joint Anglo-Russian explanatory note in April 1847, stipulating that "in ceding to Persia the city, port and anchorage of Muhammara and the island of Khizr, the Sublime Porte was not ceding any other parts there may be in this region."[12]

In order to get Persia's agreement to Article 2 of the Erzurum treaty, Britain and Russia had kept quiet about the issue of this explanatory note. Yet it would be attached to the treaty when the question of ratification came up in Constantinople and Tehran. Ultimately, exchange of ratifications would take place in March 1848 and the stage was supposedly set for the enactment of stipulations set down in Article 3 of the May 1847 treaty: the appointment of a four-power boundary commission whose task was to determine conclusively the precise delimitation of the Perso-Ottoman boundary and then mark it out on the ground.

After innumerable delays, the commission set about their business during January 1850 in Muhammara. It soon became clear that the mediating commissioners would have to restrain their ambitions since both the Ottoman and Persian commissioners would play on the vagueness of Article 2 of the 1847 treaty to advance new, rather fanciful claims.[13] The Ottoman commissioner would recognize Muhammara and Abadan island to its south (referred to as Khizr at this stage) only as Persian exclaves surrounded by Ottoman territory to the north and east. Persia responded to such exorbitance by drawing a midstream boundary along the Shatt almost all of the way up to Qurnah, the confluence of the Tigris and Euphrates rivers. The response of the mediating powers would be for Colonel Williams, Britain's representative on the commission, to sketch out a line that reflected as accurately as possible the delimitation that had been introduced by Article 2 of the 1847 treaty (see map 2.2). This ran along the east bank of the Shatt, from its junction with the Jideyeh canal in the north to Gulf waters in the south.[14]

It would take until the end of the following year for the Ottoman and Persian governments to finally agree to respect the Williams line—though only temporarily, on a *status quo* basis. Before this time, the Ottomans had categorically rejected it while the Persians had asked for a precise modification to reflect practical realities on the ground. Tehran would apparently soon drop its insistence on a midstream boundary along the Shatt but would hold out for a delimitation that left the Persian bank at a point six and a half kilometres further upstream than had Williams's proposal—so as to leave tribesmen loyal to the Shaikh of Muhammara within Persian territory. When Britain countered that such an alteration might present a strategic threat to Basra, Persia insisted that the population concerned be transferred across the Williams line into Persian territory.[15]

On the face of it, there would seem little doubt about the delimitation that Britain (with Russia) had intended to introduce with the 1847 treaty, and the February 1850 Williams line reflected it accurately enough. Yet Lord Palmerston's comments of the time (see below) suggested that the whole business had been contentious, while the British government's conduct a half-century later suggested that confusion reigned over what Erzurum had ultimately introduced. For shortly before the treaty was signed, then-foreign secretary, Palmerston, would bemoan the issue of yet more explanatory assurances to the Ottoman government.

I have to state to you with reference to the pretension which has been advanced by the Porte to an absolute right of sovereignty over the Chat-el-Arab, that when the opposite

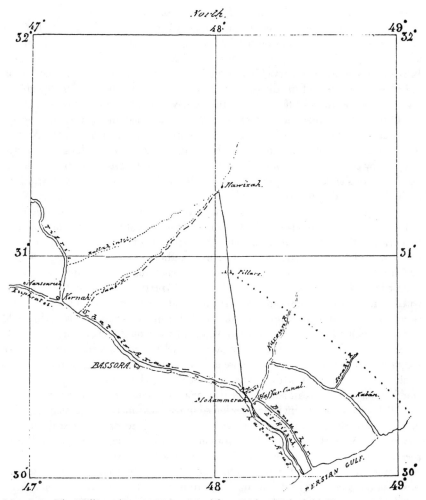

Map 2.2   The Williams line, 1850 (reprinted from Richard Schofield, "Interpreting a Vague River Boundary Delimitation . . ." in *The Boundaries of Modern Iran*, Keith McLachlan, ed., UCL Press, London, p. 81).

Note: This copy of an original hand-drawn map shows (as an unbroken line) Colonel Williams' award of February 1850. The dashed pencil line has been added to illustrate the Persian Commissioner's claim of January 1850. The dotted pencil line has been added to illustrate the Ottoman Commissioner's claim of January 1850 (originally included in FO *78/2719*, National Archives, Kew).

banks of a river belong as they will do in the case of the lower portion of Chat-el-Arab, to different Powers, it would be contrary to international usage to give to one of the two powers the exclusive sovereignty of that portion of the course of such River, and that therefore this proposal of the Turkish Government's seems to be inadmissible.[16]

The distinct lack of clarity of the Erzurum treaty's second article would be manipulated not only by the Ottoman and Persian governments in the years following that instrument's signature. Both Iran and Iraq would continue to maintain diametrically opposed interpretations of the article's reference to "free navigation rights" for Persian vessels, especially during the 1920s and 1930s but even sporadically thereafter. Most notably, in early 1935 during the League of Nations' treatment of the Perso-Iraqi dispute in Geneva, Iran argued that the reference to "free navigation rights" had the effect of dividing the river on an equal basis between the neighboring empires. Specifically, the clause relating to navigation "without let or hindrance" would be interpreted as indicating that both riparians had an equal right of sovereignty as far as the middle of the river.[17] Of course, the counter to this was perhaps the more logical interpretation of the phrase in question and one long maintained officially by Britain, the Ottoman Empire, and Iraq. For had sovereignty intended to be divided or shared, there would have been no need to single out Persian vessels in a stipulation relating to free passage.[18]

Nothing less than a full debate over the boundary in the Shatt al-Arab region was indulged in between officials of the British government and its Mesopotamian representatives in the early twentieth century. A sharp deterioration in relations between the Shaikh of Muhammara and the Ottoman authorities in Basra during 1907–08 had effectively reactivated this old concern. Yet, when the Foreign Office responded almost immediately with a statement that "His Majesty's Government are not prepared to recognise any other frontier than that laid down by the mediating commissioners in 1850 (the Williams line, that is)," the matter seemed closed.[19] Arnold Wilson, Britain's local representative in Muhammara, would however argue strongly for a revision of the Williams line just over a year later. For he had observed a local reality that rendered the 1850 line more or less obsolete. The boundary as locally recognized in 1909 ran down the center and not the east bank of the Shatt, while the land boundary left the east bank of the river at a point some 10 km. further upstream from the point indicated by the mediating commissioners in 1850 (see map 2.3).[20] In order to perpetuate the local *status quo* in a region where Britain's fast-developing commercial interests were now commensurate with its long-established political leverage, Wilson recommended that Britain distance itself from the Williams line. For a start, strict adherence to the 1850 ruling would throw the palace, courthouse, and prison of the Shaikh of Muhammara into Ottoman territory. This was an individual who had traditionally enjoyed both considerable autonomy from the Persian government and considerable support from the (British) Government of India.

Wilson was also, of course, acknowledging Britain's magnified interest in the territories subject to the shaikh's control. The Knox D'Arcy venture had discovered oil in commercial quantities near Masjid-i Sulaiman in 1908 and it was soon apparent that Muhammara's existing landing facilities on both banks of the Karun between the river's junction with the Shatt and Muhammara town proper further east were woefully inadequate for the large increase in river traffic anticipated following the oil find.[21] Only new, modern landing facilities on the Shatt al-Arab itself could accommodate the large ocean-going steamers that were required to import bulky drilling equipment for the nascent oil industry in southwest Persia. There was already a midstream anchorage of limited capacity in the Shatt that extended 4,000 meters upstream from its junction with the Karun and 1,000 meters below. This had been used ever since the Shatt had been opened to steamship navigation thirty or so years

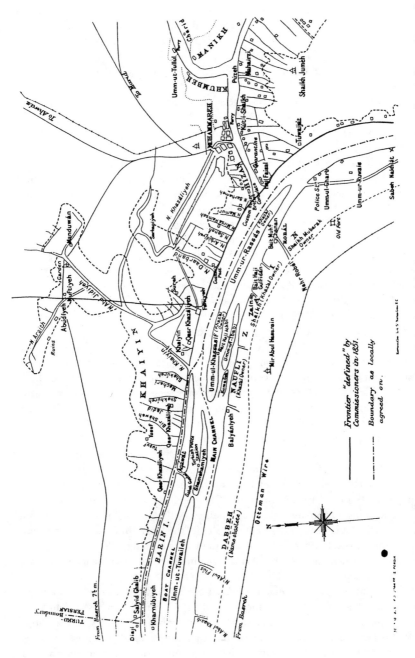

Map 2.3 The locally recognized boundary, 1909 (reprinted from Richard Schofield, "Interpreting a Vague River Boundary Delimitation . . ." in *The Boundaries of Modern Iran*, Keith McLachlan, ed., UCL Press, London, p. 84).

Note: The map shows the frontier as locally observed by Lieutenant Wilson in 1909 after the Williams line of February 1850 (originally included in FO 371/948).

earlier.[22] Its development and use did not appear to have resurrected the Shatt dispute—even though the facility lay clearly within Ottoman waters, if the Williams line was taken as the operative boundary. While there are no indications that the midstream anchorage was regarded locally as exclusively Persian, it must be presumed that most of the contacts with the facility were maintained from Muhammara. Almost certainly it was this reality that persuaded locals the boundary must lie along the midstream of the Shatt.[23]

In any event, the existing anchorage within Shatt waters was never going to provide the extended facilities now needed to handle development of oil further east. Sir Percy Cox, Britain's Political Resident in the Persian Gulf, argued in 1912 that with the projected incorporation of Muhammara into the Persian railroad system, the transfer of landing wharves from the Karun to the east bank of the Shatt was not just desirable but inevitable. Adoption of the locally recognized boundary in these parts would, of course, place not just the midstream anchorage but all of the shore-line of the Shatt at Muhammara within Persian waters.[24]

So, while the Government of India argued strongly for the adoption of the locally recognized line, the Foreign Office attempted to fudge the issue in a way that categorically refuted neither this nor the 1850 Williams line—maintaining nonetheless that the latter must be retained as the basis of all discussion on the subject. A detailed Foreign Office review of April 1912 expressed support for extending the river boundary along the locally recognized line to include the Shaikh of Muhammara's palace, courthouse, and prison. Yet it also concluded that adoption of the locally recognized midstream boundary would expressly contravene Article 2 of the Erzurum treaty. Somewhat puzzlingly (in light of the above discussion)—it declared that "British interests have nothing to gain from pressing the argument *medium filum aquae*."[25] The stance on the Williams line continued to exasperate the Government of India and India Office (their representatives in Whitehall), who were not slow to point out that the Ottoman authorities at Basra had effectively acquiesced to a midstream Shatt boundary in practice, whatever the Erzurum treaty and the Williams line had specified and however intransigent Constantinople had been in the years following the conclusion of the 1847 treaty. As the India Office had argued in June 1911, ". . . . they have allowed a situation to grow for sixty years in which the mid-channel has, without challenge, been accepted by local usage."[26] As interdepartmental battle was increasingly joined in the spring of 1912, Cox too would reinforce the arguments concerning Ottoman acquiescence, albeit with evidence that related to the point at which the land boundary left the Shatt: "the local Turkish authorities have accorded unequivocal and repeated recognition of the present (locally recognized) boundary by the erection of marks and the maintenance for many years of a permanent frontier customs post at Diaji."[27]

So it was left to Britain's foreign secretary, Sir Edward Grey, to come up with a balancing act. The scheme he advanced in July 1912 would survive unchanged to constitute the delimitation introduced by the November 17, 1913 Constantinople Protocol (see map 2.4). Unsurprisingly, the Shatt al-Arab boundary was extended ten and a half kilometres upstream from Failieh (terminus of the river boundary according to the Williams line) to coincide with the locally observed *de facto* line. This was more or less the modification to the Williams line argued for by Persia back in

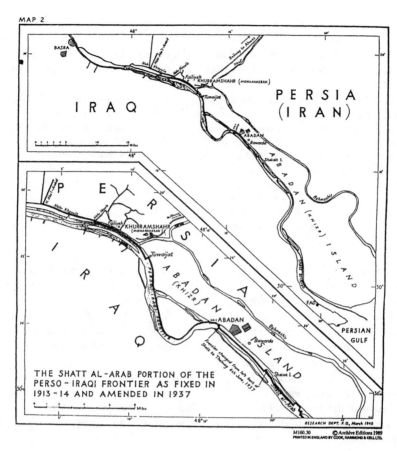

Map 2.4   The Shatt al-Arab portion of the Iran–Iraq frontier as fixed in 1913–14 and amended in 1937, Research department, Foreign office, June 1945 (originally included in *L/P & S/12/1201*, Oriental and India Office Collections, The British Library, London). Reprinted from *The Iran–Iraq Border, 1840–1958*, Richard Schofield, ed. (1989) Archive Editions, Farnham Common, Volume 11, map M160.30.

1850–51 and had more recently been urged by both the Government of India and the British Home Government. Grey seemed to accept that the major Foreign Office review of the Muhammara boundary question in 1912 had seriously underestimated the commercial incentives for adopting a mid-channel boundary alongside the port. The boundary delimitation thus was extended to the median line of the river opposite Muhammara, so that Persia might possess unimpeded control over both the existing anchorage and the envisaged landing facilities within and along the Shatt al-Arab. Persian jurisdiction would also be gained over the Karun bar—already identified as a feature that would need more or less constant dredging—while, further south, islands/mud flats in the Shatt that were attached to Abadan (Khizr) island at low tide were transferred to Persian sovereignty.[28]

Grey's proposal seemed a predictable enough compromise in the context of what was desirable for Britain and what it was likely to broker successfully in Perso-Ottoman negotiations over the course of the whole border, from the Gulf in the south to Mount Ararat in the north. He justified the arrangement in the following terms:

> [HMG] prefer to look at the negotiations in which they are now engaged as a whole, and are sincerely anxious to arrive at an arrangement which both parties can accept ex animo, and which, by removing all parts of grievance and friction not only between themselves, but also between the Sublime Porte and the Sheikh of Mohammerah, will place the relations of all concerned on a thoroughly satisfactory footing. Provided therefore that the Turkish Government will accept the frontier *status quo* from the neighbourhood of Hawizeh to the point where the Khaiyin Canal and the Nahr Nazaileh enter the Shatt al-Arab, then His Majesty's Government are prepared to use their influence with the Persian Government and the Shaikh of Mohammerah to induce them to recognise Turkish sovereignty over the whole waterway of the Shatt al-Arab [subject to the exceptions mentioned earlier].[29]

Certainly, the British foreign secretary was not blind to the manipulative worth of the compromise. In dealing with Constantinople, Britain could point to the locally recognized boundary along the Shatt's mid-channel (and informal Ottoman acquiescence to this reality) so as to underline the generosity of any deal whereby Ottoman sovereignty was confirmed over the river. Conversely, in dealing with Tehran, it would be argued that the projected territorial arrangements for Muhammara were valuable gains.

If the contextual justification for Grey's compromise seemed fair enough, its historical/legal basis seemed distinctly confused, at least in Grey's mind. It will be recalled that the Foreign Office had concluded that recognition of a midstream boundary in the Shatt would contravene Article 2 of the 1847 treaty. Yet Grey would now comment that:

> [I]f, therefore, His Majesty's Government had strict regard either to purely local considerations or to the letter of the treaties they would not hesitate to press for the frontier as locally recognised along its whole length from Hawizeh to the Persian Gulf.[30]

The whole business of establishing a boundary along the Shatt al-Arab during the mid-nineteenth century had been confused and confusing—hence the concentration in this overview. Yet it had not been that confusing. It seems likely that Grey had lost track of the detail and had made a simple error. Either that or the Foreign Office quickly recovered confidence in the effect of the 1847 treaty. For only 18 months later, the Persian government was informed by the British government that the Erzurum treaty with its explanatory notes had established Ottoman sovereignty over the river.[31] The need to issue such clarification had come about when Tehran complained that instructions to ensure that its "well-established sovereign rights on the Shatt al-Arab" did not arrive in Constantinople in time for the signature of the protocol in November 1913. Rejecting the proposition out of hand, the Foreign Office countered that Persian rights of sovereignty over the river were non-existent, as evidenced by Article 2 of the Erzurum treaty and Tehran's acceptance of the

Williams line of 1850.[32] Further damaging the Persian argument had been its unequivocal acceptance in August 1912 of the explanatory notes of April 1847 and March 1848 issued by Britain and Russia to the Ottoman government.[33]

The Constantinople Protocol specified the following as far as boundary arrangements in the Shatt region were concerned:

> From this point (the mouth of the Nahr-Nazaileh) the frontier shall follow the course of the Shatt-al-Arab as far as the sea, leaving under Ottoman sovereignty the river and all the islands therein, subject to the following conditions and exceptions:
>
> a) The following shall belong to Persia: 1) the island of Muhalla and the two islands situated between the latter and the left bank of the Shatt-al-Arab (Persian bank of Abadan): 2) the four islands between Shetait and Maawiyeh and the two islands opposite Mankuhi which are both dependencies of the island of Abadan; 3) any small islands now existing or that may be formed which are connected at low water with the island of Abadan or with Persian *terra firma* below Nahr-Nazaileh.
> b) The modern port and anchorage of Muhammara, above and below the junction of the river Karun with the Shatt-al-Arab, shall remain within Persian jurisdiction in conformity with the Treaty of Erzerum: the Ottoman right of usage of this part of the river shall not, however, be affected thereby, nor shall Persian jurisdiction extend to the parts of the river outside the anchorage.[34]

Yet even this was hardly unequivocal as far as specification of the river boundary delimitation in the vicinity of Muhammara was concerned. Paragraph b still seems a little confusing. For it implies that the port's midstream anchorage within the Shatt would remain under Persian control in conformity with the 1847 treaty. Yet the 1850 Williams line had been drawn along the eastern bank of the river at Muhammara, which ostensibly placed the facility within Ottoman waters. It would be left to the four-power Turco-Persian Boundary Commission, appointed by Section 2 of the Constantinople Protocol,[35] to put the matter to rest in 1914 (see below).

Practicalities: Oil and Access

Never again would the actual river boundary delimitation be the subject of such utter confusion. For almost the next half-century, further dispute over the Shatt al-Arab would be dominated by the functional considerations of oil development and navigation, and increasingly of access and communications. This tendency would be even more pronounced once Iraq became aware of its position as geographically disadvantaged following its admission to the League of Nations as an independent state in October 1932.

Crucial to the conclusion of the 1913 boundary settlement had been the fact that Britain and Russia were now arbitrating powers, rather than mediators as previously.[36] In this respect, Lord Palmerston's pragmatic assessment of October 1851 seemed particularly prophetic: "the boundary between Turkey and Persia can never be finally settled except by an arbitrary decision on the part of Great Britain and Russia."[37]

Following early sessions in January 1914, the official minutes (*procès verbaux*) of the Turco-Persian Boundary Commission finally provided clarification of the Muhammara (Khorramshahr) delimitation:

> . . . having followed the outline of Mohallah following always the low water mark, it reaches the point where the port and anchorage of Muhammarah begins. This point, actually known under the name of Touweidjat is situated at a distance of 4650 English feet from the outermost point of the left bank of the Karun near its juncture with the Shatt al-Arab. At Touweidjat the frontier line is transferred to the *medium filum aquae* of the Shatt, which it follows passing between the Persian shore and the island having the name of Umm al Rassas in its eastern portion and of Umm al Khassasif in its western portion.[38]

So, except for the short stretch along the median line alongside Khorramshahr (Muhammara), the Shatt al-Arab remained an Ottoman river and would become an Iraqi one when the British mandate was established over the new Mesopotamian state territory in 1920. In the years after the Great War, a number of factors would combine to produce increasing levels of Persian frustration with this state of affairs. First, the port of Basra declaration would be issued on November 8, 1919 by the occupying British military administration in Mesopotamia to formally safeguard Britain's commercial interests in the region. It held that the port of Basra extended 90 miles upstream from the mouth of the Shatt and that its authority extended over the entire river for this distance, including not only anchorage facilities at Abadan (home to the world's largest oil refinery) but also Khorramshahr, seemingly irrespective of the boundary adjustment of 1913–14. The Basra Port Directorate (later to become Basra Port Authority) had been set up in light of the declaration to administer the river.[39]

Second, the Persian state would soon bring to an end the semiautonomous rule of the Shaikh of Muhammara in the lands east of the river, thereby completing a process of imposing itself more directly along the northern Gulf shoreline that had begun during the previous century. This followed shortly after the Pahlavi dynasty's accession to power through the *coup d'état* of Reza Shah on February 21, 1921. Though Britain would continue to issue hedged promises to protect its old ally, the Shaikh of Muhammara , the writing was on the wall. As Ismael attests: ". . . this policy had become dysfunctional to British interests in Arabistan. Oil had made this a most strategic location to the British and a most valuable possession for Tehran, at the same time as Arab nationalism was developing among Arabistan's tribes. This emerging consciousness augured ill for Persian and British interests in Arabistan. Hence the British withdrew their support of Arabistan's autonomy."[40]

Third, following the Versailles peace treaties of 1919, it would be considered customary in international law for boundaries along navigable (as opposed to non-navigable) rivers to follow a *thalweg* delimitation.[41] The distinction had really arrived too late with many river boundaries adopted and defined rather carelessly during the main colonial boundary-drawing period over the previous half-century, including the Shatt during 1913–14. In any case, the logic of adopting a *thalweg* delimitation for navigable boundary rivers was sound enough. In theory, both states could thereby access the channel most suitable for navigation on an equal basis. A *thalweg* boundary therefore usually follows the main channel of a navigable river. Since such a feature does not necessarily follow the midstream of the river, the adoption of a median line boundary may leave the navigable channel wholly within the waters of one state.

It would soon become clear that reconciling itself to the possession of no legal rights in the Shatt al-Arab (save for the Khorramshahr adjustment) was a problem for Persia. Unlike in 1847, there had been no provision for Persian freedom of navigation in the 1913 settlement. As mentioned, the Basra Port Directorate controlled not only the port of Basra and its ancilliary activities but also all aspects of pilotage, navigation, and policing within all river waters south of the port, including the approaches to Khorramshahr and Abadan.[42] Until Iraqi independence, the directorate was financially independent of the Baghdad government and collected revenues from all shipping in the waterway. Here lay the crux of Tehran's frustration. For at any one time an estimated 80 percent of shipping entering the Shatt was bound for one of the Persian ports.[43]

By 1928, the basic Persian positional demand for a *thalweg* river boundary delimitation (which would ultimately only be satisfied with the 1975 package agreement) had crystallized. What was more, the balance of power politically across the Shatt had shifted from the mid-nineteenth century and Reza Shah seemed only too aware of this. As Britain's ambassador in Tehran reported in March 1929: "Persia feels that times have changed sufficiently since [the] Treaty of Erzeroum to justify her in wishing for equal rights in the river with Iraq whom we have made the inheritor of ancient Turkish privileges and who, without our aid, could not maintain them."[44] The reality of control in the river was rather different in any case from the letter of the law. Increasingly since 1926, Persian police and customs patrols had made their presence felt in the waterway, a move partially acquiesced in by the local Iraqi authorities.[45] Britain was naturally concerned that the developing functional and positional disputes not develop into a threat to the commercial health of the region. For over 90 percent of shipping using the river was British. While it considered that a relocation of the whole boundary to the midstream or *thalweg* would be extremely difficult legally (given the protracted treaty history of the river) and not necessarily desirable, the case for a revision alongside the Abadan oil refinery (where all ships were technically moored in Iraqi national waters) seemed unanswerable.

British interests in the river were also vulnerable on at least two fronts. First, any implied Persian threat to relocate port facilities away from the Shatt to the Khor Musa further east or to Bandar Abbas near the Strait of Hormuz would, if effected, eat massively into the revenues of the Basra Port Directorate, perhaps even rendering it unviable. Second, the uncontrolled flow of water (and suspended sediment) from the Karun represented a potential threat to the medium-term navigability of the Shatt.[46] Britain saw the need for an integrated regional conservancy scheme as every bit as important as satisfying Persia's more legitimate territorial grievances. Hence it tried to promote a package whereby the questions of Persian recognition of the state of Iraq (withheld until April 20, 1929), conservancy of the Shatt and Karun, and a rectification of the river boundary alongside Abadan would be addressed simultaneously. Specifically, administration of dredging, pilotage, lighting, and buoying and shipping control would be implemented by a tripartite Shatt al-Arab Conservancy Board. Britain would be an equal third member of the board, whose responsibilities would stretch as far upstream as the Persian city of Ahwaz on the Karun.[47] Yet, if anything, the combination of proposals for effective conservancy (even in far less ambitious form) and territorial adjustment would only complicate matters. From 1932 onwards, Iraq would admit the valid nature of Persian grievances over navigation and conservancy but not over the river delimitation itself, reiterating its rights to the whole of the Shatt. The prospects for any Iraqi flexibility here had not been helped by the public maintenance of the Persian positional demand for a *thalweg* delimitation for the entire length of the river boundary.[48] It had been this demand that would greet King Faisal's visit to Tehran during March 1932.[49]

All of this had to be viewed against the background of an increasing number of incidents on the waterway itself,[50] a situation that would prompt the Iraqi government ultimately to request the intervention in November 1934 of the Council of the League of Nations in Geneva to review the river boundary and the legal validity of its treaty history. Here familiar claims would be revisited and one or two new ones aired—most notably an Iraqi claim of equity to buttress its arguments that the *status quo* should persist. This held that while Persia possessed a long coastline with many ports and anchorages, Iraq remained dependent upon the Shatt as its only means of access to the sea and the only outlet for Basra, its principal dry-cargo port.[51] Persia's refusal to allow the case to proceed beyond council debate in Geneva to judicial settlement at the Permanent International Court of Justice in The Hague persuaded the two sides to adjourn the case within six months. Although the appointed rapporteur to the case, Baron Aloisi, thereby never had the opportunity to formally place his recommendations for settling the dispute on the table, there is little doubt about what they would have been: a rectification of the boundary alongside Abadan and the establishment of a conservancy board to oversee navigation in Shatt waters, essentially a trimmed-down version of recent British proposals.[52]

Though Iraq was an independent state since October 1932, its stance toward the river boundary and other regional disputes would continue to reflect British desiderata, for the former colonial power continued to exercise considerable leverage over the formulation of Iraqi policy, especially with respect to the Shatt.[53] Additionally, getting Iran (as Persia was renamed in 1935) to subordinate its wider positional claim to *thalweg* delimitation along the entire Shatt boundary to the shorter-term interest of gaining a satisfactory territorial arrangement at Abadan had to be counted as a triumph of British interests when this eventually transpired in July 1937. For it was largely British interests that had stood to benefit whereas Iran would privately regret its conduct in concluding the 1937 Tehran treaty (and thereby contradicting its basic positional demand) on many occasions before abrogating that treaty in 1969. Agreement in principle to modify the boundary at Abadan had essentially crystallized once proposed by Iraq in January 1936, though at this stage all that was contemplated was placing the actual anchorage facilities there under Iranian sovereignty. Iran countered with a proposal that the river boundary run along the *thalweg* for a stretch of 12 miles above, alongside and below Abadan and thereafter along the median line of the Shatt until it reached the waters of the Persian Gulf. This would occasion an Iraqi rejoinder in which Iran would be given a quarter of the width of the Shatt at Abadan, though the river boundary would follow the low water mark of the Shatt for the remainder of its course. Importantly, however, there were now clear Iraqi hints that a *thalweg* delimitation at Abadan was by no means out of the question, raising alarm bells for the British Admiralty (see below). By February 1937, agreement on such an arrangement had been reached in principle between Iran and Iraq. During the previous month Iran had vowed to respect the Constantinople Protocol of 1913 and the official demarcation minutes of 1914, subject to Iraqi agreement to shift the river delimitation to the *thalweg* for a four-mile stretch opposite Abadan. That was that as far as the extent of boundary rectification was concerned, though intensive negotiations ensued on the major navigational and conservancy issues—most notably, freedom of passage for merchant ships and warships.[54]

Boundary rectification and navigation rights in the Shatt had been the subjects of intense interdepartmental debate within the British government for much of 1936. Strategic and financial arguments were raised by the Admiralty and the Basra Port Directorate respectively against the adoption of a *thalweg* delimitation opposite Abadan, as it seemed increasingly likely that such an arrangement would be concluded between Iran and Iraq. Concerned over whether Iran would remain neutral in any future European war (as it would in World War II), the Admiralty argued that the Shatt's mid-channel must remain wholly in Iraqi waters and British warships therefore retain free access to Basra. Colonel John Ward had the likely diminution in the Basra Port Directorate's revenue uppermost in mind when arguing against the adoption of a *thalweg* line.[55] The Foreign Office was sufficiently exasperated to issue the following warning shot to the Admiralty in December 1936:

> We may, in fact, easily find ourselves in a position where the Iraqis are prepared to meet the Persian desire for a *thalweg* frontier, and where both parties will be able legitimately to represent that we alone are standing in the way of a settlement.[56]

Yet the Foreign Office ultimately called the shots. At the very least, they were advising the Iraqi negotiating team, at best directing them. They knew that a benign Iranian attitude during future wartime was most likely to be guaranteed if the Tehran government got what it wanted on the boundary and at this point in time it was not asking for much[57]—a *thalweg* line for four miles opposite Abadan. In any event, the Admiralty would ultimately be placated by the July 4, 1937 Tehran treaty's treatment of its concerns over navigation.

As far as the boundary adjustment at Abadan was concerned, Article 2 of the Tehran treaty specified the following:

> At the extreme point of the island of Shutait (being approximately latitude 30° 17' 25" North, longitude 48° 19' 28" East), the frontier shall run perpendicularly from low water mark to the *thalweg* of the Shatt al-Arab, and shall follow the same as far as a point opposite the present Jetty No. 1 at Abadan (being approximately latitude 30° 20' 8.4" North, longitude 48° 16' 13" East). From this point, it shall return to low water mark, and follow the frontier line indicated in the 1914 minutes.[58]

Otherwise the delimitation would follow that elaborated in the agreed minutes of the 1914 demarcation commission. Article 4 of the Tehran treaty elaborated a new navigation regime as follows:

> The provisions hereinafter following shall apply to the Shatt al-Arab from the point at
> which the land frontier of the two States enters the said river to the high seas:
>
> a) The Shatt al-Arab shall remain open on equal terms to the trading vessels of all
>   countries. All dues levied shall be in the nature of payments for services rendered
>   and shall be devoted exclusively to the coverage in an equitable manner of the costs
>   of upkeep, maintenance of navigability or the improvement of the navigable chan-
>   nel of access to the Shatt al-Arab from the sea, or to defray expenses incurred in the
>   interest of navigation. The said dues shall be calculated on the basis of the tonnage
>   of the vessels or of their displacement or both;
>
> b) The Shatt al-Arab shall remain open for the passage of warships and other non-
>   commercial vessels of the High Contracting Parties;
>
> c) The fact that in the Shatt al-Arab the frontier line sometimes follows the low water
>   mark, and sometimes the *thalweg* or *medium filum aquae*, shall not prejudice in any
>   way the right of the High Contracting Parties to utilise the entire course of the river.[59]

The last paragraph had, of course, highlighted the complex nature of the Shatt al-Arab
river delimitation introduced by Article 2 (see map 2.5). Articles 3 and 5 had

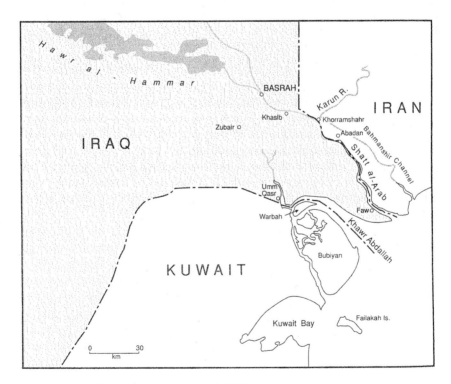

Map 2.5   Iraq's limited access to the Persian Gulf.

respectively called for the institution of a commission to demarcate the 1914 line (with the new revision concerning Abadan) and the conclusion, finally, of a bilateral conservancy convention to cover the Shatt region. The latter article read as follows:

> The two High Contracting Parties, having a common interest in the navigation of the Shatt al-Arab as defined in Article 4 of the present treaty, undertake to conclude a Convention for the maintenance and improvement of the navigable channel, and for dredging, pilotage, collection of dues, health measures, measures for preventing smuggling, and all other questions concerning navigation in the Shatt al-Arab as defined in Article 4 of the present Treaty.[60]

The treaty's six articles were given further elucidation, elaboration, and effect in an annexed protocol. Paragraph two of the protocol recognized the reality that agreement on conservancy issues was some way off but provided for such a contingency in a rather confused and unhelpful manner that would directly lead to problems in the early 1960s.

> The High Contracting Parties undertake to conclude the Convention to which Article Five of the treaty relates within one year from the entry into force of the treaty.
>
> In the event of the said Convention not being concluded within the year despite their utmost efforts, the said time-limit may be extended by the High Contracting Parties by common accord.
>
> The Imperial Government of Iran agrees that, during the period of one year to which the first paragraph of the present Article relates or the extension (if any) of such period, the Royal Government of Iraq shall be responsible as at present for all questions to be settled under the said Convention. The Royal Government of Iraq shall notify the Imperial Government of Iran every six months as to the works executed, dues collected, expenditure incurred or any other measures undertaken.[61]

In truth, it was realized that there was little chance of any conservancy convention being signed: "(i)t had become evident that the ratification and entry into force of the Treaty would leave no chance of agreement being reached over a Conservancy Convention within the stipulated year, since the Persians would not (unless they underwent a change of heart) agree to a Convention providing for British participation in the work of conservancy, etc., while the Iraqis, backed by His Majesty's Government, would not accept a Convention which did not provide for British participation."[62] There would ultimately be no real progress on this issue, Britain effectively vetoing a promising Iranian proposal of 1949 that had been forwarded for observations by the Iraqi government. Britain had balked at a clause stating that employees of the bilateral conservancy board must be nationals of the participating countries.[63]

By presenting its equity arguments before the League of Nations in 1935, Iraq had shown itself aware of its geographically disadvantaged status, though not for the first time. Shortly before independence, at an Iraqi cabinet meeting in July 1932, Iraqi Defence Minister Ja'far al-'Askari had cautioned against confirming the vague, existing boundary delimitation with Kuwait on strategic grounds. He ventured that Iraq might even consider claiming the Kuwaiti islands of Warba and Bubiyan on the geological basis that these mud flats had been created by the transport of sedimentary deposits over hundreds of years down the great Mesopotamian rivers.[64] During 1938 Iraq's first effective proposals to alleviate the access problem inevitably linked the status of its land boundaries at the head of the Gulf with Iran and Kuwait. The Iraqi Foreign Ministry had set the ball rolling with its intimation that it would like to possess an alternative outlet to the Gulf other than the Shatt al-Arab, preferably an Iraqi-controlled port on Kuwait Bay.[65]

The request would result in further heated exchanges between the various involved departments of the British government. Both the Admiralty and the Government of India strongly deprecated any suggestions that Iraq should be able to extend its railway system to a port in Kuwaiti territory, suggesting that such a project would inevitably lead to an unwelcome increase in Iraqi authority. Evidently not too dissatisfied with the prescriptions of the 1937 Tehran treaty, the Admiralty suggested that Britain's best interests would be served by Iraq maintaining all port facilities within the Shatt al-Arab. Meanwhile, only the Army Council and Air Ministry saw any virtue in establishing a new port facility on the shores of Kuwait Bay. Such enthusiasm was qualified, however, since the point about undue Iraqi influence had been well taken. Even so, the military could see the advantages of a British-controlled facility in Kuwait, which might be used successfully as the eastern terminus of a trans-Arabian route during wartime.[66]

It was now that Colonel John Ward—not only head of the Basra Port Directorate but also director-general of Iraqi Railways—would throw his hat into the ring. It will be recalled that Ward was not terribly happy with the Abadan amendment in the 1937 river boundary treaty. He now suggested to the Foreign Office that if an Iraqi link to Kuwait Bay was considered unpalatable, he could probably turn the attention of Baghdad to the Khor Zubair as another alternative to Basra. For a start, the Khor would be far less expensive to develop than Kuwait. Ward lent strong support to Iraq's arguments for extra port facilities, forwarding his own argument (a little disingenuously) that the capacity of the Shatt al-Arab was approaching saturation point. Though the Foreign Office were interested, it was realized that the southern approaches to the Khor ran along the Kuwaiti island of Warba and that this was far from ideal. Hence the suggestion that Iraq might obtain Warba and thereby secure complete control over the approaches by making territorial concessions to Kuwait elsewhere.[67] This was a simple enough idea that would prove tragically elusive in practice.

As promised, Ward turned the attention of the Baghdad government to the Khor Zubair. Soon afterwards Iraqi Foreign Minister Tawfiq al-Suwaidi released his famous *aide memoire* on Kuwait during late September 1938. In this the historical claim to the entirety of Kuwait would be invoked for the first time, though—somewhat contradictorily—so too would the Iraqi request that its vaguely defined land boundary with Kuwait be adjusted so as to allow unfettered development of a new port facility in the Khor Zubair.[68] Dissatisfaction with both the status and capacity of the Shatt al-Arab figured prominently in al-Suwaidi's reasoning. First, the reliability of the river was vulnerable to the longstanding dispute with Iran over its international status. Second, the waterway was becoming congested, principally because of the activities of the Anglo-Iranian Oil Company at Abadan.

Though it had only forsaken four miles of the Shatt al-Arab to the *thalweg* in the 1937 settlement, Iraq seemed to sense that it had lost more—that its access to Gulf waters was disproportionately less secure. By the end of 1938 the British government had effectively given its blessing to Iraqi efforts to negotiate an enhanced position for port development on the Khor Zubair. Yet negotiations never really got off the ground because of a change in government in Baghdad in 1939 and the steadfast determination of Kuwait not to yield any territory that had been recognized previously to belong to it. Iraq would have to wait until the 1960s to develop its port at Umm Qasr, although a transhipment facility, connected by narrow gauge railway, had been constructed there by the allied occupying powers during World War II. Ultimately, because the British government could not decide whether it lay within Iraqi or Kuwaiti territory, the facility was torn down in 1945, along with the Basra–Umm Qasr railway connection.[69] Still, Britain had expressed some sympathy for Iraq's access arguments in the post-Tehran treaty period, as this oft-quoted extract attests:

> . . . it is understandable that the State which controls the Mesopotamian plain should desire to have undivided control of at least one good means of access to the sea, and [British Foreign Secretary] Lord Halifax thinks that on a long view it is likely that, if Iraq were given this access, it would make for steadier conditions in that part of the world in years to come.[70]

Meanwhile a triangular territorial pattern had been set in motion whereby perceptions of Iranian gains along the Shatt al-Arab would persuade Baghdad to try to compensate itself in its dealings with Kuwait to the southwest.

Perhaps the nearest that Iraq and Kuwait came to genuinely settling the islands and access question was in the mid-1950s. At that time, the British government hit upon the idea of linking proposals for Iraq to pipe fresh water from the Shatt al-Arab to Kuwait for domestic consumption and for Kuwait to lease to Iraq the island of Warba and a strip of northern Kuwaiti land territory to finally allow unhindered development of Umm Qasr. In May 1955, Iraq had proposed ". . . to advance their frontier to a depth of some four kilometres, covering a desert strip, the uninhabited island of Warba and the waters of the Khor Abdullah which surround it."[71] In return Baghdad would consent to recent British proposals for demarcation of the remainder of the vaguely defined land boundary. Since Kuwait was looking at this time to the Shatt al-Arab as a large-scale source of fresh water (before it opted instead for extensive distillation) and any resultant pipelines would have to run over Iraqi territory via the Faw peninsula, Britain's representatives in both Baghdad and Kuwait suggested that both the Umm Qasr and water carrier schemes ought to be arranged on corresponding long-lease terms of 99 years. A significant breakthrough seemed to have been achieved when the Kuwaiti ruler gave his provisional approval to both schemes.[72]

Within a period of just six months, however, the linkage proposal had collapsed completely. No sooner had Kuwait given the linkage scheme its blessing than Baghdad professed no further interest in it, despite harboring no objections to the proposed lease agreements being signed separately. Evidently much more problematic would be a new element introduced by Iraqi Prime Minister Nuri al-Sa'id in October 1955, just as final drafts of the two lease agreements were being prepared. Iraq wanted to extend an export pipeline from the recently opened Zubair oilfield to Mina al-Ahmadi, Kuwait's principal oil port. By way of compensation, Said offered

Kuwait a 50 percent share in any new port that would materialize at Umm Qasr.[73] Though Britain considered that this might bring benefits to Kuwait, the goalposts had been moved while the al-Sabah were visibly weary of the pressure Britain was mounting to secure Kuwaiti agreement with Iraq on Umm Qasr port and the water carrier scheme. It was ultimately no surprise, therefore, when Kuwait decided against concluding the Shatt al-Arab water carrier scheme in January 1956. This led to an announcement from the Iraqi government a couple of months later that the time was not right for demarcation of the Iraq–Kuwait land boundary.[74]

While the British government may have understandably overrated the lease scheme's potential for success, a promising moment of opportunity had fallen by the wayside and Iraq–Kuwait relations would be described as "distinctly bad" in the last year of Hashimite rule.[75] Ironically, agreement to supply fresh water from the Shatt al-Arab to Kuwait, albeit on a much more limited basis, would be reached in the early summer of 1990. It is surprising how regularly many schemes and proposals repeat themselves in the history of Iraq's territorial disputes with both Iran and Kuwait. It suggests, of course, that they possess a strong logic. Nuri al-Saʿid's proposal for a joint port at Umm Qasr may well see the light of day as the "new Iraq" is returned to its region in the coming months and years.

National and Regional Rivalries

Hashimite rule was swept aside in a bloody Baghdad *coup d'état* of July 14, 1958 by the Free Officers Movement, headed by General ʿAbd al-Karim Qasim. The revolution would deprive Britain and the West of an important ally. Not only did the anti-Soviet Baghdad Pact now lie in ruins, but Britain had lost all of the considerable influence it had enjoyed in Iraq through the training of the Iraqi military and the placing of British personnel in key civil service positions. For example, when R.C. Kelt was dismissed as inspector-general of the Basra Port Authority in the late summer of 1958, Britain's long-established dominance over the administration of the Shatt al-Arab waterway came to an end. Soviet technicians would now be called in to continue the conservancy work previously undertaken by the predominantly British-staffed Authority.[76] Soviet influence over the Shatt region would, however, never begin to approach Britain's historically. For, more than ever before, control of the Shatt region and conduct of the associated disputes would now be the preserve of the local actors themselves.

Up to now, nationalism had played very little part in the history of the Shatt dispute, which had in many ways remained unpoliticized. Since the Great War the dispute had largely been dictated by functional concerns but the Shatt would now be adopted as a national symbol, as Qasim strove to prove his revolutionary credentials. At the rhetorical, rather than any official, legalistic level, the new Iraqi government denounced the 1937 treaty and claimed the Shatt as an Iraqi national river. Meanwhile, rather vague historical claims to Iranian Khuzistan (the location of the Shaikh of Muhammara's former territories) would be invoked in the Baghdad media.[77]

This marked the beginnings of the Iraqi nationalization of the dispute—in which even established physical facts would soon become the subject of contention. For example, the proportion of the Karun river's contribution to the Shatt's discharge into Gulf waters at Faw would now be disputed. Traditionally, it was accepted that up to two-thirds of the Shatt al-Arab's water volume south of Khorramshahr derived from the Karun. To admit as much for an Iraqi would be increasingly less acceptable politically from this time onwards; the facts were therefore revised so that an Iraqi national river was represented as containing predominantly Iraqi water.[78]

Yet the Shatt dispute also needed to be viewed within a context of developing regional rivalries, increasingly defined on an Arab-Iranian basis. For one thing, the nomenclature of the water body to the south was becoming a heavily politicized issue. The more or less wholescale adoption of the term Arabian Gulf by the shaikhdoms of the western Gulf littoral had been encouraged more by Egyptian President Nasser than Qasim but had a real nuisance value, in practice, for the conduct of day-to-day business in the ports of the Shatt region. Some (primarily western) businesses not familiar with the region would now be confused as to the correct nomenclature of the water body. For example, in August 1959 the Iranian customs authorities at Khorramshahr would refuse to unload consignments addressed to "Tehran, via Khorramshahr, Arabian Gulf."[79]

Developing national and regional rivalries left the Shatt, and its regulation under the 1937 treaty and protocol, ever more susceptible to functional disputes. The furor during 1959 over the small Iranian port of Khosrowabad was similar in character—but much smaller in scale—to the previous ones over the Muhammara anchorage before the 1913–14 settlement and the Abadan anchorage before the 1937 agreement. Clearly, the 1937 treaty and protocol had failed to clarify the issue of free navigation within the Shatt al-Arab. This small landing facility, which lay roughly halfway between Abadan and Gulf waters, had been constructed in 1937 by the Anglo-Iranian Oil Company but remained largely idle until 1959, when the Tehran government authorized the Iran Pan American Company's use of the port as a station for drilling operations. Iran issued a proclamation on June 9, 1959 announcing that Khosrowabad was administratively subordinate to the Khorramshahr Port Authority, in a similar manner to the way in which Britain had defined Faw as an outpost of Basra in the declaration it had made as occupying power some 40 years earlier. Adhering to the letter of the 1937 treaty, Iraq officially protested the Iranian move, pointing out that the international boundary in this area embraced the entire waters of the river up to the low water line of the Iranian bank.[80]

With Iran and Iraq having failed, crucially, to implement Article 5 of the 1937 treaty and actually institute a functioning Shatt al-Arab conservancy convention, the complex river boundary delimitation introduced by the treaty provided endless possibilities for disputes, both functional and symbolic. For every time Iran–Iraq relations soured—and the period between 1959 and 1971 was one in which relations were almost "uniformly poor"[81]—this reality would tend to manifest itself with incidents and mini-crises in the Shatt. On one level, failure to conclude a conservancy convention in the post-1937 period had ostensibly placed very real restrictions upon Iran. For the 1937 protocol had specified that until a convention was signed, Iraq would remain responsible for all of the concerns that would likely be regulated by such a treaty. On the other hand, there had been a one-year deadline specified for its conclusion and a stipulation that this time period could only be extended by express bilateral agreement. Neither requirement had been met, leaving a very unclear picture by the turn of the 1960s.

The effect of the Khosrowabad dispute had been the hardening of stances by both governments not just toward the question of conservancy but the river boundary delimitation itself. In December 1959, the Iraqi government upped the ante by suggesting (not terribly convincingly) that the 1937 adjustment in Iran's favor opposite Abadan had been a lease rather than a cession.

> In the past, in 1937 . . ., when the then Government of the late Bakr Sidqi . . . was in power, at that time strong pressure was exerted against the Iraqi Government, which needed funds, and neighbor Iran was granted about five kilometres of our Shatt al-Arab; this was a grant and not an agreed right.
>
> . . . The grant was given to Iran under pressure with the hope that the border problem between us and Iran might be solved. . . . These borders and these problems have not so far been solved. If they are not solved in the future, we shall be absolved from this grant and shall restore it to the motherland.[82]

In the early days of January 1960 Iran would respond with a rather equivocal demand that the river boundary be adjusted to the *thalweg* for the whole of its course.

> It is an open secret that the principles of international law and international justice and equity required that provision should have been made in the 1937 treaty for the thalweg to become the basis for determining the border of the two countries throughout the Shatt al-Arab and not only before Abadan. . . . the Iranian government does not regard any criterion or standard except the thalweg as conforming to international principles, and international justice and equity, for the determination of its boundary line in the Shatt al-Arab.[83]

While calling somewhat dispassionately for a wholesale revision to the *thalweg*, the statement also admitted the validity of the 1937 agreement, if also Iranian dissatisfaction with its shortcomings. If the two sides were now some way apart on the delimitation issue itself, it would be navigational and conservancy issues that would raise their head seriously in early 1961 with the harbor masters' dispute at Abadan. After an Iranian demand for sole, uninterrupted control of port operations at Abadan had met with Iraqi inflexibility, the Tehran government issued a ruling on February 10, 1961 by which vessels entering its waters or ports would have to be guided home by Iranian pilots. For by default, the failure of the two sides to conclude a conservancy convention following the 1937 treaty had meant that Iraq was still left in effective control of many issues relating to navigation in Iranian waters off Abadan itself. The Iranian ruling would itself be met with a Basra Port Authority strike, launched by Iraq to effect a nine-week standstill in the waterway, preventing the export of refined products from Abadan and other Iranian ports along the Shatt. On this occasion Iran backed down, agreeing to return the situation to the *status quo ante* in advance of negotiations that never in fact materialized.[84]

Iran would not, however, back down in 1969, occasioning Iraq once more to cast its gaze upon the Kuwaiti borderlands to the southwest. The Iranian government was more exasperated than ever with the continuing failure to sort out conservancy issues. In addition, Shah Mohammad Reza Pahlavi had made no secret of Iran's desire to play a more assertive role in the Gulf following the announcement in January 1968 that Britain would depart the western Gulf littoral as protecting power within four years. Against such a background, Iranian calls for a *thalweg* Shatt al-Arab delimitation had intensified during the late 1960s and matters came to a head in the spring of 1969. On April 15, 1969 the Iraqi government announced that all Iranian ships in the Shatt al-Arab would have to lower their flags, while all Iranian nationals on board ships in Iraqi waters would have to disembark. Iranian Foreign Minister Amir Khosrow Afshar responded four days later by unilaterally abrogating the 1937 Tehran treaty.[85] He argued that Iraq's consistent failure to respond to Iranian overtures for a conservancy convention had effectively rendered the whole 1937 treaty and protocol obsolete: ". . . since that (the Iraqi) Government has abrogated the essential clauses of the 1316 (1937) Treaty and further, since the efforts of the Imperial Government to cause the Iraqi Government to fulfil its obligations have come to no tangible result, the Imperial Government considers the 1316 treaty is abrogated, valueless and null in accordance with the principles of international law."[86] Placing heavy reliance on the legal principle of *rebus sic stantibus*, Iran also claimed that the special circumstances in existence when the 1937 treaty was concluded no longer applied: "When the treaty between Iran and Iraq was concluded in 1937, the position of the two parties was unequal. Iraq was the protégé of the imperialist Power dominant in the region which enabled Bagdad to press Iran into accepting the iniquitous boundary provisions of Articles I and II. The only return to be received by Iran for this, a return which was little enough, was acknowledgement of its vital interest in the navigation of the Shatt-al-Arab."[87]

Afshar's abrogation statement had left no doubt that Iran would not only claim a *thalweg* delimitation for the whole course of the Shatt boundary but would also enforce its jurisdiction within the estuary on that basis: ". . . the Imperial Government does not recognize and accept in the whole of Shat-ul-Arab any other principle but the internationally recognized one, i.e., the Talweg or median line principle, and it therefore will prevent with all its might any encroachment upon its sovereignty in Shat-ul-Arab waters and will not allow anyone to resort to aggressive action there."[88] While holding to the same line, Iran's communication to the Security Council of May 1, 1969 was considerably more conciliatory in tone: "The Government of Iran remains ready, as in the past, to settle the matter by friendly negotiations. These negotiations must be based on general practice of international law with regard to frontier rivers."[89]

With its superior air and naval forces on high alert, Iran also announced that all Iranian and Iran-bound shipping in the Shatt would now receive a military escort. Under these conditions Iraq took no action to ensure that its recently announced regulations were observed by Iranian shipping and, with the status of the Shatt more insecure than ever, Baghdad turned its gaze once more to Umm Qasr and the Khor Zubair. For during the last week of April, a high-ranking Iraqi delegation headed by its defense and interior ministers had been dispatched to Kuwait. It advised the

Kuwaiti government of an impending Iranian attack upon Iraq and appealed in the name of Arab solidarity to be allowed to station forces on both sides of the unde-marcated Kuwaiti–Iraqi land boundary to protect the recently constructed port of Umm Qasr. The Kuwaiti government claimed that by the time the request had been made, Iraqi troops had already advanced a few miles into Kuwaiti mainland territory south of the port. Since Arab opinion would demand that Kuwait give some support to a fellow Arab state under threat from Iran, the emirate claimed that it had no alternative but to tacitly acquiesce in the *fait accompli*. Once positioned, however, the Iraqi troops would not leave Kuwaiti territory until the thaw in relations between those states during 1977.[90]

By this stage, Iran and Iraq had agreed upon a *thalweg* delimitation for the whole course of their river boundary under the Algiers Accord and follow-up bilateral agree-ments of 1975 (see map 2.6). So, after 130 years of confusion and dispute, the Shatt al-Arab had evolved from being an Ottoman (Iraqi) river to being shared along the mid-channel, as was customary in international law. The longstanding Iranian positional demand had thereby been satisfied in a package agreement lauded for its sophistication and built-in safeguards against the recurrence of any disputes over the status and align-ment of the river boundary. It seemed and was too good to be true. Less than six years later, after the first few months of the 1980–88 Iran–Iraq War, the Shatt al-Arab was blocked by the wreckage of burnt-out or abandoned vessels and Iraq was effectively landlocked. As a prelude to prosecuting war, Iraqi President Saddam Hussein had uni-laterally abrogated the river boundary agreement—in fact tearing his copy of the accord to pieces before an Iraqi television audience. He had sensed, albeit incorrectly, that in the aftermath of the Islamic revolution in Iran, the balance of power across the Shatt had shifted and circumstances were ripe for the return of the river to its rightful owner. The territorial concessions of 1975 had only been made to quell the shah's support for the Kurdish rebellion in northern Iraq. Certainly, Iraq had not been convinced of the 1975 arrangements on their own merits and the whole package, regarded as the alternative to disintegration of a heterogeneous state, had only been concluded as a last resort.[91] As Saddam Hussein would reportedly comment himself in December 1979:

> . . . the signing of the 1975 accord is the only step I have ever regretted in all my polit-ical life . . . This accord was forced upon me . . . but I had no other choice . . . Due to the battle at the northern front our army was in disarray . . . I had to sign it. But at the very moment I was signing it, I was thinking of a day when I could tear it to pieces and retrieve Arab rights from the marauding Iranians.[92]

There is no more graphic illustration that the status of an international boundary is subject to fluctuations in the relationship between the states that share it. The theme of boundaries as political footballs would only be embellished two weeks into Iraq's invasion of Kuwait, when Baghdad suddenly seemed ready to recognize the validity of the 1975 package all over again (see section below).

Since the agreements of 1975 presumably regulate the Shatt al-Arab today, they are obviously worth a closer look. During an OPEC summit meeting in Algiers, Algerian President Houari Boumédienne presided over two lengthy sessions with the shah of Iran and Iraqi Vice-President Saddam Hussein, in which the following basis

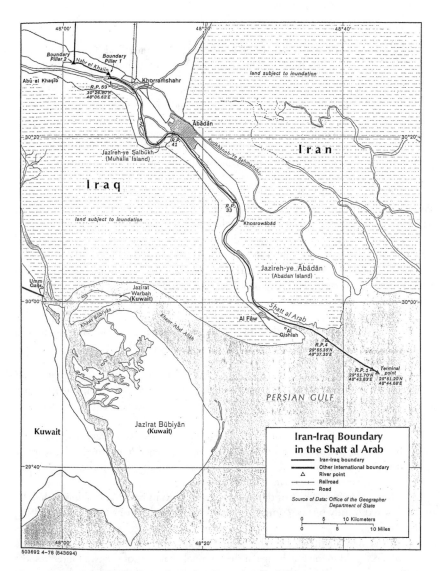

Map 2.6 Iran–Iraq boundary along the Shatt al-Arab following the agreements of 1975 (reprinted from *International Boundary* Study no. 164 [Iran–Iraq], United States Department of State, p. iii, July 13, 1978).

of an agreement was thrashed out:

> In accordance with the principles of territorial integrity, the inviolability of frontiers and non-interference in internal affairs, the High Contracting Parties took the following decisions:
>
> 1) They will proceed with the definitive demarcation of their land frontiers on the basis of the Constantinople Protocol of 1913 and the minutes of the Frontier Delimitation Committee of 1914;
> 2) They will delimit their river frontiers along the thalweg;
> 3) By so doing, they will restore mutual security and trust throughout the length of their common frontiers. They thus undertake to exercise strict and effective control over the frontiers with a view to the complete cessation of all subversive infiltration from either side;
> 4) The two Parties agreed to regard the above provisions as indivisible elements of an overall settlement and, accordingly, a breach of any of its component parts would clearly be incompatible with the spirit of the Algiers Agreement.[93]

Pursuant to the scheme agreed upon in Algiers during March, Iran and Iraq concluded a new river boundary agreement in Baghdad some three months later on June 13, 1975. In Article 1 it was declared and recognized that "the State river frontier between Iran and Iraq in the Shatt al-Arab has been delimited along the thalweg"[94] (see map 2.6). This had been calculated by a mixed Iraqi-Iranian-Algerian committee in the intervening period on the basis of surveys they had undertaken and the subsequent production of charts, upon which the river delimitation was marked. Like all good modern river boundary agreements, the *thalweg* was defined in exacting terms in Article 2 of the treaty while the contingency of physical change in the river was catered to in some depth—to a potentially ridiculous extent in paragraph 5 (emphasis added):

1. The frontier line in the Shatt al-Arab shall follow the thalweg, i.e., the median line of the main navigable channel at the lowest navigable level, starting from the point at which the land frontier between Iran and Iraq enters the Shatt al-Arab and continuing to the sea.
2. The frontier line, as defined in paragraph 1 above, shall vary with changes brought about by natural causes in the main navigable channel. The frontier line shall not be affected by other changes unless the two Contracting Parties conclude a special agreement to that effect.
3. The occurrence of any of the changes referred to in paragraph 2 above shall be attested jointly by the competent technical authorities of the two Contracting Parties.
4. Any change in the bed of the Shatt al-Arab brought about by natural causes which would involve a change in the national character of the two States' respective territory or of landed property, constructions, or technical or other installations shall not change the course of the frontier line, which shall continue to follow the thalweg in accordance with the provisions of paragraph 1 above.
5. Unless an agreement is reached between the two Contracting Parties concerning the transfer of the frontier line to the new bed, *the water shall be re-directed at the joint expense of both parties to the bed existing in 1975*—as marked on the four common charts listed in article 1, paragraph 3—should one of the Parties

so request within two years after the date on which the occurrence of the change was attested by either of the two Parties. Until such time, both Parties shall retain their previous rights of navigation and of user over the water of the new bed.[95]

Article 6 of the river boundary treaty committed the two sides to jointly survey the main river channel afresh every ten years, or even more frequently should one of the parties request as much. Such an undertaking is now desperately needed for, as mentioned at the outset, the 1975 delimitation (i.e., the median line of the *thalweg* as it existed in 1975) is now blocked by sandbars.

Article 7 spelled out the new navigation regime in which all categories of Iranian and Iraqi vessels (commercial and military) would enjoy complete freedom of navigation in any part of the Shatt al-Arab and its approaches. Trading vessels from third-party states would enjoy similar rights, unless in a state of belligerency, armed conflict, or war with either of the two signatories. Article 8, the treaty's last, stipulated that a bilateral commission should draw up rules for navigation in the river while another would be set up to prevent and control pollution—here were the spiritual successors to the elusive conservancy convention of old. Given that both states now enjoyed complete freedom of navigation in the river, the need to address conservancy issues was demonstrably less urgent than before. War would intervene before any real progress was made in any case.[96]

This chapter is not concerned with identifying the causes of the 1980–88 Iran–Iraq War,[97] though it was clear by the end of the 1970s, following the Islamic Revolution of 1978/79, that Iraq was unhappy with both the existing territorial arrangements and Iranian compliance with the package of agreements that had introduced them. True, the two sides had re-demarcated their land boundary before this time in compliance with another bilateral treaty concluded in pursuance of the Algiers Accord.[98] Yet, by late 1979, Iraq was already talking about revising the river boundary delimitation. Its ambassador to Lebanon had suggested during November that an improvement in relations with Tehran would be contingent *inter alia* on a revision of the river boundary delimitation introduced by the 1975 Algiers Accord.

Iraqi abrogation of the 1975 agreements was not far off in light of the countdown to war in September 1980. On September 17, 1980 the Iraqi Revolutionary Command Council announced such a move, justifying its decision in the following terms:

In accordance with the provisions of paragraph a) of Article 42 of the Provisional Constitution and in view of the Iranian Government's violation of the letter and spirit of the 6th March 1975 agreement and the protocols attached by not honouring the relations of goodneighbourliness, by blatantly and purposefully interfering in Iraq's domestic affairs and by failing to return the usurped Iraqi territories to full Iraqi sovereignty under the aforementioned agreement, which shows that Iran considers the March 1975 agreement null and void, the Revolutionary Command Council, meeting on 17th September 1980, has decided to consider the agreement abrogated and to restore complete legal and effective sovereignty over the Shatt al-Arab.[99]

Although Iraq had clearly decided upon war by this point, measures announced on the following day to restore its control over navigation in the river had a familiar ring to them, echoing back to the 1960s. For all ships now wishing to navigate the Shatt would have to fly the Iraqi flag, utilize Iraqi navigation pilots and pay Iraq for such services.[100]

The Shatt during wartime is not of major relevance to the themes of this chapter. Yet, the regional support lent to Iraqi territorial claims by neighboring Arab states both during and after the conflict is worthy of attention. So, too, is the triangular territorial relationship at the head of the Gulf and the effect of a blocked Shatt al-Arab upon Iraqi policy toward the Kuwaiti borderlands.

The Gulf Cooperation Council (GCC) was never slow to condemn Iranian territorial advances or actions taken by the Tehran government which appeared to threaten the territorial stability of the Gulf. Throughout the course of the Iran–Iraq War, the GCC protested Iranian advances into Iraqi territory proper, consistently demanding an immediate withdrawal to recognized international boundaries. The stance was never expressed more strongly than following the Iranian capture of the Faw peninsula in 1986. A statement released by the Ministerial Council in Riyadh during March 1986 was typical.

> The council reviewed the dangerous situation in the region in view of Iran's occupation of parts of Iraqi territory which is a violation of international charters and principles of good neighbourliness and an assault against Iraq's sovereignty and the integrity of its territories. The council condemns this occupation and calls on Iran to immediately withdraw its forces to the international boundaries.[101]

Generally, however, the GCC stopped short of extending unequivocal support to Iraq's claim to full sovereignty over the Shatt al-Arab river.[102] Unsurprisingly, the short-lived Arab Cooperation Council—set up in 1988 by Iraq as a counter regional grouping to the oil rich monarchical club that was the GCC—had no such qualms. As Iraq contemplated the basis of any final peace settlement of its eight-year war with Iran in the summer of 1989, the council (also comprising Egypt, Jordan, and Yemen) issued the following typical reservation of rights as far as the Shatt was concerned:

> They emphasised their full solidarity with Iraq in safeguarding its territorial integrity and historical rights and sovereignty over the Shatt al-Arab. They expressed their support to clear the Shatt al-Arab to render it navigable and safe.[103]

Yet the leaders of the GCC states were present at the Extraordinary (Arab League) Summit of late May 1990 in Baghdad, putting their names to a fairly unequivocal closing statement, which called for UN-sponsored Iran–Iraq negotiations to "guarantee Iraq's rights and sovereignty over its territory, particularly its historical right to sovereignty over the Shatt al-Arab."[104] This went quite a bit further than any other GCC pronouncements on the subject, provoking indignation in Iran and the Foreign Ministry's issue of a broadside at Arab capitulation to Iraqi desiderata, in which the symbolic language of Arab-Iranian rivalry was very deliberately employed (emphasis added):

> The attempts by the Iraqi regime at the extraordinary meeting of the Arab Summit to drag the Arab countries to adopt a partial stand towards the regime's expansionist claims on *Arvand Rud* [using the Iranian term for the Shatt]—a claim which was the pretext for launching the imposed war—and also the submission of the Arab heads of state to that illegitimate request, crystallised in the final communiqué of the summit, bring to attention the destructive role of these countries during the war as well as their worthless role in the peace process.[105]

Ironically and despite such solid Arab support for its claim to sovereignty over Shatt waters, Iraq was already relaxing or contemplating relaxing its own stance on the issue at around this time, just a couple of months before making the disastrous move on Kuwait (see next section).

How had the war with Iran and its rendering of the Shatt useless influenced Iraq's attitudes to its borderlands with Kuwait? During the one and only meeting of the Kuwaiti-Iraqi Common Boundary Committee in February 1981, Iraq professed a readiness to demarcate the land boundary if Kuwait would agree first to the lease of Warba and Bubiyan upon which it wished to develop military facilities for use in the war with Iran. Kuwaiti resistance to such a proposal was only reinforced when Iranian Foreign Minister Mir-Hosein Musavi announced shortly afterwards that the emirate would be dragged into the conflict if it leased the islands to Iraq.[106]

Renewed overtures beginning in the spring of 1984 would meet with a similar fate. A lengthy interview with the Iraqi president in the Kuwaiti daily *al-Watan* during May raised once again the question of demarcating the Iraq–Kuwait land boundary. If Kuwait seriously sought demarcation, Saddam Hussein suggested, Warba and Bubiyan ought to be leased since they were urgently required for naval purposes. After the Kuwaiti National Assembly implored the Iraqi leader to come up with proposals to settle the border question once and for all, Kuwaiti Crown Prince and Prime Minister Shaikh Saad were invited for talks in Baghdad in November. At the time of the visit, the Kuwaiti media carried speculative reports that Saddam Hussein's territorial proposals would be linked to longstanding, but as yet unimplemented, joint economic schemes, such as the establishment of a railway link between Kuwait and Basra, the Shatt al-Arab water carrier scheme and the extension of the Kuwaiti national grid to provide Iraq's southern borderlands with electricity.[107] This would have been a return to the imaginative schemes proposed in the mid-1950s (see earlier section), which, for a short time, had seemed to have some chance of prevailing. There was obvious disappointment when, despite all the public optimism, the meeting achieved very little. Not all interested parties were quite so sure that the meeting had failed, however. Ali-Akbar Hashemi-Rafsanjani, then speaker of the Iranian *Majlis*, was evidently concerned that Kuwait had agreed to lease to Iraq the two islands of Warba and Bubiyan. He cautioned Kuwait that, if leased to Iraq, the islands would be attacked by Iran and not necessarily ever returned.[108] In fact, Iran's warning only encouraged Kuwait to take more steps to physically assert its sovereignty over the islands, with rockets and anti-aircraft batteries installed on the features during December 1984.[109]

A Settled River Boundary or a Dormant Dispute?

Saddam Hussein's apparent abandonment of territorial claims to the whole of the Shatt al-Arab river two weeks into Iraq's move on Kuwait surprised many observers and understandably raised questions as to how, if at all, the two events were related. By the late spring of 1990, as already intimated, the Iranian and Iraqi heads of state were already engaged in the series of correspondence that would culminate in the Iraqi action, a climbdown that would implicitly lend Iraqi recognition to the river boundary introduced by the 1975 package agreement once again. In other words Iraq would effectively abandon its claim to full sovereignty over the Shatt al-Arab, having just fought eight years of war for the restoration of the Shatt to its "rightful owner." Were there any clues in the Hussein–Rafsanjani correspondence during the second quarter of 1990 that the Iraqi president had resigned himself to accepting shared sovereignty over the Shatt al-Arab and had turned his gaze southwards toward Kuwait as a means of improving access to Gulf waters?

The short answer is that there seems to be no conclusive evidence to substantiate such a thesis. As early as January 5, 1990 Saddam Hussein had attempted to launch an initiative "to achieve a comprehensive and immediate peace" by addressing Rafsanjani indirectly in the Iraqi media. This was followed by a personal letter of April 21, 1990, containing suggested schemes for a comprehensive peace and the proposal that presidential-level talks be convened in Saudi Arabia.[110] One source credits Hussein's letter of April 21 (combined with a later one of May 19) with not having wholly discounted the 1975 agreements as a basis for discussion. Importantly, however, Iraq would reserve its rights on the subject of the Shatt al-Arab, over which full sovereignty was still claimed. It also underlined that there would have to be major amendments to the 1975 agreement in this and other respects.[111] In reply Rafsanjani (in his letter to Hussein of May 4, 1990) suggested that exploratory sessions might be convened in Tehran and Baghdad within the framework of UNSCR 598 in advance of any presidential summit. Before these had any chance of taking place, however, Iraq would be required to withdraw fully from Iranian territory. Meanwhile, an Iranian National Security Council meeting had taken place in Tehran to consider Hussein's April 21 communication. It had reportedly concluded that the *thalweg* boundary introduced by the Algiers Accord was non-negotiable and that there was no point in going back to the 1975 package of agreements as the basis of discussion unless the Iraqi government first accepted them in advance in their entirety.[112]

Despite the furor in Iran caused by the Arab League's unequivocal support in late May for Iraqi claims to full sovereignty over the Shatt, Saddam's second letter of May 21, 1990—which had hinted at greater Iraqi flexibility toward Iranian peace terms[113]—would ultimately succeed in bringing Foreign Ministers Tariq Aziz and Ali-Akbar Velayati to the negotiating table in Geneva by early July. Discussions would be conducted here under the auspices of UN Secretary-General Javier Pérez de Cuéllar. Even so, there were still no tangible indications that the Iraqi government was prepared to soften its line on sovereignty of the Shatt al-Arab.

Clear indications of Iraq's flexibility over the Shatt did not come until Iraqi troops were stationed on the Kuwaiti border during the latter half of July 1990. By then, with an Iraqi force some 20–30,000 strong already looking southwards to Kuwait, the Baghdad–Tehran relationship had taken some unusual turns, which suggested the possibility of major developments in the northern Gulf. Saddam Hussein had reportedly informed Rafsanjani that "certain events would take place in the northern Gulf region that Iran should not interpret in a negative way."[114] Also, and certainly uncharacteristically, the Iranian media would comment sympathetically upon Iraqi aspirations for greater access to Gulf waters at the expense of Kuwait.[115]

Formally, Iraq's softening on the Shatt al-Arab arrived in the shape of Hussein's letter to Rafsanjani of July 30, 1990. By now there were 100,000 Iraqi troops stationed along the Kuwait border and the prospect of invasion was a real one. The latest offer for a peace settlement was careful not to concede Iraqi sovereignty over the Shatt al-Arab but, nevertheless, displayed much greater accommodation of Iranian demands than had previously been the case. The Iraqi president presented Iran with a choice of three ways forward on the Shatt, the last of which involved submitting the dispute to arbitration. The sixth point of Saddam Hussein's letter read as follows:

> Dialogue on the Shatt al-Arab must be conducted under the following three headings:
>
> A) Iraq should have complete sovereignty as a legitimate historical right;
> B) Iraq should have sovereignty over the Shatt al-Arab and the *thalweg* line law should be applied regarding navigational rights between Iran and Iraq including fishing rights, joint administration of navigation, and sharing profits thereof;
> C) The referral of the Shatt al-Arab issue in arbitration according to a formula to be worked out by the two states with each committing itself to prior abidances by its ruling. Pending the resolution of the issue through arbitration, the Shatt al-Arab is to be cleared so as to make it fit for navigation in accordance with the formula to be decided by the two sides.
>
> Agreement will be on the understanding that the two sides will together decide on any of the three headings listed above, considering that the first heading represents Iraq's right and our understanding is that the second heading represents Iran's wish.[116]

The Iraqi president wrote a further letter to Rafsanjani on August 3, 1990 so as to underline that the content of his July 30 communication still held good following Iraq's invasion of Kuwait. Its urgent tone soon produced a response from his Iranian counterpart. In his letter of August 8, Rafsanjani responded to the new Iraqi proposals over the Shatt in the following manner:

> In your letter dated 5/8/1369 (30 July 1990) you made proposals concerning Arvand Rud, and, although they wavered from your previous statements, it must be clear to you that they are unacceptable to us.
> Our specific proposal is to use the 1975 accord for the peace talks, because without adherence to previous treaties, especially that treaty which bears your own signature, there can be no expectation that confidence in what is being said today will be created.[117]

Reinforcing the point, Rafsanjani closed his letter with the following words:

> We must adhere to the treaties between the two countries which have been officially recognized internationally and not demand more than our lawful rights, because it is not

conceivable that what could not be achieved in eight years of war can be achieved in talks. If we accept this, to define the borders we need only to refer to the 1975 accord, . . .[118]

Although there was admittedly an element of equivocation and qualification, Saddam Hussein would largely accept these proposals in a further letter of August 14, 1990 addressed to the Iranian president. Here it was stated that:

> We agree to your proposal in the letter of reply dated 8 August 1990 . . . stating the necessity of working on the basis of the 1975 accord which connects it with the principles in our 30 July 1990 letter, . . .[119]

It was these three lines that were taken by most authorities to signify Iraq's renewed acceptance of the 1975 package and, by extension, its renewed acknowledgment of a *thalweg* boundary delimitation along the Shatt al-Arab. To follow up, on August 15, 1990 a summarizing letter from Tariq Aziz was delivered to Pérez de Cuéllar, enclosing the Iraqi president's letters to Rafsanjani of July 30 and August 14, 1990. Similarly, de Cuellar received a letter from Velayati two days later, acknowledging Iraq's renewed commitment to the 1975 package settlement and enclosing Rafsanjani's letter to Hussein of August 8, 1990.[120] Velayati would mention international boundaries in specific terms as follows:

> With reference to the letter of 14 August 1990 of the President of Iraq addressed to the President of the Islamic Republic of Iran—in which he accepted the proposals presented by my President in his letter dated 8 August 1990 and declared Iraq's renewed commitment to the 1975 Treaty of State Frontier and Neighbourly Relations between Iran and Iraq, . . .[121]

After Iraq began to withdraw its forces from occupied Iranian territory on August 17, 1990, as had been promised by the Iraqi president in his communication of August 14, 1990, Rafsanjani completed the cycle of correspondence that had started with Hussein's letter of April 21. Obviously interpreting Hussein's letter (and actions) to have recognized the validity of the 1975 package in full, he opened a short letter with the following paragraph:

> The announcement of your renewed acceptance of the 1975 accord has paved the way for implementing Resolution 598, resolving the problems in that framework, and transforming the existing cease fire to a permanent and stable peace.[122]

Yet the Hussein–Rafsanjani correspondence of April–August 1990 would never ultimately transform ceasefire into formal peace and doubts exist about the degree to which Iraq recommitted itself to the territorial prescription of 1975.[123] For that reason it is tempting to view the Shatt dispute as dormant rather than permanently settled. However, when the "new Iraq" begins to formalize relations with its neighbors in the coming months and years, it would be astonishing if the two states were to agree on any territorial definition other than that introduced by the 1975 package settlement. For a start, as the most authoritative legal study of the Shatt produced to date attests: "in view of all the circumstances of the case," Iraq had "no right to abrogate the Baghdad Treaty of 1975."[124] Second, as we have just seen, Iraq went a very long way toward formalizing its reacceptance of the 1975 arrangements with the Hussein-Rafsanjani correspondence of 1990. Third, a *thalweg* delimitation is by far the most practical and workable territorial arrangement for the Shatt al-Arab and the 1975 treaty is a demonstrably well-conceived and appropriate settlement.

Prospects

It is largely in the context of border management, as opposed to territorial definition, that Iraq's boundaries have arisen as issues under American occupation. Amid the general insecurity prevailing in Iraq during the summer of 2004, the porosity of state limits is much more of an issue than their precise delimitation. Though accurate details are wanting, the task of securing the state's international boundaries with Syria and Iran appears to have been entrusted in the short term to a combination of U.S. forces and Iraqi militias and tribesmen.[125] Indeed, Iraq's provisional government was handed direct responsibility for patrolling (with a 1,200-strong force) a 210-kilometer–stretch of the central land border with Iran and, in particular, the Muntheria border crossing—a popular entry point for Iranian pilgrims destined for the southern Iraqi Shi'i shrines in Karbala and Najaf.[126]

The issue of delimitation of the Iran–Iraq land boundary has also arisen, albeit with a distinct lack of clarity. For, in testimony of July 9, 2003, U.S. Secretary of Defense Donald Rumsfeld charged Iran with nibbling away at Iraqi territory by shifting its border posts several kilometers westward over a 25 kilometer stretch of the borderlands in the south.[127] Iran promptly denied the charge. Though it is impossible to be sure, it seems that Rumsfeld was referring to borderlands in the vicinity of Iran's massive (though as-yet undeveloped) Azadegan oilfield in the alluvial borderland plains of Khuzistan, lying just to the north of the Shatt al-Arab river boundary section.[128] Lying adjacent to Iraq's Majnoon oilfield (and widely believed to be a part of the same transboundary field structure), Azadegan has estimated reserves of 30 billion barrels (of which 6 billion are currently recoverable) and could potentially augment Iran's total daily oil production by 400,000 barrels when fully onstream. In February 2004, negotiations with a Japanese consortium to develop part of the field were finalized, in spite of American pressure not to do so.[129]

Since other borderland localities close to Azadegan/Majnoon are also promising geologically, the precise course of the boundary delimitation in the southern plains may continue to be closely scrutinized since the commercial stakes now appear to be so high. How ironic it is that such a highly alienated, disfigured, and partially abandoned border landscape—the legacy of eight years of war— should now assume such commercial significance that control of every last square kilometer could be contested, simply for the resources it overlies. Yet pragmatism may yet prove the order of the day where exploitation of transboundary resources is concerned. Just as transboundary oilfields or hydrocarbons-rich borderlands provide potential for dispute (one only needs to look at Rumaila/Ratga (Iraq/Kuwait) in the recent past) they can also provide the basis for cooperation. Here Iran and Iraq could also look to many useful existing precedents within the Middle East region in shaping arrangements for the coordinated future development of the resource-rich Azadegan/Majnoon borderlands. In any case, the precise delimitation of the land boundary in these parts will surely be clarified as and when Iraq formalizes its reacceptance of the 1975 package of agreements.

Yet Rumsfeld's assertion that Iran had moved the border and was "not being respectful of Iraq's sovereignty" may also have been designed to demonstrate publicly that the United States will be quick to protect Iraq's national interests, particularly its territorial integrity. This would, after all, only be a continuation of efforts by central authority in Baghdad to legitimize its rule or presence by invoking territorial symbols.

Crucially, however, the traditional symbolic role played by the Shatt al-Arab in Iran–Iraq relations is likely to be far less pronounced in the future. This is because the *thalweg* delimitation introduced by the 1975 package of agreements is without doubt the most logical and workable alignment for the river boundary. It will be recalled that the logic of adopting a mid-channel boundary had been recognized locally around one hundred years ago because it was equitable and convenient. The effective joint conservancy of the river—more elusive historically than agreement on delimitation—will only be achieved with a formal reacceptance and the eventual implementation of the 1975 package. Cooperation here will pave the way for the forging of constructive management of the borderlands further north, especially in the Azadegan/Majnoon transboundary field structure, about which we are going to here a lot more in the relatively near future.

In recommitting themselves to the 1975 agreements, Iran and Iraq will have to address several of the minor shortcomings that have become apparent over the last quarter-century. One or two ambiguities remain in the land boundary delimitation itself. As far as the Shatt is concerned, the two sides need to establish precisely the present course of the *thalweg* (or the median line of the principal navigable channel as the *thalweg* was so defined in 1975) and formalize their agreement on the new delimitation by drawing up a new annex to the 1975 package.

It is not inconceivable that Baghdad will one day reclaim the Shatt as an Iraqi national river though it does seem unlikely. Iraq's reconstruction and medium-term material well-being will best be served through the integrated economic development of the northern Gulf. This is most likely to be realized by adherence to the 1975 package agreement with Iran and to the 1993 UN settlement of the Kuwait–Iraq border. The hotchpotch of a boundary delimitation that existed along the Shatt before 1975 and the bizarre and inequitable arrangements that existed for its navigation always left the river vulnerable to the incidence of functional disputes. Clearly, Iran and Iraq always need to be mindful of the history of this dispute, but the future of a river boundary that has previously served as the most important territorial symbol of Arab-Iranian rivalry is now likely to be governed by pragmatism.

Notes

1. E. Lauterpacht, "River Boundaries: Legal Aspects of the Shatt al-'Arab Frontier," in *International and Comparative Law Quarterly*, vol. 9, ser. 4 (1960), pp. 208–36 and Kaiyan Homi Kaikobad, *The Shatt-al-Arab Boundary Question: A Legal Reappraisal* (Oxford: Clarendon Press, 1988).
2. G.E. Hubbard, *From the Gulf to Ararat* (Edinburgh: William Blackwood, 1916); C.H.D. Ryder, "The Demarcation of the Turco-Persian Boundary in 1913–14," in *The Geographical Journal*, vol. 66 (1925), pp. 227–42. Beyond these secondary sources, there is really no substitute for delving into the primary record of the history of the dispute. The British Government Records respectively housed at the Oriental and India Office Collection at the British Library at St. Pancras (formerly the India Office Library and Records at Blackfriars) and the National Archive at Kew (known as the Public Record Office until May 2003) are a particularly rich source of information. Selections from these collections have been published relatively recently. See Richard Schofield, ed., *The Iran-Iraq Border, 1840–1958*, 11 vols. (Farnham Common: Archive Editions, 1989).
3. The reactivation of the dispute in the late 1960s (culminating in April 1969 with the shah's abrogation of the 1937 Tehran treaty) resulted in the appearance of a number of articles, of which Alexander Melamid's and Vahé Sevian's are the best (A. Melamid, "The Shatt al-'Arab Boundary Dispute," in *The Middle East Journal*, vol. 22 (1968), pp. 351–57 and V.J. Sevian, "Evolution of the Boundary Between Iraq and Iran," in Charles A. Fisher, ed., *Essays in Political Geography* (London: Methuen, 1968), pp. 211–23). All scholars owe a massive debt to Ulrich Gehrke and Gustav Kuhn, however, for producing their pioneering and painstakingly researched two-volume collection (*Die Grenzen des Irak: historische und rechtliche Aspekte des Irakische Anspruchs auf Kuwait und des irakische-persischen Streites um den Shatt al-'Arab* (Stuttgart: W. Kohlhammer, 1963). The Algiers Accord and follow-up agreements of 1975 generated some new but also the re-publication of older material (e.g., C.J. Edmonds, "The Iraqi-Persian Frontier: 1639–1938," in *Asian Affairs*, part 2, vol. 62 (June 1975), pp. 147–54). Predictably, however, it would be the outbreak of war in September 1980 that would spur a spate of new articles and monographs on the Shatt al-Arab: e.g., Daniel Pipes, "A Border Adrift: Origins of the Conflict" in S. Tahir-Kheli and S. Ayubi, eds., *The Iran-Iraq War: New Weapons, Old Conflicts* (New York: Frederick Praeger, 1983) and Peter Hunseler, "The Historical Antecedents of the Shatt al Arab Dispute," in M.S. El Azhary, ed., *The Iran-Iraq War* (London: Croom Helm, 1984). A more recent review is Lawrence G. Potter, "The Evolution of the Iran-Iraq Boundary," in *The Creation of Iraq, 1914–1921*, ed. Reeva Spector Simon and Eleanor H. Tejirian (New York: Columbia University Press, 2004).
4. For instance: Richard N. Schofield, *Evolution of the Shatt al-'Arab Boundary Dispute* (Wisbech: Menas Press, 1986); Majid Khadduri, *The Gulf War: The Origins and Implications of the Iran-Iraq Conflict* (New York: Oxford University Press, 1988).
5. Shahram Chubin and Charles Tripp, "Domestic Politics and Territorial Disputes in the Persian Gulf and Arabian Peninsula," in *Survival*, vol. 35, no. 4 (Winter 1993), pp. 3–27.
6. See Richard Schofield, *Kuwait and Iraq: Historical Claims and Territorial Disputes*, 2nd ed. (London: Royal Institute of International Affairs, 1993); Richard Schofield, "The Historical Problem of Iraqi Access to the Persian Gulf: The Interrelationships of Territorial Disputes with Iran and Kuwait, 1938–1990," in Clive H. Schofield and Richard N. Schofield, eds., *World Boundaries: The Middle East and North Africa* (London: Routledge, 1994), pp. 158–72.
7. See Melamid, "The Shatt al-'Arab boundary dispute"; Richard Schofield, "Positional Disputes and the Twentieth Century Utilisation of the Shatt al-Arab—International Right

or International Need," in *Boundaries and State Territory in the Middle East and North Africa*, ed. G.H. Blake and R.N. Schofield (Wisbech: Menas Press, 1987).

8. L.J. Bouchez, "The Fixing of Boundaries in International Boundary Rivers," in *International and Comparative Law Quarterly*, vol. 12 (1963), pp. 789–817; Gideon Biger, "Physical Geography and Law: The Case of International River Boundaries," in *Geojournal*, vol. 17, no. 3 (1988), pp. 341–47.

9. Hubbard, *From the Gulf to Ararat*, p. 2.

10. Text reproduced in Foreign Office, "Memorandum on the Frontier Between Persia and Turkey and Persia and Iraq, 1639–1934," January 8, 1935. Foreign Office Confidential Print No. 14514.

11. Rechid Pacha, "Traduction d'une Note officiale [sic] remise par son Excellence Rechid Pacha à Sir Stratford Canning," March 1, 1846. FO 881/10041.

12. Foreign Office, Translation of the May 31, 1847 Erzurum Treaty, June 1, 1847. FO 881/10041.

13. For greater detail see Richard Schofield, "Interpreting a Vague River Boundary Delimitation: The 1847 Erzurum Treaty and the Shatt al-Arab before 1913," in *The Boundaries of Modern Iran*, ed. Keith McLachlan (London: UCL Press, 1994), pp. 72–92.

14. Ibid., pp. 80–82.

15. Ibid.

16. Lord Palmerston to Lord Bloomfield, March 3, 1847 in FO 78/2716.

17. The same old argument was rendered to me personally by Iranian Foreign Ministry officials in Tehran as recently as November 1989.

18. Schofield, "Interpreting a Vague River Boundary Delimitation," p. 74.

19. Foreign Office, "Supplementary Memorandum Respecting Mohammerah," March 4, 1908. FO 416/35.

20. Sir Arnold Wilson to Mr. G. Barclay, May 26, 1909. FO 371/710.

21. Schofield, *Evolution of the Shatt al-'Arab Boundary Dispute*, pp. 47–48.

22. Sir Percy Cox to Sir Edward Grey, July 15, 1912. L/P&S/10/266.

23. It should be underlined that this was not the anchorage mentioned in Article 2 of the Erzurum treaty, which lay further south off Abadan or Khizr island, as it was then referred to.

24. Ibid. Cox would further note that, if mooring buoys were provided, all ships moored at the midstream anchorage could be berthed on the Persian side of the midstream channel line.

25. Alwyn Parker, "Memorandum Respecting the Frontier Between Muhammara and Turkey," Foreign Office, April 3, 1912. FO 881/14638.

26. Lord Crewe, India Office to the Foreign Office, June 3, 1911. FO 371/1179.

27. Sir Percy Cox to A. Parker, Foreign Office, May 23, 1912. L/P&S/10/266.

28. Schofield, "Interpreting a Vague River Boundary Delimitation," p. 87.

29. Sir Edward Grey to Sir G. Buchanan, July 18, 1912. L/P&S/10/266.

30. Ibid.

31. Foreign Office, "Memorandum on the Frontier Between Persia and Turkey and Persia and Iraq, 1639–1934," January 8, 1935, Foreign Office Confidential Print no. 14514.

32. Ibid.

33. Harold Shipley, "Report on the Turco-Persian Frontier Commission of 1912," March 19, 1913. FO 881/12714.

34. League of Nations, Official Journal, February 1935, p. 217.

35. This specified that "[t]he frontier line shall be delimited on the spot by a Delimitation Commission, consisting of commissioners of the four governments. Each government shall be represented on this Commission by a commissioner and a deputy commissioner."

36. Section IV of the November 17, 1913 Constantinople protocol would establish as much: "In the event of a divergence in the Commission as to the boundary line of any part of

the frontier, the Ottoman and Persian commissioners shall submit a written statement of their respective points of view within forty-eight hours to the Russian and British commissioners, who shall hold a private meeting and shall give a decision on the questions in dispute and communicate their decision to their Ottoman and Persian colleagues. The decision shall be inserted in the Minutes of the plenary meeting and shall be recognised as binding on all four governments."

37. Lord Palmerston to G.H. Seymour, October 11, 1851. FO 78/2716.
38. Translation of original French in "The Dispute over the Shatt al-'Arab" (Washington, D.C.: U.S. Department of State, Bureau of Intelligence and Research, 1960), Intelligence Report no. 8208, January 22, 1960, p. 8.
39. Schofield, *Evolution of the Shatt al-'Arab Boundary Dispute*, pp. 52–53.
40. Tareq Y. Ismael, *Iraq and Iran: Roots of Conflict* (Syracuse, NY: Syracuse University Press, 1982), p. 12.
41. Conversely, non-navigable boundary rivers would only need delimiting by a simple median line since possession of the main channel was not an issue.
42. Schofield, *Evolution of the Shatt al-'Arab Boundary Dispute*, pp. 52–53.
43. Kaikobad, *The Shatt-al-Arab Boundary Question*, p. 53.
44. Sir Robert Clive, Tehran to the Foreign Office, March 4, 1929. L/P&S/10/1229.
45. Kaikobad, *The Shatt-al-Arab Boundary Question*, p. 55.
46. Schofield, *Evolution of the Shatt al-'Arab Boundary Dispute*, pp. 53–55; Kaikobad, *The Shatt-al-Arab Boundary Question*, pp. 54–57.
47. Ibid.
48. Privately, there were already clear hints that, in practice, it was prepared to accept such a delimitation for a far more limited stretch of the river, i.e., opposite Abadan.
49. Ibid.
50. Most notably the Persian arrest in June 1933 of Captain Macleod, the British Harbour Master at Abadan (and employee of the Basra Port Authority), for boarding a Persian warship while docking at Abadan. See unpublished note by R. Michael Burrell, "Addendum: Iran and the Shatt al-'Arab" (n.d., c. 1972), p. 4.
51. Schofield, *Evolution of the Shatt al-'Arab Boundary Dispute*, pp. 53–55; Kaikobad, *The Shatt-al-Arab Boundary Question*, pp. 56–58.
52. Ibid.
53. As reflected in the title of Daniel Silverfarb's work, *Britain's Informal Empire in the Middle East: A Case Study of Iraq, 1929–1941* (New York: Oxford University Press, 1986).
54. Kaikobad, *The Shatt-al-Arab Boundary Question*, pp. 61–63.
55. Schofield, *Evolution of the Shatt al-'Arab Boundary Dispute*, pp. 53–55.
56. Telegram from the Foreign Office to the Admiralty, December 10, 1936. FO 371/20039.
57. As Kaikobad attests: ". . . there is no evidence in the records to show that Iran insisted upon the adoption of a median line in the Shatt. The evidence is quite to the contrary, namely that Iran was content with the acquisition of four miles of the thalweg boundary and the cession of the Abadan anchorage" (Kaikobad, *The Shatt-al-Arab Boundary Question*, p. 63).
58. League of Nations (1938) *Treaty Series*, number 4423, p. 241.
59. Ibid.
60. Ibid.
61. Ibid.
62. Foreign Office note on "Progress Made Towards Instituting a Conservancy Convention for Shatt al-Arab Since 1938," September 27, 1944. FO 371/40101.
63. Foreign Office Research Department memorandum entitled: "Negotiations for an Irano-Arab Shatt-el-Arab Conservancy Convention," July 1959. FO 371/133111.

64. Schofield, *Kuwait and Iraq: Historical Claims and Territorial Disputes*, p. 64.
65. Ibid., p. 76.
66. Ibid.
67. L. Baggallay, Foreign Office to R.T. Peel, India Office, August 26, 1938. R/15/5/208.
68. Aide Memoire by Taufiq al Suwaidi, September 28, 1938. FO 371/21858.
69. Schofield, *Kuwait and Iraq: Historical Claims and Territorial Disputes*, pp. 85–90.
70. L. Baggallay, Foreign Office to the India Office, December 16, 1939. CO 732/86/17.
71. British Embassy, Baghdad to the Foreign Office, May 24, 1955. FO 371/114644.
72. Gawain Bell, British Agency, Kuwait to the Foreign Office, June 28, 1955. FO 371/114644.
73. Schofield, *Kuwait and Iraq: Historical Claims and Territorial Disputes*, pp. 95–97.
74. Ibid.
75. Telegram from the British Embassy, Baghdad to the Foreign Office, November 17, 1957. FO 371/126913.
76. Schofield, *Kuwait and Iraq: Historical Claims and Territorial Disputes*, pp. 100–01.
77. Schofield, *Evolution of the Shatt al-'Arab Boundary Dispute*, pp. 58–59.
78. For example, see D.J. al Rubaiay, "Irrigation and Drainage Systems in the Basra Region of Iraq," unpublished doctoral thesis, University of Durham, 1984. Admittedly, an unchecked buildup of sediment at the Karun Bar would naturally limit the throughput of water from the Karun but at no time did this occur to such a degree that the balance of national water contribution to lower Shatt waters was altered. See Schofield, *Evolution of the Shatt al-'Arab Boundary Dispute*, pp. 27–31.
79. Letter from P.G.B. Giles, British Embassy, Tehran to Commercial Relations and Export Department, Board of Trade, London, August 20, 1959 in FO 371/140125. The actual consignments in question, sent by the British firm Stricks, contained 60 crates of whiskey and microfilm for the Irano-British bank.
80. Schofield, *Evolution of the Shatt al-'Arab Boundary Dispute*, pp. 27–31.
81. Shahram Chubin and Sepehr Zabih, *The Foreign Relations of Iran: A Developing State in a Zone of Great-Power Conflict* (Berkeley: University of California Press, 1974), p. 192.
82. Comments of General Qasim at press conference of December 3, 1959, reproduced in "The Dispute over the Shatt al-Arab," Intelligence Report, Bureau of Intelligence and Research, U.S. Department of State, January 22, 1960, p. 20.
83. "The Dispute over the Shatt al-Arab," p. 20.
84. Schofield, *Evolution of the Shatt al-'Arab Boundary Dispute*, p. 60.
85. Schofield, *Kuwait and Iraq: Historical Claims and Territorial Disputes*, p. 114.
86. Iranian statement concerning abrogation of 1937 treaty between Iraq and Iran, reproduced in Richard Schofield, ed., *Arabian Boundary Disputes*, Volume III, *Iran-Iraq, 1938–1992* (Farnham Common: Archive Editions, 1992), pp. 118–23.
87. Letter dated May 1, 1969 from the Permanent Representative of Iran addressed to president of the Security Council in ibid., pp. 126–29.
88. Iranian statement concerning abrogation of 1937 treaty in ibid., pp. 118–23.
89. Letter dated May 1, 1969 from Permanent Representative of Iran addressed to the president of the Security Council in ibid., pp. 126–29.
90. Schofield, *Kuwait and Iraq: Historical Claims and Territorial Disputes*, pp. 114–15.
91. Richard Schofield, "Borders and Territoriality in the Gulf and Arabian Peninsula During the Twentieth Century," in *Territorial Foundations of the Gulf States*, Richard Schofield, ed. (London: UCL Press, 1994), p. 4.
92. Quoted in an unpublished conference paper presented by Abbas Maleki, "Iran, Iraq and the UN Security Council," Geneva (1989). It should be pointed out that this author has seen no other sources that corroborate Maleki's report of Hussein's comments.

93. United Nations, *Treaty Series*, vol. 1017, no. 14903.
94. Ibid.
95. Ibid.
96. Ibid.
97. Many sources do, of course, concern themselves with this very issue. F. Gregory Gause III's recent reflections are worth singling out here: "Iraq's Decision to Go to War, 1980 and 1990," in *The Middle East Journal*, vol. 56, no. 1 (Winter 2002), pp. 47–70.
98. "Protocol Concerning the Redemarcation of the Land Frontier Between Iran and Iraq," signed in Baghdad, December 26, 1975.
99. Schofield, *Arabian Boundary Disputes*, Volume III, p. 189.
100. Ibid., p. 190.
101. Ibid., p. 231.
102. Richard Schofield, "Boundaries, Territorial Disputes and the GCC States," in *Gulf Security in the Twenty-First Century*, ed. David E. Long and Christian Koch (Abu Dhabi: Emirates Center for Strategic Studies and Research, 1997), p. 147.
103. Schofield, *Arabian Boundary Disputes*, Volume III, p. 857.
104. Ibid., pp. 858–59.
105. Ibid., p. 860.
106. Schofield, *Kuwait and Iraq: Historical Claims and Territorial Disputes,* p. 120.
107. Al Mayyal, Ahmad, "The Political Boundaries of the State of Kuwait," unpublished Ph.D thesis, Department of Geography, School of Oriental and African Studies, University of London (1986), pp. 195–96.
108. Schofield, *Kuwait and Iraq: Historical Claims and Territorial Disputes*, p. 121.
109. Richard Schofield, "The Kuwaiti Islands of Warbah and Bubiyan, and Iraqi Access to the Gulf," in Schofield, *Territorial Foundations of the Gulf States*, pp. 170–71.
110. The full text of the letter (the Iranian version) is included in a piece entitled "Keyhan e-Hava'i publishes leaders' letters," in *Foreign Broadcast Information Service [FBIS]*, November 1, 1990. For another source on these letters, with English and Persian texts, see Maryam Daftari, trans., *The Texts of Letters Exchanged Between the Presidents of the Islamic Republic of Iran and the Republic of Iraq 1369 (1990)* (Tehran: The Institute for Political and International Studies, 1374/1995).
111. *Iran Focus*, vol. 3, no. 6 (June 1990), p. 6.
112. Ibid. and Dilip Hiro, *Desert Shield to Desert Storm: The Second Gulf War* (London: HarperCollins, 1992), p. 81.
113. Various sources, including Ofra Bengio, "Iraq: al-Jumhuriyya al-'Iraqiyya," in *Middle East Contemporary Survey*, ed. A. Ayalon (Boulder, Colo.: Westview Press, 1991), pp. 2, 18, and 31), mention that Hussein's greater flexibility extended to the Shatt al-Arab itself. Yet, evidence for this is conspicuous by its absence. There is certainly no direct mention of the Shatt al-Arab or the 1975 Algiers Accord in Hussein's letters of April–May 1990.
114. Communication revealed by the head of the Iranian National Security Council after the 1991 Gulf War, quoted in *The New York Times*, March 20, 1991.
115. Schofield, *Kuwait and Iraq: Historical Claims and Territorial Disputes*, p. 130.
116. *"Keyhan-e Hava'i* publishes leaders letters," September 26 and October 3, 1990 in *FBIS*, November 1, 1990.
117. Ibid.
118. Ibid.
119. Ibid.
120. United Nations Security Council documents S/21528 (August 15, 1990) and S/21556 (August 17, 1990).

121. Schofield, *Arabian Boundary Disputes*, Volume III, p. 386.

122. Ibid., p. 401.

123. Shaul Bakhash concludes that Iran's belief that Iraq had caved in on the demand for a return to the *thalweg* stemmed from a misinterpretation of the Hussein–Rafsanjani correspondence itself. See "Iran: War Ended, Hostility Continued," in *Iraq's Road to War*, ed. Amatzia Baram and Barry Rubin (New York: St. Martin's Press, 1993), pp. 219–31.

124. Kaikobad, *The Shatt-al-Arab Boundary Question*, p. 99.

125. Iraq Press (Baghdad), September 12, 2003 (online).

126. "Iraqi Force Patrols in the East," *Associated Press*, September 28, 2003 (online).

127. *The New York Times*, July 10, 2003, p. A1.

128. Confidential oil industry source, September 2003.

129. *Petroleum Intelligence Weekly*, Energy Intelligence Group (New York), September 2003. Also, "Defying U.S., Japan Signs Oil Deal with Iran," in *New York Times*, Feb. 19, 2004, p. A9.

Chapter 3

Between Iraq and a Hard Place: The Kurdish Predicament

M.R. *Izady*

At the beginning of the twenty-first century, Kurds find themselves as fragmented and embattled as at the beginning of the twentieth century. They are also as restless as they were one hundred years earlier, except they now find themselves divided not into three states as they were then, but into eight.[1] If the prospect of Kurdish independence seemed not too unlikely in 1900, it is increasingly remote today (see map 3.1).

The Kurdish aspiration for independence, which lasted until 1848 in the form of independent principalities, has emerged as a perennial stumbling block to the peace, stability, and prosperity of the states that incorporate portions of the Kurds' ancient homeland. Iran and Iraq are just two of many affected states.

In the past, both Iran and Iraq have had to deal with and suppress the Kurdish desire for national independence, demand for local autonomy, or even a simple expectation of ethnic cultural survival. In the process, they have done much to harm themselves through the squandering of state funds and energy in violently putting down and keeping under control the restive Kurdish population. On occasion, they have sided with Kurds across the border in their enemy's territory in order to weaken it through internal strife. For example, in the clash between Iran and Iraq in the 1980s, both sides encouraged the Kurds to commence military activities and promised them much in return when they won the war against the enemy state. Kurds, particularly those in Iraq, cheerfully fell for this recurring ruse, and ended up paying horribly when the war ended with neither state vanquishing the other.

Kurdish Geopolitics

The geopolitics of Kurdistan has effectively precluded the formation of an independent Kurdish state in the last century. Currently stretching over seven international boundaries (with detached pockets in two more states), Kurdistan resembles

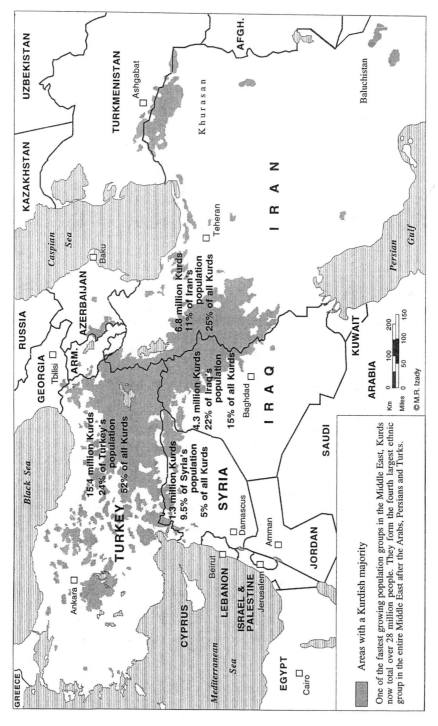

Map 3.1 Demographic distribution of Kurds in the Middle East, 1996.

The labels and text visible on the map include:

- GREECE
- UZBEKISTAN
- KAZAKHSTAN
- TURKMENISTAN
- Ashgabat
- AFGH.
- Khurasan
- Baluchistan
- RUSSIA
- GEORGIA
- Tbilisi
- ARM.
- AZERBAIJAN
- Baku
- Caspian Sea
- I R A N
- Teheran
- Black Sea
- 15.4 million Kurds 24% of Turkey's population 52% of all Kurds
- TURKEY
- Ankara
- 6.8 million Kurds 11% of Iran's population 25% of all Kurds
- 4.3 million Kurds 22% of Iraq's population 15% of all Kurds
- I R A Q
- Baghdad
- 1.3 million Kurds 9.5% of Syria's population 5% of all Kurds
- SYRIA
- Damascus
- KUWAIT
- SAUDI ARABIA
- Persian Gulf
- CYPRUS
- Mediterranean Sea
- Beirut
- LEBANON
- ISRAEL & PALESTINE
- Jerusalem
- Amman
- JORDAN
- EGYPT
- Cairo
- Km 0 100 200
- Miles 0 50 100 150
- © M.R. Izady

Areas with a Kurdish majority

One of the fastest growing population groups in the Middle East, Kurds now total over 28 million people. They form the fourth largest ethnic group in the entire Middle East after the Arabs, Persians and Turks.

an arching shield of highlands, which until 1991 separated the Middle East from the militaries of the Soviet Union in the Caucasus. With the dissolution of the Soviet Union, and the receding power of Russia, an unclear future looms on the northern horizons of the Middle East, where Kurdistan continues to serve as a buffer zone.

The Kurds have the dubious distinction of being the only ethnic group in the world with indigenous representatives in four contending world geopolitical power formations: the Arab world (in Iraq and Syria), NATO (in Turkey), the former Warsaw Pact and the Soviet bloc (in Armenia, Azerbaijan, and Georgia), and the South Asian–Central Asian bloc (in Iran and Soviet Turkmenistan). The Kurdish question and their fate in the twentieth century must be understood within the context of power politics among these world blocs and their shifting interests.

For world powers to help the Iranian Kurds meant to indirectly but seriously press Turkey's eastern flank with the USSR, with clear ramifications for NATO's security. To help the Iraqi Kurds is to assist Iran and Syria indirectly in their longstanding antagonism toward Baghdad, and again worry Turkey. The Arab bloc, for their part, has found it unacceptable to have non-Arab minorities in Iraq or Syria wooed by outside forces. For the West, not to help the Kurds at all left them with the option of seeking aid from the Soviet Union, or pushed them toward terrorism as the only other alternative for furthering their cause. The demise of the Soviet Union has removed this northern card from the Kurdish leaders' deck, but the present fluid situation can easily lead to terrorism, as it already has with some Iraqi Kurds in the form of the small but lethal Islamic terror group, Ansar al-Islam.[2]

Kurdistan as the primary watershed in an otherwise parched Middle East is of critical importance to the states that now administer it. Further, nearly all the Syrian and Turkish petroleum deposits are in Kurdistan, while the old Kirkuk fields in Iraq constitute about one-third of that state's total petroleum reserves. In fact economic concerns likely were the principal reason Britain chose to short-circuit the process set in motion by the Treaty of Sèvres for an independent Kurdistan after World War I. Because of the importance of the oil-bearing territories of central Kurdistan, Britain incorporated them in its Mandate of Iraq, allowing the rest to be annexed by Turkey in return.

Let us examine the political and sociopsychological events of the twentieth century to better understand the Kurdish predicament today, the role they have played and will continue to play as pawns in the geopolitical game between Iran and Iraq.

Kurds in Iraq and Iran

Kurds in Iraq

Almost from the moment of Iraq's formation as a British mandate, the British had to deal with Kurdish unrest in the north. However, the Kurds there were never a match for the technologically and numerically superior imperial troops. In fact, the Iraqi Kurds became one of history's first civilian targets of bomber aircraft, when the British Royal Air Force in Iraq routinely bombed villagers in central Kurdistan.[3]

In Iraqi Kurdistan an independent Kurdish kingdom was proclaimed in 1922 by Sheikh Mahmoud, under the banner of the "Free Kurdistan Movement." Although he had no connection with the old Kurdish princely houses, Mahmoud sprang from an illustrious Qadiri Sufi religious order, that of Barzinja (Barzanja). He thus enjoyed supreme religious status when he sought political station as well. His power base was in the Sorani-speaking, less tribal and more urbane, southern portion of Iraqi Kurdistan, where he was a precursor of Jalal Talabani and his political party, the Patriotic Union of Kurdistan (PUK).

Mahmoud was originally chosen by the British authorities to help them in administering the Kurdish regions of their newly acquired Mandate of Iraq. He soon proved to have other ideas and priorities, the least of which being to hand over his homeland to a European potentate. He was quickly arrested and sent to exile in India, only to be brought back a year later. True to the problem facing every Kurdish leader in the twentieth century, throughout his 12-year struggle Mahmoud had to fight as much against Kurdish tribal chiefs and political aspirants as the British forces, and could claim real authority only in his home district of Sulaymania. He was a representative of the old society, and aroused considerable animosity among the modernist Kurdish intellectuals, who blamed the Kurdish predicament on just those values that Mahmoud and traditionalists like him stood for and promoted. Meanwhile, the local tribal chieftains for their part did not see much difference between giving up their semi-independence to Mahmoud or to London and Baghdad. Mahmoud's strong and specific religious background could not have helped his cause among those Kurds who were not Sunni Muslims of the Qadiri Sufi order. Yet despite all these handicaps, Mahmoud and his aspirations for an independent Kurdish state remained popular.[4]

In 1926, the League of Nations Commission, citing the cruel treatment of both the Assyrian Christians and the Kurds at the hands of Turkish troops, awarded the former Ottoman province of Mosul (the Mosul Velayet) to Iraq. The League required Iraq to allow cultural and social autonomy in the Kurdish regions.

Having hoped to receive central Kurdistan as his independent kingdom from the League of Nations, the disappointed Mahmoud went into action again. First he moved his headquarters across the border into Iran to commence a new round of struggle from relative safety. There, Mahmoud staged a revolt in the town of Marivan, hoping to wrest the territory from Persia and use it as a staging ground against the British in Iraqi Kurdistan. Beaten back by Persian forces sent by the new Pahlavi monarch, Reza Shah, he moved once again across the border to Sulaymania, where he was suppressed one more time by the British in the spring of 1930.

As early as 1927, the Kurmanji-speaking[5] northern section of Iraqi Kurdistan was the scene of another, rather peculiar, uprising led by the charismatic religious leader of the Barzani clan, Sheikh Ahmad. He was the elder brother of the well-known Kurdish political leader, General Mustafa Barzani, and a leader of the influential Naqshbandi Sufi order. Ahmad took on the British, Turks, and Arabs, as well as fellow Kurds (the rival Baradost clan). As if that were not enough, Ahmad also challenged traditional Islam by instituting a new religion, which was to bring together Christianity, Judaism, and Islam in one. Possibly hoping to unite the religiously fragmented Kurds, he also included elements of Yazdanism by declaring himself the new avatar of the Divine Spirit.[6]

Ahmad's forces were put down by British and Iraqi troops after several years of fighting. They were supported by Royal Air Force bombers, whose appearance stunned the Kurdish villagers more than the destruction their bombs wrought on their lives and property.[7] Defeated, Sheikh Ahmad escaped to Turkey, but later was arrested and sent into exile in southern Iraq. His legacy within the Barzani clan was passed on to his brother Mustafa, who raised the specter of Kurdish home rule (as early as 1940, but mainly in the course of the 1960s), which stretches to this day.

An unfortunate result of Mahmoud's and Ahmad's fierce and long struggles against the British in central Kurdistan was that it weakened British resolve to grant local Kurdish autonomy, as called for in the League of Nations' articles of incorporation of central Kurdistan into the State of Iraq. The Anglo-Iraqi Treaty of 1930, which provided for the independence of Iraq in 1932, did not include any specific rights of autonomy, or in fact rights of any other kind, for the Kurds.

Protesting the terms of the treaty of Iraqi independence, the seemingly unsinkable Mahmoud rose one last time in 1931. Having finally scaled down his expectations following a dozen years of fruitless struggle, Mahmoud this time asked for only an autonomous Kurdistan. The British refused, and by December 1931, Mahmoud had been broken for good. But his tenacity and dogged struggle for the rights and aspirations of his people bore fruit nonetheless in an unexpected manner. The Iraqi independence treaty of 1932 provided for the teaching of Kurdish in the schools and for the election of local Kurdish officials in Iraqi Kurdistan. After 1932 a relative calm descended upon the ravaged countryside of central Kurdistan, for the first time since 1914. But now the game was being played with increasing ferocity in Turkey and soon in Iran as well.

Kurds in Iran

As an independent state, Iraq did not exist before its invention by the British following their takeover of the region in 1918. Therefore, Kurds have been part of Iraq since 1926 and the inclusion of the Kurdish-inhabited Ottoman Velayet of Mosul in the British Mandate. In contrast, there are no clear beginnings in Iran—Persia until 1935—an ancient state that finds its name mentioned even in the Old Testament. There have been myriad dynasties representing scores of ethnic groups that have ruled Persia, Kurds included. On occasion, Persia/Iran has been divided into many independent states, while at other times, it has been unified and brought under a powerful central government that expanded its borders into Asia, Africa, and Europe.

One may place the beginning of the modern state of Iran/Persia to A.D. 1501 and the emergence of the Safavid dynasty. Henceforth, the state we recognize today as Iran came to be a permanent and a primary political actor of the Middle East. The Safavid dynasty itself was a hybrid of Kurdish and Turcoman bloodlines, with the root being fully and completely Kurdish.[8] On another occasion, a hybrid of Kurd and Lur elements ruled Persia under the Zand dynasty, A.D. 1750–94. Despite this, at all times until relatively recently a number of ancient Kurdish dynasties ruled autonomously (and occasionally, independently) over Kurdish lands and paid the

Map 3.2 Republic of Kurdistan in the context of Kurdish inhabited lands, 1946.

scantiest fealty to the imperial government of Persia. Not until 1867 did the writ of Tehran run directly in Kurdistan via governors appointed from the capital.

The last of the Kurdish autonomous principalities, the ancient house of Ardalan, was overthrown in 1867 by the central government of Persia, ruled at the time by the (Turcoman) Qajar dynasty. Smaller Kurdish chiefdoms, meanwhile, lasted until the late 1920s. Then came the unique phenomenon of a short-lived Kurdish republic.

By the autumn of 1940 and as a result of the Allied invasion of Iran, the Iranian Kurds initiated an independence movement. Having suffered from a lack of security, the interference of Soviet forces in the local economy, and the resulting famines, in 1945 Iranian Kurds established an independent Kurdish republic in Mahabad. Republican forces quickly expanded their domain south toward Sanandaj and Kirmanshah. Beaten back at the battle of Divandara, they retreated to a tiny enclave behind the Soviet defense lines in the zone they occupied in Iran (see map 3.2). Democratic elections held with an admirable absence of ballot fraud resulted in the formation of a national parliament and state ministries, election of a president (Ghazi Muhammad) and a cabinet. Technically, the Republic lasted for one year (from December 1945 to December 1946), during which time Kurdish state apparatuses and ministries were formed and functioned, until their destruction at the hands of the Iranian forces. The memory of the Republic is held supreme in Kurdish national consciousness.

The Republic of Kurdistan (or the Mahabad Republic, as it is often known to Western writers) was, nonetheless, a by-product of the Soviet occupation of northwest Iran (the Soviets also helped with the creation of a neighboring Azerbaijan Democratic Republic centered on Tabriz). The Republic would have had no chance of emerging, had the central Iranian government not been evicted from the area by Soviet forces. Both the Kurdish and Azerbaijan republics unquestionably were marked by the Russians for incorporation into the Soviet Union when World War II ended. This was so, although the historical records of the time and the recently opened Soviet archives prove that the Kurds' republic was not a Soviet creation.[9]

It is rather naive, however, to believe there would have been any chance of survival for this brave Kurdish experiment with a democratic independent state, once the Soviet Union withdrew its supportive military umbrella. Iranian troops took Mahabad with ease, and the Republic's government surrendered without resistance. President Ghazi Muhammad refused to abandon ship when the day of reckoning for his people had arrived. The president and many of his cabinet members remained, and were hanged by Iranian forces in the city's main public square at the site where they had taken their oath of office nearly two years earlier.[10] The Kurdish republic was disbanded, one week short of its first anniversary.[11]

Postwar Developments

Kurds in Iraq

The relative calm that descended upon Iraqi Kurdistan due to the progressive articles included in the Iraqi Constitution, which guaranteed the rights of the religious and ethnic minorities, was to last until the fall of the monarchy in Iraq in 1958. Kurds viewed this new, republican period with much hope. In fact, the military regime of 'Abd al-Karim Qasim between 1959 and 1963 placed the Kurdish sun disk (a yellow disk surrounded by seven red rays) as the central emblem on the Iraqi state flag. Qasim is believed to have been an assimilated, arabized Kurd himself, even though his adversarial policies toward the Kurdish leadership did not endear him or his government to them, resulting in a few, rather minor, insurgencies. After toppling Qasim's military junta in Baghdad, the Baath party leaders who replaced him reached a comprehensive settlement with the Kurds. The Kurdish sun disk was, however, now dropped from the Iraqi state flag.

On March 11, 1970, Saddam Hussein (then vice-chairman of the Revolutionary Command Council, the second most powerful man in the regime) negotiated a deal with General Mulla Mustafa Barzani, the Iraqi Kurdish Democratic Party (KDP) leader.[12] The agreement explicitly declared, "The people of Iraq are made up of two principal nationalities, the Arab and the Kurdish." The Iraqi flag, meanwhile, carried three stars as its centerpiece: one for the Shi'i, the other for the Sunni Arabs, and the third for the Kurds, representing the three largest groups of the ethno-religiously diverse country (see map 3.3). Kurdish was to be accorded the status of the second national language alongside Arabic, and an autonomous Kurdish Region was to be established within four years of the signing of the treaty. Only Kurdish-speaking government officials would be appointed to serve within the autonomous region. A Kurd was actually appointed the vice-president of the Iraqi Republic. But the agreement was not destined to stand.

Each side seemed to think it could have gotten a better deal, and that it had been tricked by the other party. Both sides, the following events showed, were just buying time. General Barzani escaped an assassination attempt on September 29, 1971, less than a year after signing the agreement. This event did not diminish his misgivings as to the intentions of Baghdad, and of Saddam Hussein, whom he suspected as the mastermind of the attempt.

By the beginning of 1973 the KDP's publications were already bitterly dismissing the agreement and sincerity of Baghdad. They complained of the continued Arabization program, the arming of the KDP's rival Kurdish groups, and attempts against the lives of its leadership. A widely circulated official publication dated June 1973 summarizes these grievances:

> The present policy of Arabization which is being diligently pursued inside Kurdistan is a perfect example of how sincere efforts for the implementation and practice of Kurdish autonomy have been replaced by sinister and systematic plans to arbitrarily detach parts from the area of the proposed Kurdish autonomy and to cut up and divide the population of Kurdistan. One has only to follow the progress of this hateful policy in the areas of Kirkuk, Khanaqin, Sinjar and parts of the province of Nineveh [Mosul] and Duhok to see in use such measures as the bringing of Arab tribes from outside to settle them in Kurdistan; the deliberate creation of antagonism between the Kurds and the ethnic and religious minorities living in Kurdistan; the resort to terror and the arming and financing of suspicious and pro-government elements [among Kurds]; the mass deportation of Kurdish families and clans;[13] and the pursuit of a definite policy of discrimination against the Kurds of these areas by refusing them government jobs and by

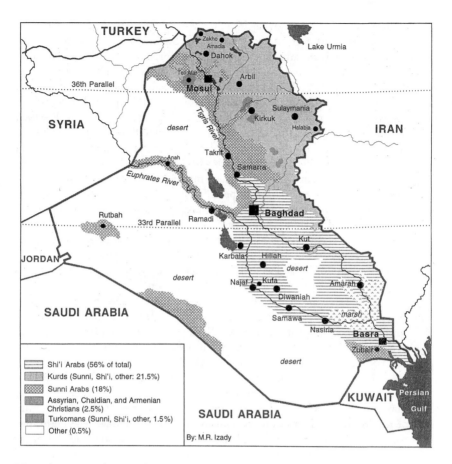

Map 3.3   Iraq and its peoples.

arbitrarily transferring Kurdish civilian and military officials to the southern part of
Iraq. All this is done to make life miserable for the original Kurdish population of these
parts and consequently to force them out . . . All this is in addition to the plots that are
organized against the life of Barzani and the local military attacks which have been carried out against such areas of Kurdistan as Aqra, Barzan and others.[14]

Barzani repudiated the agreement later in 1973. He quickly established ever more
cordial relations, overt and covert, with the three archenemies of Iraq—Iran, Israel,
and the United States.

In 1974, at the end of the four-year interim period, Baghdad published the details
of the law that would govern the Kurdish autonomous area. While it provided for
Kurdish executive and legislative local councils, real power over the internal affairs of
the autonomous region was held in Baghdad.[15] The restrictive law conformed with
neither the word nor the spirit of the 1970 agreement.

Both sides were itching to show their military muscle, and this provided them with ample excuse. Kurdish forces, under Iraqi KDP direction, within a few weeks commenced massive guerrilla attacks on government forces and installations. Their alliance with Iran became more and more conspicuous, as cash and arms from the shah were augmented by U.S. and Israeli intelligence and funding. Seeking regional supremacy and an upper hand in his territorial dispute with Iraq, the shah found the Iraqi Kurds a suitable thorn to press in the side of Baghdad. He did not, however, want an outright Kurdish victory, as he would then need to deal with the heightened aspirations of his own Kurdish minority. The shah shrewdly profited from the Iraqi Kurdish uprising, increasing aid to the Kurds when they were in trouble, and decreasing it when they were gaining ground. Barzani, meanwhile, appeared oblivious to this.

Armed with these "allies," Barzani appeared to have the Iraqi government at a disadvantage. He then committed a strategic mistake by ordering a switch from guerrilla to conventional warfare against the central forces. The Kurdish *peshmerga* guerrillas, adept at elusive warfare in the mountains since at least the time of the Medes and the conquest of Assyria, were no match in a conventional war against the clearly superior Iraqi forces, and were soon cut to pieces. By 1975, the Kurdish forces had been chased to within a few miles of the Iranian border and then over it.

Realizing the fast-approaching defeat of Barzani's forces, and that the war gave him the opportunity to press Baghdad into a treaty on terms favorable to Iran, the shah correctly concluded that the Iraqi Kurds' day in the sun had passed. He agreed in Algiers (March 6, 1975) on the terms of a treaty of friendship with Iraq, and, for turning his back on the Kurds, received all the land and sea concessions he had wanted. Saddam Hussein signed for Iraq. Mustafa Barzani ended up in exile in Tehran on a meager Iranian government stipend.[16]

Triumphant, Baghdad embarked on a systematic program of reducing the influence of Kurdish political parties in its domain, while pouring financial and human resources into rebuilding the devastated Kurdish countryside. It hoped to co-opt the Kurdish citizens by giving them a fairly reasonable "piece of the pie." A small "Kurdish Autonomous Region" was created in Iraqi Kurdistan under Baghdad's strict supervision and control (see map 3.4). It included about half of the Kurdish-populated lands in Iraq. Meanwhile, a government-sponsored program of Arabization of certain Kurdish regions gained momentum. This last program, however, appears in retrospect to have been in vain, despite many population transfers, deportations, and the enticement of Arab immigrants from as far afield as Sudan and Mauritania to settle the Kurdish highlands.

Kurds during the Iran–Iraq War

The start of the war between Iraq and Iran, and the open siding of the Iraqi KDP with Iran, did not help the Kurdish case in the eyes of average Iraqis. This was to have been expected, however, since the KDP had its headquarters in Iran and had derived a good deal of its budget from Iranian sources since Barzani's 1975 flight from Iraq. While the war was going well for Iraq, Baghdad cared little what the Iraqi KDP was doing in Iran. After the reversal of its fortunes and the invasion of Iraqi

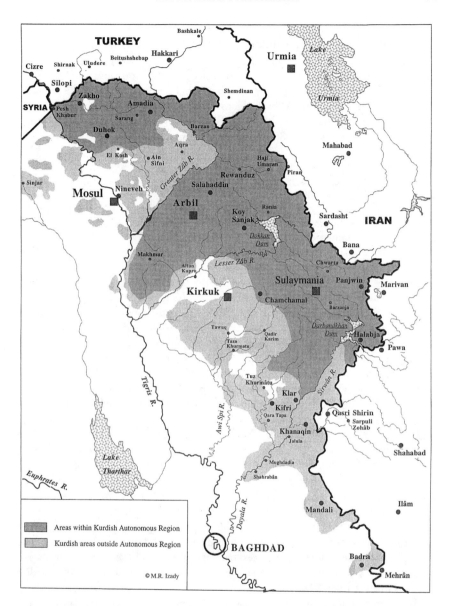

Map 3.4   Kurdish autonomous region of Iraq, 1974–91.

territories by Iranian forces in the summer of 1982, it began to care much more. Failing to co-opt the KDP with a number of peace offerings, in 1984 Baghdad struck a deal with the other Kurdish political party, the PUK, led by Jalal Talabani.

As the war with Iran went ever more awry, Baghdad was forced to sue for a settlement with the Kurds, at almost any price. Talabani succeeded in extracting from

the desperate Saddam Hussein concessions that were much more generous than in
the original 1970 agreement with Mustafa Barzani. The Autonomous Region was to
expand to include all of the disputed areas, and Kirkuk. The degree of local autonomy was to be strengthened, to include free elections for local councils. The region
was also to be allocated 25–30 percent of the overall Iraqi state budget. Nonetheless,
since the agreement was made by Saddam under duress, it is doubtful that, had it
been signed and ratified, Baghdad would have adhered to it without major alter-
ations after the ceasefire of 1988. As *The Economist* observed,

> The break [in Talabani-Baghdad negotiations] came when Turkey's foreign minister
> arrived in Baghdad to assert that the Kurdish autonomous area with the proposed
> expanded powers was too autonomous for Turkey's liking, and that the agreement, at
> that point awaiting signature, should not be implemented. Dependent on the pipelines
> through Turkey for its oil exports, Iraq complied with its big neighbor's wish and
> dropped the Kurdish deal. It also, the same year, granted Turkey the right of hot pur-
> suit of dissident Turkish Kurds across the frontier.[17]

Fighting between Kurdish and Iraqi troops resumed, lasting for another four
years, but now with a sinister dimension. The Iraqi military had used chemical
weapons with caution on the Kurdish fighters and then on civilians since 1985.
Having been encouraged by the silence of the international community and the
United Nations while using them regularly on Iranian forces, in March 1988 the
Kurdish town of Halabja became the site of the first extensive use of chemical
weapons on civilians since they were outlawed after the horrors of World War I. Up
to 5,000 people were reported to have perished in Halabja. Between March and
August 1988, Baghdad finally put down the insurrection by the use of chemical
weapons on civilians and guerrilla fighters alike.

On August 20, 1988, a ceasefire took effect between Iran and Iraq, ending their
eight years of war. Free to act against Kurdish rebels, Baghdad resorted to much more
extensive use of chemicals. In the same month, an area to the north of Mosul was
victimized. The affected region is a triangle located on the Iraqi borders with Syria
and Turkey. The Kurdish towns of Zakho, Duhok, and Amadiya mark the corners of
this triangle. Through this region pass the Iraqi–Turkish oil pipelines to the
Mediterranean and the highway connecting Iraq to Europe via Turkey. By any measure this area is of extreme economic importance to Baghdad. Gas canisters dropped
from planes and helicopters on villages, hamlets, and farms in the region were apparently meant to flush out or kill every inhabitant. Approximately 65,000 Kurdish
civilians lost their lives.[18]

To enforce better control over the Kurdish populace and deny civilian logistical
support to the Kurdish guerrillas, after 1988 Baghdad embarked on a scorched earth
policy reminiscent of the Persian policy of the sixteenth and seventeenth centuries.
An astonishing amount of work was dedicated to the destruction of hundreds of villages and infrastructure supporting life in central Kurdistan. Buildings were first
blown up and then bulldozed. Cement was poured neatly into wells and irrigation
works to choke them. Power transmission towers were pulled down and burned, if
of wood, or dynamited if of concrete. Witnessing such an admirably efficient, and

costly, effort in even the far corners of Iraqi Kurdistan, one cannot help remark on the irony. The Kurdish countryside was long in want of just such attention, and such meticulous feats of engineering, as the Iraqis were lavishing on it—but it was needed for construction, not, as it was now receiving, for destruction.

Kurds versus the Iranian Government

In Iran, the relative calm that had taken effect after the fall of the Kurdish Republic and the heavy-handed repression by Iranian military and security forces broke down with the country-wide disturbances and bloodshed that followed the "White Revolution" of Shah Mohammad Reza Pahlavi starting in 1962. Benefiting from the diversion of attention of Tehran from Kurdistan to more dangerous hot spots around the country, Kurds took up arms again. But now, and for the first time, they had the United States to answer to.

In March–April 1963, operations began in Iranian Kurdistan under the supervision of the American Green Berets and Air Commandos (commanded by USAF Major Arnie Tillman and Captain Richard Secord). At the direction of the U.S. Military Assistance and Advisory Group (MAAG) compound in the Kurdish city of Kirmanshah, Iranian T-6 planes were modified by the Americans with powerful and deadly Gatling guns and wing-racks for Zuni aerial rockets and light bombs. One C-47 "psychological warfare" aircraft was even fitted with a loudspeaker! A crash retraining of the Iranian "junkyard pilots" (as the American trainers referred to them) was also put into effect. Aerial missions to support the ground operation commenced immediately. In his memoirs, Captain Secord describes the details of this successful air campaign against the Iranian Kurds:

> Both the ground and air campaigns were aimed at building the sinews of war . . . good real-time combat intelligence, and a sound doctrine for coordinated air-ground activity. With that infrastructure, the war becomes much easier.[19]

Within several months,

> the positive results of these efforts began to show themselves. The Iranians began winning more than they lost. So much so that by the fall of 1963, less than a year after arrival, the Kurdish threat to the Shah's government was virtually nil.[20]

Debatably, no other means of combat has been as successful in suppressing the Kurds as aerial warfare. After these early experiments produced impressive results, the use of air war on the Kurds became the sine qua non of any military operation in the Kurdish mountains. In one instance in 1997, the Turkish air force employed over 150 planes of various types to carry out around-the-clock raids on Kurdish guerrilla strongholds in northern Iraq, resulting in a sustained major reduction in operations by the main (Turkish) Kurdish guerrilla group, the Partiya Karkerana Kurdistan (PKK).

Following the fall of the Iranian monarchy in February 1979 and until the Islamic government could tighten its grip on the country, the grievances of several ethnic groups were transformed into armed uprisings. In Kurdistan, long-suppressed political organizations such as the Kurdish Democratic Party of Iran (KDP-I) and the Komala, a Marxist organization founded during the time of the Kurdish Republic,[21] quickly moved to secure a form of local autonomy while Tehran was still weak and willing to compromise. As the Iranian government regained strength, it used Kurdish demands for extensive autonomy as "proof" of the Kurdish goal of dismembering the state. It declared all-out war on the Kurds.

Supplied by competing Kurdish groups, particularly Iraqi Kurdish expatriates, with information and volunteers, Iranian forces stormed Kurdish strongholds. The brutality that ensued led to many international awards for the photographers and journalists who captured scenes of Kurds being executed en masse by the government forces. (Some wounded Kurds are seen in these photographs being executed while on hospital stretchers.) At the height of the Iran–Iraq War in 1983, Tehran's Prosecutor General Ayatollah Khalkhali (the notorious "hanging judge") justified draining the blood of the condemned Kurds before their execution by noting that it could save a soldier wounded in the war, and thus gain divine forgiveness for the soul of the executed Kurd. In a few years' time, most Kurdish regions were captured by Iranian government troops, using land and aerial bombardment of towns and villages to flush out the activists, including KDP-I, Komala, and members of Sunni Islamist groups.

The area and number of Kurds controlled by the leaders of Komala and the KDP-I (as well as by a new Kurdish religious movement and its leader, Sheikh Izzidin Husayni, who supported the uprising) was rather limited and at no time included more than one-quarter of Iranian Kurdistan. As a result, the overall number of Kurdish casualties and deaths was relatively small, perhaps in the range of a few thousand.

By 1983, the uprising had diminished to just a minor headache for Tehran, which, except for some remote mountain hideouts, had the Kurdish territories firmly under its control. Faced with these reverses, and following the end of the war with Iraq, the general secretary of the KDP-I, Abdul Rahman Ghassemlou, sued for peace talks with the Iranian government in 1989. However, after arriving in Vienna to meet with an Iranian delegation, he and his colleagues were machine-gunned on July 13 by the "peace negotiators" at the appointed hotel. His successor, Dr. Sadeq Sharafkandi, sought a new round of peace negotiations and made conciliatory gestures. His eloquence and urbanity, however, did not however awaken honor and decency in his enemies in Tehran or across the border in Iraq. Dr. Sharafkandi was gunned down by assassins in Berlin in 1993.

The transition this time did not go as smoothly as before. The new KDP-I leader, Mustafa Hijri (Hedjri) demanded revenge on the government forces in Kurdistan. This was a desperate move out of sheer anger, as the KDP-I forces were no match for their enemies. The new leadership of the KDP-I—in fact all those party members who had returned to Iranian Kurdistan during Sharafkandi's conciliatory term of office—were hunted down by government troops and the dreaded Revolutionary Guards (the *Pasdaran*). Many escaped to Iraq, where Iranian long-range artillery, surface-to-surface missiles, and aerial bombardment kept the KDP-I functionaries on the run even on the other side of the border. Much damage was inflicted on their hosts, the Iraqi Kurdish villagers, whose territory they used as a staging ground to attack Iran. The Iraqi PUK leadership gave its support to the refugee KDP-I members, while the Barzani-led KDP was paralyzed with indecision. At one point in early 1994, the Iranian air force was taking daily turns with the Turkish air force in bombing the Iraqi Kurdish territories in pursuit of their own respective Kurdish insurgents. And in all of this, the Iraqi Kurdish civilians paid their customary toll in death and destruction.

Kurdish "Democracy" in Iraq

In August 1990, Iraq invaded its small, but rich neighbor, Kuwait, prompting an international military coalition to expel the Iraqi forces seven months later. In March 1991, less than a week after the announcement of the Allied powers' ceasefire, the Kurds staged a general uprising in Iraqi Kurdistan. While the elite Iraqi Republican Guards were battling a Shi'i revolt in the south, the Kurdish forces, which had gathered under a coalition of all major Kurdish political parties in Iraq, took over all Kurdish-inhabited areas of Iraq, and more. On March 20, Kirkuk, the jewel in the crown of their "victory," was won. This proved to be, however, an empty victory and a cruel illusion.

After putting down the Shi'is in the south, the battle-hardened, dreaded Republican Guards advanced into Kurdistan. A massive flight ensued. Nearly half of all Iraqi Kurds fled to the borders of Turkey and Iran, as a horrific drama of mass starvation, freezing, epidemics, and harassment by Iraqi and Turkish troops unfolded. Nearly 1.5 million Kurds passed into Iran. Another 500,000 massed on the Turkish border, with only about 200,000 being allowed in by the Turks, who closed their borders after two days.

Allied forces (mainly British and American) were sent into northern Iraq to protect the Kurds. They also declared the area north of the 36th parallel off limits to the Iraqi air force. This was a little strange. The ethnic line separating Kurds from Arabs in Iraq runs almost north–south. The area thus included a large Arab population, and the multiethnic Mosul, the second largest city in Iraq. Although the designated area also included Arbil and a score of smaller towns, it left out over two-thirds of Iraqi Kurdistan, including Sulaymania, Kirkuk, Kifri, Khanaqin, and Badra. Allied forces also occupied a "Security Zone," a sliver of land north of Mosul that included the Kurdish towns of Zakho, Amadiya, and Duhok—exactly the same area that had been extensively gassed by Baghdad in August 1988. The creation of the Security Zone was designed to entice Kurdish refugees to return to Iraq and the area was later handed over to Kurdish forces.

Iraqi government functionaries were eventually chased out of the area by the Kurds, prompting a quarantine of all Kurdish-occupied areas by Baghdad. As of the end of 1991, this Security Zone had grown to include almost half of Iraqi Kurdistan, and to stretch from the Syrian borders, along the Turkish and Iranian borders to the Diyala River (see map 3.5).

The Iraqi Kurds then ushered in what appeared to be democratic rule for their liberated region, complete with general elections, a parliament, and a government. Elections were held in the summer of 1992, in which the two main Iraqi Kurdish parties, the KDP and PUK, were joined by a dozen other smaller ones to solicit

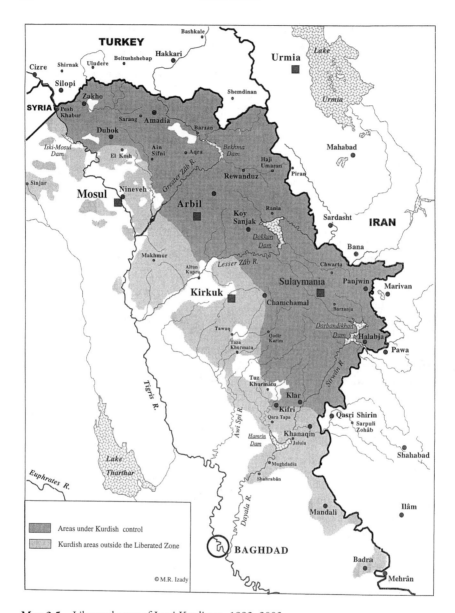

Map 3.5   Liberated areas of Iraqi Kurdistan, 1992–2003.

Kurdish votes. After the primary, a suspiciously equal 48 percent of the votes were
reported to have been cast for each of the two major parties. Surprisingly, no runoff
followed. A runoff would of course have allowed for a winner, and then a government to be formed by the winner—all at the expense of the losing parties. But

neither the KDP nor the PUK was prepared to be the loser, no matter what democracy's dictum. They muzzled any call for a runoff.

A parliament was, however, formed in Arbil, and a cabinet divided up conveniently between the candidates of these two main parties (plus a token few from the others) was seated. This was as much for the benefit of Western governments and human rights groups—those who were providing protection and doling out money to the Kurdish regional government and political leaders—as for the average Kurd.

Struggle between the KDP and PUK

As one ethnic region after another declared its independence, from Slovakia to Tajikistan, and was greeted with open arms by the international community, blind luck had also delivered Iraqi Kurdistan from its tormentors in Baghdad. Georgia, Armenia, and Azerbaijan—regions that actually border on Kurdistan—declared their independence and were admitted immediately into the United Nations. However, the Iraqi Kurdish leaders missed this historic alignment of local and international factors conducive to their independence.[22] The facade of cooperation between Barzani and Talabani was soon to shatter, as their differences led beyond verbal disagreement and into bloodshed.

Iraqi Kurdish "democracy," trumpeted with much fanfare in 1992, was as dead as it was unreal from the beginning. Domestic affairs in Iraqi Kurdish territories were abominably mishandled by the autonomous Kurdish "government." The continuing feud between the two warlords-turned-politicians, Massoud Barzani of KDP and Jalal Talabani of PUK, had by 1995 increased from low-intensity assassinations and murders to open warfare. The main cause was money. Having been deprived of a cut in the lucrative smuggling and sanction-busting business taking place across the border between Turkey and Iraq, Talabani put his close relationship with Iran to good use. By the beginning of 1995, PUK forces had pushed the KDP out of the autonomous capital at Arbil and in fact all the way up against the Turkish border.

Realizing the gravity of the situation, Barzani played the only card left in his deck: he appealed for help to President Saddam Hussein and his military—the same man and force who had poisoned Kurdish children at Halabja and in the Northern Triangle in 1988. President Hussein now issued a general amnesty to all Iraqi Kurds, inviting them back. In return, he declared there would be free movement of Kurds in the "autonomous region" (that which was recognized by Baghdad in 1975, not the one established by force in 1992). He also promised to lift the economic embargo (which was an empty gesture, realizing it was Kurdistan that was smuggling its ample surpluses into Iraq and not the reverse), and begin communication and exchange with the "rulers of the autonomous area."

The invasion of the "safe" autonomous zone of Kurdistan by Baghdad's forces in 1996, even if by the personal invitation of one of the Kurdish leaders, offended and baffled the United States, leading to cruise missile attacks on Baghdad and a stiff warning to withdraw. Iraqi forces did so after having reinstalled Mr. Barzani, but they remained clandestinely to help Barzani regain his fief and incur more favors to Baghdad. It was now his turn to corner Talabani between a rock and a hard place—the

Iranian border. As the city of Sulaymania fell to the KDP forces who were reinforced by Iraqi regulars, nearly 80 percent of the population fled in well-justified fear toward their usual place of refuge: Iran.

By 1996, the little town of Penjwin on the Iranian border had become another scene of mass suffering for the fleeing Kurdish civilians. Rupert Colvill of the UNHCR in Geneva estimated 75,000 had huddled into Penjwin, formerly a town of 5,000, on their way to the ever-present refugee camps in Marivan, Iran.[24] Iranian officials estimated that 250,000 refugees were pushing up against their borders, stating they would be allowed to cross only if their lives were in danger. Iran hoped to avoid a repeat of the humanitarian crisis of 1991.

The United States, of course, would not allow the current reversal and the entry of the Iraqi forces into Kurdistan to stand. American opposition ultimately prevented the continuation of this cozy relationship between Mr. Barzani and his newfound friend, President Saddam Hussein. The warlord was ordered to remove himself from the territories of Talabani, and allow the latter to restore his fief at Sulaymania. The words of an exasperated Kurdish refugee woman summarized the predicament that Kurds have faced in the past and are facing today: being stuck between the rock of many external enemies and the hard place of their own incompetent, often criminal, political leadership. "Massoud Barzani is no better than Saddam Hussein," stated Media Kareem to the reporters on the Iranian border, complaining that Iran was not an inviting place for the Kurds either. "We don't like the system there," she said. "They are worse than the Iraqis."[25]

U.S.-sponsored talks between the warring parties took place at Drogheda, Ireland in August of 1995, where the representatives of the PUK and KDP agreed to end their 15-months' long bloody conflict. (The signing of the agreement by Turkey raised quite a few eyebrows.) Their battles had cost the lives of nearly 2,000 of their guerrilla forces and an untold number of civilians. The Drogheda agreement provided for the cessation of verbal and physical hostilities between the two parties, release of the prisoners, and the demilitarization of Arbil, the capital of the Iraqi Kurdish free areas and the seat of its parliament. The parties agreed at Drogheda to share the proceeds from the border tariffs (mainly on illegal oil shipments). These were then collected solely by the KDP, which controlled the primary border crossing between Turkey and Iraq at Khabur-Silopi on the Tigris. However, provisions for the division of income between the two warlords could not be enforced. A withdrawal of KDP forces, however, ultimately took place and the territorial status quo ante was restored by 1998.[23] The flow of a large portion of revenue from Iraqi oil sales to the Kurdish region by the Allies starting in late 1996, however, satisfied the financial needs of Barzani and Talabani, leading to a relative calm between the two sections of "liberated" Iraqi Kurdistan. From 1996 to the autumn of 2002, Kurds in both sections prospered and luxuriated in the peace thus purchased.

Meanwhile, rampant human rights abuses carried out by various Kurdish political groups against fellow Kurds in Iraq were noted in a special report by Amnesty International (February 1995), and international sympathy for the plight of the Kurds dissipated. The window of opportunity for Kurdish independence was nailed shut.

Prospects of Kurdish Independence

Should Iran or Iraq, or in fact anybody, worry about the emergence of an independent Kurdistan any time soon? Nearly all the evidence leads to a negative answer. There are numerous internal and external factors that militate against creation of an independent Kurdistan, in Iraq or elsewhere. These include the prevalence of despotism, the legacy of regionalism, and geopolitical factors.

Despotism

There is no satisfactory model to prescribe the right method to inculcate the desire for political democracy in a population that has not experienced it in their living memory. Kurds and Kurdish leaders are as much novices when it comes to political democracy as the rest of the Middle East. What there is of democracy in that vast area is at best democracy in form, but never in substance. More often, even the form is missing. In a nonelective, nondemocratic environment, only the most crafty or ruthless climbs to the position of leadership.

The engulfing of Kurdistan by satellite communications and its connection to cyberspace in the past few years has brought about a profound realization about the nature of their leadership among average Kurds. A good example is Abdullah Öcalan, chairman of the PKK. After his arrest and trial in Turkey in 1999, he pleaded passionately for his own life, while unabashedly offering to short-circuit the entire Kurdish movement in Turkey in return. It is hard to fathom the mental anguish of a Kurdish public who have given tens of thousands of lives and 15 years of suffering, willing to follow Öcalan's lead, only to find the *Serok* or "Leader" selling them off summarily. Broadcast live on their televisions, the Kurdish viewers could not help but witness the self-evident fact that Kurdistan is not just a victim, but a den of self-serving tyrants.

Most Kurds, however, have been loath to denounce the despotic and self-serving leaders among them. Some are honor-bound by family and clan ties. Others simply are worried about embarrassment in the eyes of the outsider. The intellectuals have more commonly covered up the evils of the leadership than pronounced them. In doing so, they have perpetuated the abuse of the trust placed by the people in their leaders. In fact, the leaders fully expect such a cover-up by their subjects and all Kurds for the sake of saving the national "face."

To achieve any improvement in the Kurdish leadership, the level of Kurdish political and social awareness needs to be elevated by inculcation of love for truth. This decisive feat would require the Kurds' enlightenment about the foundation blocks of a representative democracy. No nation can expect the establishment of priorities and the keeping of commitments by its leaders without first cultivating such virtues in individual citizens. In this regard, in 1820 Thomas Jefferson wrote, "I know of no safe depository of the ultimate powers of the society but the people themselves, and if we think them not enlightened enough to exercise that control with a wholesome discretion, the remedy is not to take it from them, but to inform their discretion."[26]

Regionalism

For pan-Kurdish aims to be achieved, a major chasm, or series of chasms, in Kurdish political culture must be spanned, that is the wide variations in "weltanschauung" and social ideals of the five regions of contiguous Kurdistan.

The reason for the divisions between the political culture of the Iranian Kurds and those of Iraq are obvious, though not widely known. So much attention has been focused on the modern, post–World War I division of Kurdistan that most scholars have come to neglect another, far older dividing line in Kurdistan, separating the Iranian Kurds from the rest. The Iranian Kurds have been living in that country since ancient times. In the process, they have absorbed from—and contributed much to— the Iranian national political culture and social ethos more than to the larger Kurdish political culture. The contact between the Iranian Kurds and their ethnic kin was and remains through central Kurdistan in Iraq, an area that traditionally has served as a crucial bazaar of ideas from various segments of Kurdistan.

Different styles of political leadership evident in Kurdistan naturally tend to reflect the predominant subculture of their respective area. In fact, reviewing the Kurdish political parties, their leadership, and their style of conduct is the quickest way of discerning the character and strength of regional differences within the Kurdish nation.

In northern Iraqi Kurdistan, the Barzani-led KDP represents an ethos embodying the northern Kurdish tradition. It is familial, with firm grassroots connections through tribal and local elders and community clan leaders. The Barzanis are religious, with their followers being traditionalist and inward-oriented people. In consulting tribal elders on all important decisions, they continue the time-honored tradition of tribe-based democracy. They treat their followers as members of the same extended family.

In central Kurdistan in Iraq, the Talabani-led PUK represents a more urban, modern, and outward-looking populace, with a strong connection to southern Kurdistan in Iran. The party is less religious, as is characteristic of these parts of Kurdistan, and its leaders less often consult local clan, tribal, or religious leaders. They view the KDP and its followers from a position of sophistication and modernity, scorning the tribal, religious, and peasant affinities of their northern counterparts, the *goundi* (hillbillies) who never cease to be an embarrassment in any undertaking, political or social.

This PUK viewpoint is shared by many average Kurdish citizens of this area, who populate some of the most ancient urban centers of Kurdistan and pride themselves on a clear and venerable history stretching back for thousands of years. Meanwhile they never fail to confess their admiration for the honesty, valor, generosity, and the "natural looks" of their rougher northern compatriots.

The northerners' view of Talabani's party is equally contradictory. They consider the PUK to be an effete organization, more concerned with looks than substance, and led by people whose preferred means are treachery rather than valor and who seldom are willing to give their lives for their honor. Nonetheless, they admire the sophistication and cosmopolitanism of these southerners, and envy the very same "sophisticated looks" they spend so much time smearing.

The Iranian KDP, with its base in eastern Kurdistan, is less clannish, and while counting on support from local patricians and clan leaders, is elitist. Reflecting its constituents' feelings, the party leaders bear an unflattering view of the neighboring Kurds of central, and particularly northern, Kurdistan. They regard them as basically hard-minded, barely educated tribal people whose long association with the alien Arab and Turkic cultures has rendered their social behavior an embarrassment and their culture adulterated. They "authenticate" this by noting that most Kurds of Turkey and Iraq have no grasp of the meaning or background of Kurdish culture and history. The Iranian Kurds regard themselves superior in all elements of culture and believe their subtlety sets them apart from the "unpolished hillmen." At the same time, these eastern Kurds look for political leadership from the crude and rough, but also trustworthy, solid, witty, and can-do Kurds of Iraq.

The southern Kurdish political elite distance themselves from other Kurds even farther. Most, if not all, find Kurdistan too small and unpromising a place to "waste" their political or cultural talent, and find Baghdad or Tehran, if not Vienna, Paris, or New York, to be preferable locales. Even today, there is no exclusively Kurdish political party to speak of in the south, as the elite find outlets for their political ambitions outside Kurdistan. For example, Karim Sanjabi (d. 1995), an unassimilated Kurd from Kirmanshah, long headed the important Iranian National Front Party (founded by Mohammad Mosaddeq). The political culture of the southern and eastern Kurds is Iranian in outlook, and far more easily understood in the context of the state's political culture than any pan-Kurdish one.

Kurdish Geopolitics

A further impediment to their national well-being is that the Kurds lack natural friends in their immediate vicinity. In this respect they contrast markedly with the Palestinians, who are surrounded and generally supported by other Arabs and serve as a unifying cause for pan-Arabists. The Kurds share an ethnic identity with none of their sovereign neighbors. The Kurds are thus victims of their own strategic location and world geopolitical concerns. They remain friendless locally and internationally.

At the same time the Kurds, due to their dispersal, are divided into many geopolitical blocs, each with a distinct state culture and weltanschauung whose influence they cannot entirely escape. Today the eastern and southern Kurds are expected to follow the Islamic, traditionalist ideology of Iran, while the Iraqi and Syrian Kurds, on the other hand, have been obliged to adapt their heritage and justify their existence under the radical Arabism of these two anti-Western states. In Anatolia, Kurdish culture faces a Turkey with a southeast European outlook and a staunchly pro-Western, modernist government.

These cultural, economic, and political forces are pulling the segments of the Kurdish nation in various directions. If not stopped, in the long run they will undoubtedly undermine the cultural coherence and national identity of the Kurds, creating new nations out of the single old one. One may in fact ask: Would Kurds still form a nation today if the common element of suffering under foreign prejudice and oppression were to be removed?

Based on the experience of other nations, three types of independence for Kurdistan are possible, and examined below:

A pan-Kurdish state. A nearly all-inclusive, pan-Kurdish state is the most elusive of all options, not just for external reasons, but internal ones as well. This option entails the dismemberment of four Middle Eastern states, including its two most populous and powerful ones, Iran and Turkey. Middle Eastern societies are far from that level of social maturity that allows for the Quebecois or the Slovaks to divorce Canada and Czechoslovakia by simply voting for it. None of the states administering portions of Kurdistan are about to allow such a luxury to the Kurds or any other group living under their jurisdiction any time soon. In view of the effectiveness of modern weaponry, a protracted bloody war between the Kurds and these states will surely result in destroying more than would ever survive to become part of that pan-Kurdish state. Short of a cataclysm of the magnitude of World War I and the breakup of the all local states' structure, one cannot see how else the Kurds can extract all their people and territories from these states.

A pan-Kurdish state may not even be feasible or desirable for internal Kurdish reasons. Kurdish society's cultural cleavages are as vast as those that normally exist among all large, far-flung nations. To politically unite the Kurds of Marash and Antep with those of Sanandaj and Kirmanshah may be as awkward and impracticable as uniting under the same flag the comparably distanced Arabs of Iraq, Kuwait, and Syria, or Germans of Austria, Switzerland, and Germany. The only possible way would be through undemocratic force. (Recall that it was the Prussian military that forcefully united over a score of German principalities and polities into a single German state by 1871. Even then, Austrian and Swiss Germans remained outside and independent.)

But, in the event that such a pan-Kurdish state did come to be formed, it should in the long run fare well. Economically, it would have vast water and agricultural resources. Its petroleum reserves are already well developed, with its own refineries, pipelines, and exporting facilities on the Gulf of Alexandretta in place. It would be one of the biggest countries in the entire Middle East, and potentially one of the wealthiest. It would border at least seven sovereign countries, and would by necessity be a major player in Middle Eastern affairs.

Many Kurdistans. Why should Kurdish statehood mean a Greater Kurdistan or none? In fact, why should there be only one Kurdistan, small or large? Let us not forget that in the very neighborhood of Kurdistan there are now over a score of Arabic-speaking countries, and three Persian-speaking states. Farther afield, there are four German-speaking independent states, a score or so Spanish, and a dozen English-speaking countries. Each group of these countries has much in common historically and culturally in addition to the element of language. National identity needs more than just a common language or a common culture to translate into a voluntary uniting under the same flag. None of the above-mentioned states are rushing to unify with their brethren. Such a feat requires either brute force or a plain and immediate profit to compel the average person to opt for it. Lacking these, the prospect of a unified, pan-Kurdish state emanating solely from a common Kurdish national identity is as unlikely as a pan-Arab, pan-German, or a pan-Persian state. In the case of

Kurdistan, even now when there is no immediate prospect of independence, the various Kurdish political parties are often compelled to settle their differences through open warfare against one another. How realistic is it to expect that these same groups will put their differences aside for the sake of a unified greater Kurdistan when and if such a prospect presents itself? What would possibly prevent the far-flung, heterogeneous Kurdistan not to go the way of all these other nations given as examples above, splitting into many "Kurdistans"?

Mixed Option. A Kurdish state need not even contain most of the Kurds. The republics of Azerbaijan, Armenia, Israel, and Laos, for example, contain only a minority of the Azeris, Armenians, Jews, and Laotians alive today. Kurdish leaders like Barzani, Talabani, or Öcalan may, realistically, legitimately, and morally aim their aspirations at only their own respective portions of Kurdistan. Presently, all shun such a divisive pronouncement, banking instead on a more popular, but unrealistic position of viewing themselves as pan-Kurdish leaders and advocating a Greater Kurdistan.

In any scheme to create one or many independent Kurdistans, vast numbers of Kurds will remain outside its (their) territories. By the very verdict of geography, Kurdish-inhabited regions of Khurasan, central and western Anatolia, and the Caucasus cannot be connected to an independent Kurdistan(s) without transferring more non-Kurds populating the intervening lands to "Kurdistan" than Kurds. Kurds of central Anatolia and Khurasan have not been connected to contiguous Kurdistan since classical times. Those in the Caucasus (the territories of "Red Kurdistan") have been effectively detached from it since the middle of the nineteenth century, following the massive influx of Armenians into the khanate of Erivan (Republic of Armenia). These regions cannot be expected to join an independent Kurdistan, but the inhabitants could choose, however improbably, to emigrate in their millions and settle in such a hypothetical Kurdish state(s). These immigrant populations will have a hard time sympathizing with such a state when a real prospect of secession emerges. Being left behind, they would need to bear the brunt of the secession and demand for their speedy departure or assimilation.

In addition to these major exclaves, there is also the issue of the Kurdish diaspora. An independent Kurdish state in eastern Turkey would be an anachronism, since roughly 60 percent of the Kurds in Turkey now live outside the traditional Kurdish territories. The burgeoning Kurdish population in that state has steadily left the native Kurdish regions of eastern Turkey for the prosperous and labor-poor western Turkey, including cities such as Istanbul, Izmir, and Ankara. The two populations are now in the process of geographical integration. Kurds and Turks are now condemned—or privileged—to live together for good.[27]

Although the figures are less alarming, there are also large numbers of Kurds in Iran, Iraq, and Syria who live in the major industrial magnets and cities. These all will have to be left behind in the event of the emergence of an independent Kurdistan. Few will find it attractive to move immediately or eventually into an economically depressed new state. The example of the Jewish diaspora vis-à-vis Israel comes to mind. People grow used to and form attachment to their new lives, particularly when a new generation is born in such a diaspora. If they were subject to overt prejudice or persecution, many might move into independent Kurdistan, no matter how disadvantageous it might be economically. Many others will move on, but to similar economically developed societies, continuing their lives in diaspora, as long as they can maintain their preferred lifestyle. An independent Kurdistan will never contain all Kurds.

American Involvement and Role in Kurdistan

As the only world superpower, the United States has now inherited the Kurdish question and thus is actively involved in Kurdistan. In the past, American–Kurdish interaction was sporadic and incidental. In 1919, the European colonial empires offered a mandate over Armenia and Kurdistan to the United States, which was promptly rejected by the U.S. Senate. That august institution saw the true reasons behind Europe's offer of this "choice foothold" in Asia: using the United States and these mandates as a buffer between Soviet Russia in the north and British Iraq and French Syria in the south.

Immediately after World War II, U.S. pressure helped to evict the Soviet Union from northern Iran and thus terminate a presence that had provided the vacuum in which the Kurdish Republic had been declared and maintained at Mahabad. The entry of Turkey into NATO in 1952 placed over half of the entire Kurdish population worldwide inside the American-dominated world order. The outcome was and remains disastrous for the Kurds. Having proved to be a valuable and trustworthy ally of the United States, Turkey has been getting away with proverbial murder within its own territory and even in the territory of its neighboring states with tacit American silence if not overt support.

Nonetheless, and despite its public pronouncements to the contrary, the United States has maintained contact with the main Kurdish elements in Turkey.[28] The placing of the PKK on the U.S. State Department's list of terrorist organizations occurred only after Israel and Turkey reached a strategic military alliance in 1997. The alliance soon checked and then decisively turned back the rising tide of PKK power in eastern Turkey.

The United States need not support the Kurdish aspiration for independence in Turkey, however, because the practicability of such a desire is slowly disappearing, if not already gone. The United States is improving the lot of the Kurds in Turkey via the pressure exerted on that state by the European Union to ease up on suppressing every vestige of Kurdish identity and cultural rights. Such improvements should lead to eventual cultural and local autonomy for the Kurds in a federal Turkey if it is ever to be admitted into the European Union. Only the United States can assuage the paranoia of the Turkish generals regarding any such arrangements.

Following the advent of the Islamic Republic in Iran in 1979, the United States stopped helping that state to suppress its Kurds. Prior to that, the United States supported the Iranian government in all steps taken to maintain its full control over the Kurds, including, as mentioned above, direct bombardment of Kurdish targets by U.S. Air Force personnel in 1963. Although the Islamic Revolution effectively terminated American support for the Iranian government, it did not lead to support for the Kurdish insurgency, since no American government wants to see Iran disintegrate.

Iraqi governments, from the overthrow of the monarchy in 1958 until the onset of war with Iran in 1980, always had to worry about American plans for the Iraqi Kurds. This sometimes translated into support for the Kurdish insurgencies in northern Iraq. The most glaring of such actions was American support for the Kurdish uprising of 1974–75 already reviewed here. The Iraqi attack on Iran was seen as a positive step by the United States and the West, since it could sap Iran's revolutionary energy. All support for the Kurds in Iraq, therefore, ceased.

When the Iraqi occupation of parts of southwestern Iran was rolled back in 1982 and the prospect of Iranian occupation of the whole of Iraq became conceivable, the United States and the West threw their lot behind Baghdad to prevent just such a prospect. Sensing the same, the Iraqi Kurds sided with Iran and commenced a new insurgency against the Iraqi government. Baghdad, finding it increasingly impossible to fight the Iranians at the borders and the Kurds within its borders, resorted to extreme measures by using chemical weapons against both, beginning in 1985. The United States and the world kept their silence, even after the massive gas attacks on Halabja (March 1988) and in the Northern Triangle (August 1988).

In the 1980s, therefore, the United States was seen as the enemy of the Iraqi Kurds by suppressing any international assistance or outcry that may have saved them from being gassed by the Iraqis with total impunity. The invasion of Kuwait by Iraq in August of 1990 turned the picture upside-down once again. Now, it was the turn of Baghdad to become the pariah and the Iraqi Kurd the international darling.

As reviewed earlier, the United States established and enforced a military exclusion zone over Iraqi Kurdistan from the spring of 1991 until the Coalition invasion of Iraq in March 2003. This served two purposes from the point of view of the United States: (1) it weakened Iraq; and (2) it weakened the Iraqi Kurds. The first was of course desirable as long as the Iraqi president needed to be restrained. The second was also equally desirable, because the protection was preconditioned on the Iraqi Kurds not suing for independence at that most opportune time in their recent history. A strong Kurdish voice could have demanded independence from Iraq and throw the geopolitical balance of power in the area off kilter. None of the neighboring states wishes to see an independent Kurdistan on Iraqi territory, since it could lead to similar demands by their own Kurds. The United States does not want to see an independent Kurdistan because of the same reason. Further, a declaration of independence by the Kurds presently under American control in northern Iraq would lead to a crisis in international law, which the United States is actively preserving.

To prevent the Kurds from contemplating such an option, the United States continues to encourage the persistence of a dual political leadership in Iraqi Kurdistan. The credibility bestowed on Barzani and Talabani by their frequent entertainment in Washington and other Western capitals, and the distribution of Iraqi oil revenue to both, have indeed rendered them two kings in one realm. As long as the duo exist, no fear of Iraqi Kurdish independence need be entertained. The murderous past encounters between the two are ample proof of their inability to work together or step aside to allow for the emergence of a single common voice among the Kurds to call for independence. Moreover, the problem extends far beyond these two individuals, who represent a tribal/dynastic ruling class that will be hard to unseat, leaving little room for new voices.

War on Iraq, 2003

Following the terrorist attacks of September 11, 2001 on the United States, the new American policy of preemption led to renewed U.S. concern for Iraq. By the fall of 2002, the president of United States was preparing for an invasion of Iraq. By total serendipity, the Iraqi Kurds now found themselves on the side of the United States.

The invasion of Iraq by the Coalition Forces on March 19, 2003, has to a large degree changed the role and influence of the United States on Kurdish affairs. Today, about 15 percent of the Kurds—that is, all the Iraqi Kurds—are the wards of the United States. By pure accident, they find themselves in the most amicable and cordial relationship with America, symbolized by the tumultuous welcome of General Jay Garner, the first American military governor of Iraq, into Sulaymania in April of 2003.

The Kurds and their leaders have suddenly found themselves for the first time since the mid-nineteenth century on the side of the winner, in this case, the mother of all winners: the United States of America. Except for some small, forgivable aberrations (such as the brief occupation of Kirkuk and Mosul), they have behaved admirably, and have rendered every assistance asked of them by the U.S. forces. The Governing Council of Iraq formed in July 2003 included 5 Kurds, including representatives of Barzani and Talabani, in its membership of 25. In fact a Kurd, Mr. Hoshyar Zebari, served as the interim Iraqi foreign minister and after June 2004, as foreign minister. Oddly, he also served as Iraq's representative to the Arab League. The fortunes of the Iraqi Kurds seem to have taken an upturn.

Conclusion

How long this "Arbil spring" lasts depends not just on the United States and its geostrategic and logistical needs, but also on how long the two Kurdish warlords or their heirs refrain from commencing their usual and murderous fratricidal infighting. If that resumes, all bets will be off. Governors will be appointed by a new government in Baghdad to run the Kurdish "provinces," and incorporate the region fully into the traditional Iraqi administrative structure, not as a federated and unified Kurdish province that the Kurds are hoping for. Only the future can tell whether the Iraqi Kurds will be lucky or will fall victim once again to the whims of their unelected, unrepresentative, and uncaring leaders.

It has been said that the Kurds have only two problems: their enemies and their friends. If past events are any indication, the Kurds will continue to remain an internal nuisance to the states in which they reside. Both Iran and Iraq can find the suppression of their respective Kurds a point to bring the two together. Conversely, they can continue as in the past to encourage strife among the Kurds outside their own borders to score points with the opposite side. Lacking any natural allies, the Kurds shall continue to seek help from self-serving outside powers, and thus continue to play the pawn in the game of power-politics played by local and international actors. The sole prospect for an independent Kurdistan is through the default of others. A complete collapse of local states, coupled with a lack of objection by the United States, is the only conceivable mode by which it can be achieved, not through any endeavor of the Kurds themselves. The history of the past 150 years bears witness to this.

Notes

1. In A.D. 1900, Kurdistan remained divided between the empires of the Ottomans, Persians, and Russians. In A.D. 2000, Kurds found their homeland divided between Turkey, Iran, Iraq, Syria, Armenia, Azerbaijan, Georgia, and Turkmenistan. Large numbers of Kurds are also to be found in Lebanon, where they form about 5 percent of the population; in Germany, where they form about 1 percent of the population; and in many Central Asian and Middle Eastern countries. Russia is also home to nearly 100,000 Kurds.

2. The Ansar al-Islam is a terrorist organization founded around the towns of Penjwin and Khurmal on the Iranian border by one "Shaikh Krakar," who was imprisoned in October 2002 in Norway for his violent activities. The Ansar have already killed many Kurds and a number of American personnel in the area.

3. The dubious distinction of being among the first civilian casualties of aerial warfare, however, goes to the Sanjabi Kurds of Iran, who summered in Iran and wintered on the Iraqi side of the border. In the spring of 1918 they came under heavy British air strikes at Dasht-i Hurr with a direct loss of nearly 500 civilian lives; many times more people died attempting to ford the flooding Zamkan river in shock after having seen for the first time these new, destructive flying machines.

4. Sir Arnold Wilson, the British Civil Commissioner in Mesopotamia, verifies this by stating: "in Southern Kurdistan, four out of five people support Sheikh Mahmoud's plans for independent Kurdistan." See his book, *Mesopotamia, 1917–1920: A Clash of Loyalties; a Personal and Historical Record* (London: Oxford University Press, 1931), p. 137.

5. Kurmanji is one of the four main dialects of Kurdish, the others being Sorani, Gurani, and Dimili/Zazaki.

6. Yazdanism was the pre-Islamic, native religion of most Kurds. It survives today mainly in its denominations of Alevism, Yezidism, and Yarisanism/Ahl-i Haqq. For more on the religion of the Kurds, see Mehrdad R. Izady, *The Kurds: A Concise Handbook* (Washington: Taylor & Francis, 1992), chapter 5.

7. The use of air power against Kurdish civilian and military targets was only to expand from these landmark beginnings. Both Iranian and Turkish governments used their tiny air force against the Kurds. Turkish use of air strikes was initiated in 1931–32 at Mt. Ararat, but with negligible results. It was put to more effective use from March 1937 to October 1938 against the Kurdish district of Dersim, where the Turkish aircraft were fitted with chemical and incendiary weapons. An untold number of civilians lost their lives when they were gassed in their villages or set alight by aerial bombardment in the Dersim forests. World War II brought some initial bombardment by the British and Soviet air forces on Iranian military targets located in Kurdistan, which caused some "collateral" casualty among civilian Kurds. These attacks, however, soon ceased.

8. The putative ancestor of the dynasty, Shaikh Safi al-Din Ardabili, was of pure Kurdish descent (Ibn Bazzaz Ardabili, *Safwat al-Safa*, trans. and ed. Ahmad Kasravi (Tehran, 1927)).

9. See Olga Jigalina, "The Lessons of Mahabad," in *The International Journal of Kurdish Studies*, vol. 11, nos. 1–2 (1997).

10. For a refreshingly intimate and candid review of the Republic by current Kurdish political leaders, see "The Republic of Kurdistan: Fifty Years Later," Special Issue of *The International Journal of Kurdish Studies*, vol. 11, nos. 1–2 (1997).

11. True to his race, half a century after these tragic events, the new leader of the Iranian Kurdish movement, Dr. Sadeq Sharafkandi, was also to misjudge his foe. And like his illustrious predecessor, President Ghazi Muhammad, Sharafkandi paid with his life for his trust in the decency of his enemy.

12. Following the lead of the Iranian Kurds and their Republic, in 1941 the Iraqi Kurds established a branch of the Kurdish Democratic Party (KDP)—one of the two primary political parties of the Republic of Kurdistan—in Iraqi Kurdistan. After the demise of the Republic, the Iraqi Kurds made their own KDP independent of the Iranian main body, which continues as such to the present day.

13. This refers to the Fayli/Pahli Kurds of the lower Diyala river basin, near Baghdad.

14. "On the Kurdish Movement in Iraq," *Know the Kurds*, no. 1. The Information Department of the Kurdistan Democratic Party, June 1973, pp. 8–9.

15. Edmund Ghareeb, *The Kurdish Question in Iraq* (Syracuse: Syracuse University Press, 1981), pp. 156–70.

16. He died of cancer while receiving treatment in Virginia in 1978.

17. *The Economist*, April 27, 1991, 46.

18. U.S. Senate Foreign Relations Committee Report, 1988.

19. Richard V. Secord with Jay Wurts, *Honored and Betrayed: Irangate, Covert Affairs, and the Secret War in Laos* (New York: William Morrow, 1986), p. 50.

20. Michael E. Haas et al., *Air Commando: 1950–1975, Twenty-Five Years at the Tip of the Spear* (A USAF publication, n.p., 1994), p. 39.

21. The Komala's main area of operation is the city of Sanandaj and surrounding districts. It has been a rival to the KDP of Iran ever since.

22. When questioned by this author in New York in August of 1992 about their reason for refusing to deliver independence and salvation to the beleaguered Iraqi Kurds, Messrs. Barzani and Talabani announced before a group of reporters that "the international conditions were not right." Barzani added it was out of deference to the foreign allies, while Talabani pointed to the fear of neighboring armies marching into their territories.

23. The Drogheda agreement and the revenue-sharing deal held until the Coalition invasion of Iraq in 2003. The new, provisional constitution, adopted on November 15, 2003, does not distinguish between the Iraqi provinces in the budgetary context, so the three Kurdish federated provinces will not get a set portion of the national budget or oil income set aside for them automatically.

24. *CNN*, November 19, 1996.

25. *CNN*, November 19, 1996.

26. It is unreasonable to expect enlightened political leadership when the general population is largely unlettered and politically illiterate. This point was once made by the shah of Iran in an interview in 1972 with the Italian journalist, Oriana Fallaci. When he was asked why he did not treat the Iranians as decently as the King of Sweden treats his citizens, he replied, "I'll treat them like Swedes when they behave like Swedes." For a further assessment of this issue, see M. Izady, "The Sphinx's Beard: Notes on Kurdish Political Naiveté," in *Kurdish Life*, no. 15 (Summer 1995).

27. Personal communication by the late President Turgut Özal of Turkey during his visit to Harvard University, 1992. Also, Kaya Toperi, a spokesman for the government of Turkey, asserted in a (U.S.) National Public Radio interview on March 1, 1991 that of "about 7–12 million people of Kurdish origin living in Turkey, two thirds live outside the southeastern regions." For more information, see the section on "Demography" in Izady, *The Kurds*, pp. 111–20.

28. In mid-2004, a PKK office was still open and active in Washington, albeit with a different name. This is despite the fact that the PKK was placed on the list of terrorist organizations in 1997 and remains so today.

Chapter 4

The Antinomies of Iran's War Generation*

Farideh Farhi

I told my wife that the front has such purity and joy (safa). It takes over people. You cannot let it go.

—Dr. Houshmand, a war veteran
and physician (*Zan-e Ruz*, August 20, 1987)

Cannon, Tank, and Basij no longer have any effect.

—A campaign chant at a youth rally
during the 2001 presidential election

Oh God! Be witness that the children of our war have never been as wronged as they are now.

—*Ya Lessarat* (June 27, 2001)

I belong to a generation mostly born in the 1960s. This generation was faced with a variety of turbulences; it is a generation that saw the revolution, saw the war. Some of my friends became martyrs; some became disabled and prisoners of war. A number of them escaped from the border, became political refugees, social refugees. In any case, the generation I live with was a very different generation. Some became complete nihilists, some full-fledged idealists. In other words, it was not a generation that became indifferent to its time.

Khosrow Hasanzadeh[1]
A war veteran and painter

The difficulty of grappling with the subject of the war generation in Iran became evident to me as I posed my questions to Iranians of various backgrounds and ideological orientations.[2] The immediate response was: "Which war generation? The one that went to war or the one that was born during the war?" I wanted to know about the contemporary sociopolitical position of the one that experienced the Iran–Iraq War either at the front or elsewhere. But the initial reaction pointed to a fundamental fissure that seems to rend Iranian society, a society in which at least part of the population, voluntarily or involuntarily, went through a very intense experience of war. Yet it also contains a much larger segment of the population that, for good or bad, apparently wants to leave the war and the values propagated during the war period behind. Seemingly, in this confrontation, on the one side stands a generation born during the eight-year war[3] that declares with confidence that Iranian society can no longer be controlled or cowed by cannons, tanks, and reference to the vestiges and values of the people's militia (*Basij*) that helped to "win" the war.[4] On the other side stands a generation that sacrificed its life and livelihood in order to save the nation from Iraqi aggression. As such, in the official ideology, it is represented as the austere and yet benign guardian of values that helped Iran survive in spite of international aggression and collusion. It watches with distressed, and at times angry, eyes those whose memory of the war is either amnesiac or, even worse, blemished. Furthermore, it sometimes has to act violently, but only because no one else does and because essential values are violated. Its dilemma remains one of figuring out a way to pass on the memories, experiences of, and lessons learned during the war to the next generations.

This fundamental split, at least at the level of ideology, was abundantly clear in a public exchange that was publicized immediately after the 2001 presidential election. In an accusing letter to President Khatami, and while articulating a series of grievances about the dire economic condition of her husband and family, a reported wife of a "neurologically and psychologically disabled war veteran" (*Janbaz-e asab va ravan*)[5] bluntly asks whether Khatami has an explanation for the political rallies with "dancing and celebrations" that are held for him.[6] She further questions Khatami's motives for visiting "this sacred place" the day before the election, referring to Shahrak-e Shahid Mahallati, a large urban complex near Tehran designed to house members of the Revolutionary Guards Corps and veterans of the Iran–Iraq War. She accuses the president of "duplicitous words" and reproducing the "acts of the hypocrites," admonishing him to remain true to the Prophet and Imam Ali and stop "the excessive freedom given to young women and men in order to remain loved by people."

A reader unschooled in Iranian politics may find this letter odd in its juxtaposition of the economic difficulties of war veterans and the government's neglect of their problems, and the presumed freedom given to young men and women to dance and party at political rallies. But for Khatami the connection is clear enough. Thanking the woman for her sense of social responsibility, he is equally blunt in defending the young folks, who despite having what may be an "un-Islamic appearance," are still "attracted to the system." He then goes on to say:

> Dear sister must continue to be concerned about how, in the name of Islam and values, the name of people (which is more honorable than their blood) is easily and unfairly compromised. [She must be concerned with] how corrupt and murderous bands have found a place in organs that are supposed to be providers of security to the society but use power to kill, and engage in financial and economic abuse . . . My dear sister should continue to be concerned about how some with the support of a number of governmental institutions and organizations, by offering lies and misrepresentation of realities . . . attempt to undermine a public servant and a government that is trying to serve under the most difficult of conditions, portraying it as anti-Islam and the source of insecurity and ruin. And in this path, alas, they do so in the name of the blood of the martyrs, and the dignity and honor of the freed prisoners of war (*azadegan*), those who

sacrificed (*isargaran*) and were disabled in the war (*janbazan*) and their cherished families, which is the biggest sin because of the lying and slander it entails and doubly more so because of hiding behind the esteemed name of martyrs and values.[7]

Khatami's reference to what in Iran has come to be considered the "instrumental use" (*estefade-ye abzari*) of those who went to war (*razmandegan*)[8] in order to deny the aspirations of others is not accidental. It is a deliberate attempt to point to the controversy that surrounds the war generation and its presumed values, and the difficult terrain the reformist president must navigate in order to acknowledge the decisive contribution of that generation to Iran's recent history and yet not fall into the trap of separating that generation from the rest of society.

Meanwhile, those who went to war, in all their diversity, are faced with contradictions of their own. On the one hand, they have every reason not to be happy about the societal amnesia about the war and values that were celebrated during the war. At the same time, the imposed official rendition of what the war and the war generation were about must also be a source of concern for war veterans for a variety of reasons. To say the least, as hinted by the quotation from Khosrow Hasanzadeh cited above, it undermines the diversity that characterizes the generation born in the 1960s from which most of the war combatants were presumably drawn. More importantly, the official rendition posits the war veterans in an idealized time warp from which they can never escape or evolve. Finally, it places them at odds with the rest of society, particularly the youth, who may be ready to honor the sacrifices made but not if those sacrifices are constantly reiterated and used to block the aspirations of others. In fact, it could easily be argued that the constant harping on the values generated at the battlefront and the valor exhibited there not only does not advance the cause of cherishing the memory of those who served (and for that matter the cause of giving their families and other veterans the social services or opportunities needed for upward social mobility usually afforded to war veterans throughout the world), it actually creates resentment and backlash. After all, if indeed the "sacred defense" (*defa'e moqaddas*) of Iran was made possible *only* by the quiet and self-effacing sacrifice of countless men and women fully committed to the idea of the Islamic Republic as an expression of Divine will on earth, isn't this idea itself wholly and immediately negated by the act of propagating the fact of that sacrifice and demanding political and economic rewards on the basis of the sacrifice?

In this chapter, I attempt to delve into the contradictions faced by and imposed on the war generation in Iran. I begin with an analysis of the official representation of those who went to war. The chapter then discusses the problems this idealized representation poses for this generation, which even during the war was a much more diversified lot than acknowledged. It ends by referring to a rich array of voices that have begun to sabotage the "official version" of the war generation.

The Official Representation of the War Generation

As many students of comparative historical analysis have pointed out, revolutions have a closely knit relationship with wars.[9] Mobilization for wars and against security threats has historically offered emerging post-revolutionary state-builders an important instrument for maintaining popular support as well as an indispensable alibi for domestic clampdown and crushing of dissent. Needless to say, fighting wars requires massive material and human resource mobilization. But it is the necessary ideological and cultural groundwork for mobilizing and sustaining a war that proves more long-lasting. The Iranian post-revolutionary dynamics are no exception to this rule. The Iran–Iraq War became the basis of a new political milieu that has remained even after the war, despite the rise of other ways of thinking about and conceiving politics.

Mohammad-Javad Gholamreza Kashi identifies emphasis on Shi'i values, Shi'i-generated epic aspects of the war, mourning, opposition to existing values in the city, martyrdom, action as opposed to words, purity and devotion, and spiritual rewards in the afterlife as the most important elements of the culture of war propagated by the war machine in Iran.[10] There is no doubt that this discourse was a useful one in giving legitimacy to the war efforts and the necessary war mobilization that accompanied it. To be sure, the propagated ideal type of behavior was not completely distinct from the images generated for an ideal Islamic revolutionary during the revolution.[11] However, while the revolution brought out a multiplicity of voices, at times emphasizing contradictory aspirations (e.g., submission to Islam and the spiritual leader as well as democracy and freedom), the war offered a univocal venue for both crushing domestic opposition to the newly emerging political order as well as "sacred defense" against international aggression. According to Kashi:

> On the basis of this unitary consciousness the essence of life is worship of God, and the most important evidence of worship is war and defense of Divine values. In this model, Satan has a powerful presence both at the internal—passions—and external—temporal vices—levels. Accordingly, the true worshipper is at war both against his or her self and temporal transgressions. Of course neither of these battles can become realized merely through the pious individual. God always has proof on earth and both of these wars take place with His guardianship on earth . . . This discourse has specific practical implications, the most important of which are emphasis on war and courage, worship, control of passions, avoidance of fame and material interests, unconditional adherence to the leadership and avoidance of any questioning in this regard.[12]

Moreover, what was developed during the war engulfed the society far beyond the war front. In the cities, the locale from which volunteers were sent to war and stations for the mobilization of basij forces, the broadcast of war chants from radio, television, and loudspeakers, the "narrative of conquest" (*ravayat-e fath*) produced by a cultural foundation of the same name (the largest film production unit connected to the Islamic Revolutionary Guards Corps (IRGC) that literally brought the details of the war into peoples' living rooms every night), and ceremonies held for the funeral of war martyrs together reflected the encroachment of the values of the war front into the daily life of all Iranians. This encroachment was facilitated by the nature of the war itself, initiated by Iraq's entry into Iranian territory, eliciting a defensive response on the part of the Iranian population. So long as the war was perceived to be a defensive war and so long as Iranian resistance showed signs of success in pushing back the Iraqi military, the war and all the ideological and cultural groundwork that was needed to keep it at the center of Iranian political discourse remained extremely compelling.

At the same time, it is interesting to note that despite the prevalence of the "war mood," the war itself did not engulf the whole society in terms of the mobilization of personnel. Questions related to how many people went to war and from what age group they were drawn are actually not easy ones to answer for a war heavily dependent on volunteers, many of whom served at the front repeatedly after multiple injuries. In fact, I have yet to find an official written source identifying the number of people who went to war, including the volunteers and draftees. The numbers given to me by various sources varied from 1.5 to 3 million people for the eight year period, which even at the high end is not a large figure in light of a population that counted a little less than 50 million in 1986 (of which about 8.5 million can be counted as men between 15 and 35 years old).[13] Clearly the data given about the number that served at the front and the ratio in relation to the larger population pool from which they were drawn is problematic. First of all, using 1986 as a benchmark year for identifying the available pool is problematic for a war that lasted eight years. Also, the lack of concrete information about the age of volunteers in the war, which according to anecdotes and occasional reports by journalists included volunteers as young as 13 as well as some older than 50, makes the whole notion of "war generation" a tricky concept for Iran.[14] Nevertheless I think it is sufficient to give us clues, contrary to general perceptions, about the limited nature of mobilization for the war.

Several reasons can be enumerated for this relatively low level of war mobilization. The first and foremost is its essentially volunteer nature. To be sure, Iran has relied on a longstanding tradition of conscription developed during Reza Shah's period to satisfy the needs of its military. Universal conscription for men occurred at different stages, beginning at the age of 18 but also later depending on the level of education. But during the Iran–Iraq War, at least for the first several years, the voluntary mobilization went a long way in replenishing troops on the war front. This is not to say that mandatory conscription was not practiced. Many served despite the fact that they would have preferred not to. But active and widespread resistance did not occur. Some resisted the draft by leaving the country, while others who remained resisted it simply by not showing up to be inducted.[15] Again, this is not to say that no one was drafted against his will, simply that the government never developed a systematic mechanism for identifying draft-resisters and enlisting them, probably because it did not feel the need.[16]

Instead, and this is perhaps the second reason for the relatively limited nature of the war mobilization, given the political situation in the early post-revolutionary years and the intense conflict that surrounded the establishment of a full-fledged Islamic republic, governmental communiqués suggested a desire to limit the number of Iran's defenders to hard-core supporters of official values. For instance, on December 21, 1980 the government issued a communiqué dividing political parties and groups into four basic categories and clarifying its stance toward each category:

The ones which back the Islamic revolution, the ones which agree with it, the ones which are against it, and the ones which fight against it. . . . The state will benefit from the good ideas of the first group and even ask their help for executive tasks. The second category will sometimes be asked to cooperate. The groups which are against us but don't fight us have permission to be active, but there will not be any compromise, alliance, engagements and cooperation between us. . . . their actions could not be in support of the Islamic revolution, and even if so, we consider them as limited, tactical and dictated for political reason.[17]

The immediate post-revolutionary political and military struggles for the control of the country were indeed the most important determinants of the way the war was fought against Iraq. On the one hand, the initial failures of the established armed forces, under the leadership of President Abolhasan Bani-Sadr, undermined his claim that the war needed to be fought by professionals. On the other hand, the fluidity of the revolutionary situation made clear that whichever political group was able to mobilize popular forces would be in a better position in the power game being played. In this process, the IRGC, an institution initially organized to fight against domestic opponents in Kurdistan, Khuzistan, Torkaman Sahra, and other areas, proved to be the most proficient at organizing and mobilizing popular forces for the war.[18] In the process, it gained the upper hand as the most adept institution in defending the country and establishing internal order. It did so by developing a military doctrine that to its mind was a response to the "existing vacuum and exigencies."[19] It made a decision in favor of continuation of the war on the basis of limited operations designed according to a full understanding of the terrain, with emphasis on the use of infantry forces during night operations. Moreover, as mentioned above, the emphasis on infantry forces was made possible by an overarching policy of attracting popular forces and militia, expanding the military organization of revolutionary forces, and emphasizing in a coordinated and intense campaign values such as unity, faith, and love of martyrdom.

The popularity of this approach was dependent on the character of the war and success on the battleground. So long as the war was seen as a defensive one against Iraqi aggression, a situation that changed after Iran freed the city of Khorramshahr in May 1992, it was bound to remain popular even if the number of battleground successes were few. Even after Khorramshahr, the war remained popular because of a series of important victories, including the occupation of the abandoned Iraqi oil port of Faw in 1986, which was considered to be a logistical triumph. However, with increasing setbacks on the battleground, the human cost of continuing a strategy of achieving peace through a decisive battleground victory became increasingly debated within the regime and in society, particularly in the cities and among the educated strata.[20] The more the rationality of continuing the war became an issue, the more difficult it became to sustain the high level of volunteers, forcing the war machine to heighten the emotive content of its strategy. Rather than responding to the questions that were raised, it began to rely more and more on sacred symbols, religious lamentations and mourning ceremonies, and rigid understanding of religious duties. The war and associated self-sacrifice and quest for martyrdom, originally conceived as a means to an end, itself was presented as sacred. More importantly, sharper lines were drawn that were to be carried down to the postwar period.

On the one hand stood those who were defenders of the values of the "sacred defense": values that brought order, purity, and brotherhood to the war front. On the other hand stood the cities, void of the same values, full of women who did not cover themselves properly, people who were in pursuit of material things, young men and women who did not follow rules of "proper" conduct in their relationships, commercial advertisements on walls and billboards, and art works that were not in keeping with art sanctioned during the sacred defense. These were things that the volunteers and fighters at the war fronts were presumably aware of even during the latter part of the war.[21] But like everything else they tolerated them and, because of their commitment to a sacred war, did not made them a concern. With the end of the war, however, opportunity was afforded to the cities to make the sacred values of the war their own. Newspapers and journals reflecting the values of the front, such as *Shalamcheh* (name of an important battleground in which many Iranians were killed), *Jebheh* (*The Front*), and *Sobh* (*Morning*) began to appear with heavy emphasis on the memory, writings, and wills of those who were killed in the war as well as attacks against those who had gained economically during the war and were continuing to do so afterwards. Centers such as the Bureau for the Literature and Art of Resistance (*Daftar-e Adabiyat va Honar-e Moqavemat*) of the Islamic Propaganda Organization also began to produce numerous war memoirs and stories.[22]

More ominous, but clearly made possible by the dichotomization mentioned above, was the development of paramilitary groups, such as *Ansar-e Hezbollah*, which assumed for themselves the responsibility of "cleansing" the cities from moral and political corruption, in the name of war veterans. No systematic study has been done about the social makeup of such groups, the funding for them, and the relationship they have to institutions that prospered during the war, such as IRGC and Basij. Neither is it clear the extent to which these organizations draw from the war generation, since as reported many of their club-wielding members appear too young to have experienced the war. What is clear however is their reliance on war values to attack political opponents and perceived cultural foes.[23]

Cracks and Variety

Despite the omnipresence of the official representation of the war generation, the dichotomy created could not exist unchallenged for at least two reasons. First, contradictions began to arise at the level of official policy in the immediate postwar period. The acceptance of Resolution 598 was itself a major cultural shock in so far as it undermined the whole notion of "war, war until victory" that had been the most important motto and motivating ideal for the most diehard believers of the Islamic Republic. This is what Sa'id Tajik, the author of the very interesting war memoir *Jang Dust-dashtani Ast* (*War is Lovable*) has to say about the day Resolution 598 was accepted:[24]

> With the hearing of this news [acceptance of Resolution 598], it was as though the whole world crashed over my head. I was choked with tears. We went to see Fazel. When he saw us, he put his head down and began to cry . . . We talked of the way Imam was wronged (*mazlum*). We talked about Imam and the martyrs and we cried. That day Dokuheh [barracks] was the house of sadness and sorrow. Everyone was lost and crying . . . The smell of oppression and loneliness/exile (*ghorbat*) had taken over. That day was the worst day of our lives! In utmost disbelief, we were hearing the news that we could not have imagined.[25]

The abruptness with which peace with Iraq occurred was manifested in the fact that during its announcement slogans about the necessity of continuing the war until Saddam's demise and the conquest of Jerusalem were still not erased from city walls and billboards. Complicating the situation was lack of an explanation for the sudden change of mind on the part of Ayatollah Khomeini and the rest of the leadership. To be sure a promise was given for a later explanation, but that is still to come. In fact, the ending of the war, along with the question of whether the war should have continued after Khorramshahr, remain the Iran–Iraq War's most important puzzles or question marks and a source of debate in Iranian society.[26] The following misgivings echoed in *Fakkeh*, a journal dedicated to the concerns of rank-and-file veterans, reflect the continuing existence of unanswered questions for those who served:

> In any case, the apparent end of the war came with the acceptance of Resolution 598 in Tir 1367 by the Islamic Republic of Iran. Two years later the prisoners of war came back, but many unspoken and ambivalent points remain hidden in this eight-year file. What happened to the remainder of the captives?[At that time] Imam told people that the main reason for the acceptance of the resolution would be explained by the national authorities later . . . [these are] issues that 11 years after the end of the war are not bad for authorities to explain to people. After all it was the same people that, following their leader and Imam for eight years, rubbed the noses of their aggressors to the ground and at the end came home with empty hands and a calamity-stricken nation.[27]

Even more devastating for the presumably pure and self-sacrificing veteran, still celebrated by at least one part of the official ideology, was the sudden change of direction during the presidency of Ali-Akbar Hashemi-Rafsanjani that began immediately after Ayatollah Khomeini's death in 1989. The declaration of an "Era of Reconstruction" by Hashemi-Rafsanjani clearly suggested the end of other eras, specifically the revolution and war eras. Acknowledging the "epic" nature of the war, given the sacrifices made in not allowing "an inch of Iranian territory to be lost," Hashemi-Rafsanjani now talked about the problems and ruins left from the war era that needed to be overcome.[28] Suddenly, in this version of official ideology, the families of the martyrs, the disabled war veterans, the freed prisoners of war, and those who sacrificed for the war, rather than being the source for the moral revitalization of the cities or places beyond the war front, became "victims" and social categories that needed to be taken care of. They were of course constantly acknowledged and thanked for their sacrifice, their grand and perfectly sketched faces adorning most of the walls of the cities. But their values and the kind of spiritual selflessness that made warriors legends were essentially relegated to storybooks and memoirs.[29]

The values that were not relegated to storybooks and memoirs spoke of a pervasive materialism that was manifested in the increasing corruption of the system and easy riches that were accrued by those who were willing to use the war values as well as the war industry to enrich themselves. Compounding this situation has been the fact that the institutions originally designed to give service to war victims and their families, such as *Bonyad-e Shahid* (Foundation for the Martyrs), *Bonyad-e Mostaz'afan va Janbazan* (The Foundation for the Oppressed and Disabled War Veterans), *Setad-e Azadegan* (Headquarters for the Freed POWs) or *Setad-e*

Markazi-ye Baz-sazi-ye Manateq-e Jang-zad-ye Keshvar[30] (Central Headquarters for the Reconstruction of the Country's War-Stricken Areas) simply were not able to give the kind of service that would reduce the economic difficulties the war veterans were experiencing in the light of increased materialism of the society. This difficulty mostly stemmed from the fact that many of the organs designed to pursue the interests of war veterans became increasingly engaged in economic activities not supervised by their presumed clienteles. This predicament has led to the clear separation of economic and service activities of organs such the Foundation for the Oppressed and Disabled War Veterans, but the general problem continues for most organs.[31]

The second reason for the crack in the official ideology was the fact that the war generation was never a uniform entity to begin with. Despite the prominent presence of the volunteers, the so-called war generation included those who resisted going to war as well as those who were drafted. Even among the volunteers there was variety, including a number of distinct volunteer "waves." According to Mohammad Dorudian of IRGC's Center for War Studies and Research, the first wave occurred at the beginning of the war with the tensions arising from Iraq's invasion.[32] The people who volunteered for the war were from all social strata and political orientations.[33] In terms of characteristics, this wave was similar to the last wave of volunteers that went to war during Iraq's last incursion (along with the incursion made by the Iranian opposition group based in Iraq, Mojahedin-e Khalq) into Iranian territory immediately after Iran accepted Resolution 598. The second wave occurred after the fall of Bani-Sadr and when Iran began to claim victory in the battlefield, particularly after it forced the Iraqis to retreat in Operation *Fath-ol Mobin* (Operation Undeniable Victory) in March 1982. Again, according to Dorudian, this wave included volunteers from all walks of life. This situation began to change after the regaining of Khorramshahr in May 1982. The changed character of the war, from a defensive one to one of pursuing a decisive victory inside Iraq as well as the high number of casualties, ultimately affected the characteristics of the volunteer forces as well. These forces became more "professional," and consisted of repeat volunteers. This situation continued until the last stages of the war, which as mentioned above, because of Iraqi incursions inside Iranian territory saw the mobilization of volunteers from all strata of society. Dorudian maintains that the very last stages of the war even included a number of "opportunists" who, realizing the potential benefits of identifying themselves as war veterans, made it a point to show up at the war front.[34]

The variety present at the war front was noted by others as well. One field commander, who himself was a repeat volunteer in the earlier stages of the war, suggested to me that the roots of distinction between the fundamentalist and reformist readings of Islam in Iran could be found at the front.[35] As far as he was concerned, the first wave of volunteers, despite their commitment to Islam, went to the front for a purpose beyond the war, either to defend Iran/Islam or liberate holy cities. For them the front was an occasion to live the ideal life for which the Islamic revolution of 1979 was made. Brotherhood, equality, simplicity, purity and joy (*safa*), as well as spiritual cleansing were important values, none of which went against the simple pleasures and duties of everyday life that could even be found and cherished at the front. The second set of repeat volunteers, which began to gain the upper hand as the war progressed and with the governmental emphasis on martyrdom and sacredness of the war experience itself, understood faith in a much more doctrinaire fashion. From them emerged a more austere and joyless version of Islam that rejected any kind of compromise with life appearances. For them the war itself was sacred, while the continued public support of the war by many others took the form of not wanting to back away from the support they felt obligated to give to many friends who had lost their lives in the war.[36] The latter group supported the war not because they did not understand its shortcomings or because they thought of it as sacred, but because they were faced with a dilemma. Whatever success the Iranian forces were having at the war front, under very adverse conditions, was made possible, they believed, by the commitment to the idea of righteous war until victory and lack of questioning of the leadership of the war, so they felt that any questioning, even when justified, might rob the Iranian forces of the only asset they had. The choice was ultimately to withdraw from the front and leave the scene to the "true believers of the Imam's path." Added to their dilemma was the sobering reality that any public questioning of the "Imam's path" was simply not a possibility and had very dire consequences until very recently.

In any case, despite the imposed silence, the diversity among the war volunteers could not go unnoticed for long given Iran's competitive political climate. The war that came immediately after the revolution, not surprisingly, turned out to be a training ground for many of Iran's political players. Hence, with the increased contentiousness of Iranian politics between reform and antireform forces, discussions about the varying political proclivities of the war volunteers were also bound to surge. Not only can many older contemporary political and military leaders of the Islamic republic, such as Ali Khamenei, Ali-Akbar Hashemi-Rafsanjani, Mohammad Khatami, Mohsen Reza'i, Rahim Safavi, and Ali Shamkhani point to their role in the running of the war in various capacities, but many others who are a bit younger, can trace their role to direct battlefront experience. Of course, given the way the legacy of the war has been appropriated by those who are against democratic reform, the impression given has been that most of the people who went to war are against reforms, with reform being defined as a move toward a loose and corrupt liberalism. This impression has been reinforced not only by the instrumental use of the war generation by the antireform forces but by the reformists themselves who seem rather hesitant to talk about their war experience perhaps, as mentioned above, for fear of "betraying martyred friends" but also because they do not want to be guilty of the same instrumentalism that characterizes the antireform discourse.

But even here, there have been times that the political variety of the war generation could not be suppressed. For instance, when Hossein Loqmanian, a reformist Majles deputy from Hamedan, was charged and arrested in late 2001 for insulting the head of the Judiciary in a speech given in the parliament, it was difficult to ignore the crucial information that he had lost a leg at Shalamcheh, one of most gruesome battle arenas of the Iran–Iraq War. In a Majles speech, printed in the daily *Nourouz*, a fellow reformist deputy from Malayer laid out the facts that Loqmanian spent more than five years at the front, was a search and destroy commander, lost his left leg by hitting a mine, never discussed his sacrifices in the war in his campaign appearances and speeches, and never accepted any financial help from the Martyrs Foundation (the last two points made as implicit criticism of those who have used their participation in the war for political and financial gains).[37]

The implicit narrative here is of course one of pointing to the absurdity of questioning the loyalty of one who has sacrificed so much for the republic. The uses of war memories and badges are again instrumental, but this time for defensive purposes, for establishing one's loyalty, rather than aggressively questioning/undermining the loyalty of others.

Contemporary Public Battles and the War Generation

So far I have tried to show that the idea of the war generation, conceived in a one-dimensional fashion, has played a very important role in the framing of postwar politics in Iran. It has been an instrument through which attempts to reform the harsh application of Islamic codes of conduct have been attacked and silenced. In other words, it has been an easy instrument to hurl against opponents in Iran's factional politics. Of the importance of the values propagated in the war years, it suffices to say that none of the categories introduced to celebrate the gallantry and self-effacing heroism of the men who went to war and the women who supported them have been "retired," so to speak. In fact, in today's Iran you can still be martyred, fall into the category of war disabled, and become a member of Basij forces.

But having said this, I have also tried to argue that this idea of the self-effacing war hero also from the beginning bore within it its own negation. The negation has come in the form of variety that has characterized the war generation itself. But it has also come in the form of governmental policies that have moved away from the values propagated during the war era. Not willing to abandon the propagation of war values, the postwar governmental policies of emphasis on economic growth and private enterprise have simply made the contradictions faced by the war generation evident for everyone to see. The contradictions are even difficult to avoid in the streets where the giant pictures of war martyrs uncomfortably stand next to advertising billboards for domestic and foreign products.

But the contradictions, more than anything else, have come to be evident in the abuse and overuse of the categories developed during the war. These contradictions become evident every time forces connected to the Basij are identified as somehow being involved in violent acts against societal groups, every time a regular government worker who dies in the line of duty is identified as a martyr, and every time a government worker who is injured is put in the same category as a disabled war veteran (*janbaz*), entitled to all the benefits that are accorded to that category. In fact, the contradictions have become so evident that not even Masud Dehnamaki, a war veteran and one of the editors of *Shalamcheh*, *Jebheh*, and *Sobh* publications that have trumpeted war values on a regular basis, can ignore them. This is what he had to say recently about the values associated with the war:

> When I saw that they demonstrate in religious schools because of the caricature of so and so Ayatollah [reference to Ayatollah Mesbah Yazdi, who has become known as the most important proponent of a harsh interpretation of Islam] in *Azad Daily*, when I see

that all cities are spinning because of the dancing of a woman in Berlin, when I see that
with Aqa's speech [reference to Ayatollah Khamene'i] regarding the enemy's foothold,
20 newspapers are closed in one night but nobody comes into the streets for the implementation of Aqa's 8-Article order [about combating economic corruption] and the
judiciary does not even hang one Aqazadeh [reference to the sons of those in power
who are making money] from the electric poles in Azadi Square, and nothing moves
for the sake of justice, then I am revolted by all the slogans about values from this or
that. I prefer to be a laborer in this land than to be, for instance, a bearer of values.[38]

But not all reactions to the abuse of war values in light of the pervasive materialism of Iranian society are so drastic. I would like to end this chapter by pointing to
some of the variegated attempts to deal with the legacy of the war that I have come
across. My intent is not to claim analytical comprehensiveness, but rather to point
to the variety of responses that are developing to give the war its "proper" place
within contemporary Iranian history—to make it a milestone reflecting the Iranian
national character, nothing more and nothing less. More importantly, to make it
something through which generations of Iranians can engage in conversation in
order to find answers and some sort of national consensus about questions that are
creating divides within the society. After all, one of the most important ways of keeping the war experience alive is through the expansion of debate about the experience.

The historiography of the war is one of the areas in which interesting attempts
are being made to frame the conflict in less political ways. As Kaveh Bayat, an independent Iranian historian points out, while the early historical productions about the
war all were essentially propaganda tracts, increasingly there is an attempt to present
the war in ways that will ultimately allow more independent judgments to develop
about the important strategic decisions taken at various junctures.[39] In particular,
Bayat points to a series of work that has been produced by the IRGC's Center for
War Studies and Research, focusing on different stages of the war and the historiography of important battles, as well as a detailed multi-volume daily chronology of the
war. What is interesting about this center, as reported in a brochure describing it, is
the intention from the beginning of the war among some sectors of the IRGC to
develop a cadre of "narrators" (ravian) to accompany the troops and their leaders at
the war front to take note of events as well as engage in interviews with the people
there.[40] The result of course is a vast archive of material that is bound to be increasingly used. This is why Bayat thinks, "the historiography of the war in comparison
to the main body of the historiography of contemporary Iran is a highly advanced
and distinct phenomenon."[41] To be sure, there is much more to be done but a
process is in place that will hopefully allow important questions, particularly regarding the beginning of the war and its continuation after Khorramshahr, to be raised
and debated. Indeed, the fact that various serious publications by an IRGC-funded
unit have been subjected to critical commentary and analysis by an independent historian writing for a journal committed to civil dialogue should itself be considered
an important, even if small, step in loosening the hold of stale and propagandistic
commentary on the war.

As mentioned, the Center for War Studies and Research was initiated within
the IRGC and interestingly continues to blossom in unexpected ways. So far it
seems free from involvement in factional conflicts, within the confines of IRGC.

A different trajectory can be laid out for another IRGC-funded project. Research about the history of the war has not been the only area in which the IRGC has been involved. Another area of immense importance is filmmaking about the war. In fact, there is no doubt that the IRGC, through what in Iran is called "sinema-ye defa'e moqaddas" (sacred war's cinema), was a very important force in shaping the post-revolutionary film industry in Iran, both in terms of training capable filmmakers and in terms of production support. The most celebrated unit of this support came together under a complex called Ravayat-e Fath Foundation. It was able to produce along with other things a very important, and some say attractive to all sectors of the society, documentary television series during the war.

Despite the IRGC's strong footprint on post-revolutionary cinema, however, its influence has not proved lasting. In fact, many of Iran's most important directors, such as Ebrahim Hatami Kia, Rasul Molla Qolipour, Mojtaba Ra'i, and Ahmadreza Darvish, who were products of this system of support, have increasingly moved away from the war movies promoted by the IRGC. The situation has reached a point where an important war movie director, Ebrahim Hatami Kia, who learned about filmmaking through the IRGC's resources, now publicly criticizes the interference of military personnel in cultural and artistic activities.[42]

Voices of opposition are raised even among those who are engaged in documentary filmmaking about the war. This is what Reza Borji, who suffered a chemical weapons attack while filming during the war and still suffers from its consequences, has to say about his made-for-television documentary *Medal-ha-ye Shekasteh* (Broken Medals), which relies heavily on the words of Iraqi prisoners of war in Iran:

> Before we saw that the hero has to stand until the last moment. No, it is not like this. We were defeated. We retreated. One of the Iraqi officers said it very nicely: "You show in your movies that an old man goes out with a stick and in an absurd fashion imprisons an Iraqi and comes back. At least give him a weapon. Iraqi soldiers have been trained to use a Kalashnikov for at least one year. If this was the way, why didn't you come all the way to Baghdad?" In our movies, we showed Iraqis as fools (*halu*), and then a young person would say if this was the case, why did you fight for eight years and besides Faw and Halabcheh you couldn't capture any other place? No, sir, it wasn't like that! You went behind an embankment and you saw that the people that made you wait for three hours were one-fifth of the battalion that was fighting. The opposite could also happen. Everything was two-sided. If we do not show these realities about the war, then we have wronged our own history. When the future generations want to read this history, they will realize that it has been written in a one-sided and one-dimensional way. In places like Shalamcheh we gave a martyr every one-and-a-half meters; that is, the whole place was covered with [the bodies of] martyrs and this is the way we kept the place. Or they lost many more times than us so that they can do an operation. This war was sacred for us. Was it sacred for the Iraqis? We don't know. Even today whenever I remember Shalamcheh I begin to cry that I had to go over the corpses of friends (*bache-ha*) with a motorcycle to get a job done. Now if many of the leaders want to say that the whole war was victory for us, let them say it. They can offer whatever thesis they want, but the reality was something else. We were both victorious and defeated . . . We said all these things in the film. War is two-sided and we cannot hide realities. And so long as it does not undermine national security we have to say it. We must be objective since for the young generation, talking about the war is difficult. There has to be support.[43]

Indeed, connecting to the young generation and making them understand and respect the life experiences of their elders, and yet not be hampered by them, seems to be a daunting task with which the people who experienced the war are faced. Let me end with an excerpt from a letter to the editor of the journal *Fakkeh* (again the name of a war front area), a monthly that is just a few years old and is dedicated to the "propagation of the culture of sacrifice and martyrdom in the Islamic Revolution." While acknowledging its debt and allegiance to Ayatollah Khamene'i, it is also dedicated to being "an independent publication with no affiliation with any party, group, or faction." Here is a letter from a reader:

> I know for publishing this journal you suffer many difficulties. But the result of your work is nothing but the past. Fakkeh attracts those that have seen Fakkeh, have set foot in the soil of Shalamcheh, and are after the memories of those days. But I am thinking about why you have not become a companion of the present? What are you afraid of? Of politics? From being banned, from whom? Listen Fakkeh, I don't want your only audience to be your friends. I want you to make those who are [no longer able] to find your path to accompany you, and to do this your efforts [so far] are not enough. From the inner folds of your memories make yourself a companion of the landscape of your time so that I know what to do in this muddle. Either I have to be merely happy with memories or be witness to the increasing number of your ignorant opponents; the youth that because of the absence of your words have become intoxicated with the words of unsuitable friends against whom you can stand up. Don't be afraid of politics; your source of imitation was and is a man of politics. I don't want to convince you to follow this approach. I want to convey the thirst of a generation that when you were fighting was writing, in his first-grade handwriting, "I like the warriors."[44]

What else does this writing suggest but a keen awareness that the fate of the generation that went through war and its historical legacy will not be determined by the current propaganda about it. Those who served in the war have to reconnect to the rest of society, in spite of the bad billing they have received. This is indeed a daunting task, it seems to me, not only for those who went to the warfront and/or conducted it from headquarters outside the war zones but also the whole country. Wars and revolutions offer important founding narratives for nations in search of stability and states in search of popular legitimacy. Without a narrative that connects all sectors of the society to a somewhat commonly acceptable history, social and political cohesion will remain a far-flung aspiration. Whether or not the Iranian struggle for reform will be successful will depend as much on the increasing influence of reform-oriented forces in the political arena as on the ability of various members of civil society to rewrite the history of the war. It must be done in such a way that, while acknowledging mistakes made, still the "important and vital" contributions made by the revolution to the "defense of Iran" will become the nation's common heritage. For now, like the 1979 revolution itself, the legacy of the "sacred" war in defense of Iran continues to divide rather than unite despite its genuinely popular roots. Not surprisingly, the answer to the question of why this is so must be found less in the historical event itself but in the uses of history.

Notes

* I would like to thank Gary Sick and Lawrence Potter for suggesting this topic to me. I am also very grateful to Alireza Alavi-Tabar, Mohammad Dorudian, and Alireza Kamari for their generous sharing of time, memories, and expertise. This essay should be considered an initial foray into a very large and complicated topic, in all its political, cultural, ideological, economic and sociological manifestations.

1. "Paint No Matter What: The Life and Times of Khosrow Hasanzadeh." A documentary directed by Maziar Bahari, and produced by Fariba Nazemi and Maziar Bahari.

2. The research for this study was conducted in the summer of 2001 with the help of a grant from the United States Institute of Peace for a project on the changing public sphere in Iran.

3. Varied figures ranging from 60 to 70 percent have been reported regarding the percentage of the Iranian population that is young, depending on the cut-off age used. According to *Iran Statistical Yearbook 1378/1999* (Tehran: Statistical Centre of Iran, Winter 2001), which is based on the 1996 census, approximately 60% of the Iranian population in 1996 was under 24. A person born in 1981, at the beginning of the war, was eligible to vote in the 1997 presidential election (won by the reformist Mohammad Khatami). According to the same source, in 1986 there were a little more than 9 million people (out of the population of 49.5 million) that were under 4 years of age (7.5 million were between five and nine years of age). This was the height of population explosion in Iran as the numbers began to taper off after 1986, instead of continuously increasing. This group of war babies, between 15 and 19 years old in 2001, constitutes the largest voting bloc among the Iranian population. The next group of upcoming voters, the ones under four in 1991, is a little more than 8.1 million strong and the ones under four in 1996 are approximately 6.1 million.

4. The ironic, and I think intended, similarity to the revolutionary slogan *tup, tank, mosalsal digar asar nadareh* (cannon, tank, machine gun no longer have any effect) should not be missed here.

5. *Janbaz* refers in Persian to someone who lays down his life for some cause. But in the post-revolution period it has been specifically used to refer to a disabled person from the Iran–Iraq War, and so I have given the equivalent of "a disabled war veteran" for it.

6. This letter and Khatami's answer were printed in most of the reformist dailies such as *Nourouz, Hayat-e Now*, and *Iran*, on 26 Khordad 1380/June, 16, 2001 as well as *Ettela'at*, the government-subsidized daily that focuses more on straight and non-controversial news.

7. *Azadeh* is the word used to refer to a freed prisoner of war. *Isargari* technically means giving selflessly and *isargar* refers to someone who gives selflessly to a sacred cause, but now it has been adopted for a specific meaning, namely somebody who has sacrificed in the cause of the Islamic revolution. In the sense that is being used by officialdom to designate people who have contributed their own or their beloved one's life to the defense of the regime, it has no English equivalent.

8. The term *Razmandegan* (singular *Razmandeh*), which literally means combatants, refers to those who voluntary served at the front as members of the Basij or Islamic Revolutionary Guards Corps for at least nine continuous months or one year discontinuously, allowing those identified as such to enjoy certain privileges along with *isargaran, janbazan, azadegan*, and the families of the martyrs in the areas of education and employment. It is also increasingly the general term used for war veterans. But such usage is not yet formalized. Researchers at the Janbazan Foundation Research Center told me that attempts have already begun to substitute "razmandeh" for "veteran" in the translated literature on veterans' affairs. There is however resistance to the translation, presumably on the basis that acknowledging that there were those who sacrificed in wars elsewhere denigrates the

particularly intense sacrifices made in Iran. This resistance, however, seems to be receding. In 2004, a bill creating the Ministry of Welfare and Social Security became law. Once operational, along with other responsibilities, this ministry is expected to address the needs of all veterans (*razmandegan, azadegan, Janbazan*) and the families of martyrs. Previously the needs of each of these categories were addressed through disparate foundations and organizations.

9. See e.g., Theda Skocpol, "Social Revolutions and Mass Military Mobilization," in *World Politics*, vol. 40, no. 2 (1988), pp. 147–68; and Stephen M. Walt, "Revolution and War," in *World Politics*, vol. 44, no. 3 (1992), pp. 321–68.

10. Mohammad-Javad Gholamreza Kashi, *Jadu-ye Goftar: Zehniyat-e Farhangi va Nezam-e Ma'ani dar Entekhabat-e Dovvom-e Khordad* (The Magic of Discourse: Cultural Consciousness and the System of Meanings in the 2 Khordad Election) (Tehran: Ayandeh Pouyan, 1379/2000, pp. 326–34).

11. For a comprehensive analysis of revolutionary images see Peter J. Chelkowski and Hamid Dabashi, *Staging a Revolution: The Art of Persuasion in the Islamic Republic of Iran* (New York: New York University Press, 1999).

12. Kashi, *Jadu-ye Goftar*, p. 336.

13. This figure is gleaned from a compilation from *Iran Statistical Yearbook, 1999* (Tehran: Statistical Centre of Iran, 2001), pp. 55–57. It is reached by adding the number of men who were between 25 and 45 in 1996. However, a clearer picture, although by no means authoritative, may be developing regarding the number of casualties in the war. In a Friday sermon given in 1996, Ali-Akbar Hashemi-Rafsanjani spoke of 200,000 killed, 200,000 injured, and 1 million internal refugees (*Resalat*, 20 Bahman 1375/ February 9, 1996). Unofficial figures from *Bonyad-e Janbazan* suggest that as of 2000 there were 403,748 *janbaz* of various degrees. It is not clear how many of these are served by Bonyad-e Janbazan. I understand that perhaps as many as 30% of those injured in the war refuse to seek any help from the government because the pursuit of "material rewards" undermines of the whole notion of serving at the front for the sake of God's pleasure. These figures were given to me by someone who did not want to be identified and should not be considered an official source.

14. No official figures regarding the age of combatants exists. Again, some clues can be gleaned from various casualty figures. According to Mohammad-Hasan Rahimian, then the director of the Martyrs Foundation, 72 percent of those killed were ages 14–24, and 7,000 were under 14 (reported by *AFP*, March 13, 1998). According to figures given by the Martyr's Foundation in 2000, 44 percent of those who died were aged 16–20, 30 percent were between 21 and 25 and 8 percent were between 26 and 30, leaving 18 percent either under 16 or over 30 (reported in *Iran Times*, November 10, 2000, p. 4).

15. This is why in contemporary Iran there are still quite a few people who have difficulty applying for government-related jobs because they have not cleared their military service record. Recognizing this predicament, through the decree of the Leader a new amnesty law came into effect in September 2003, giving general amnesty to all high school and college graduates born before 1975. Those with higher degrees were also given amnesty, but with variations in their year of birth. According to the director of the Armed Forces Draft Board, Sardar Musa Kamali, about 10 million men born between 1955 and 1975 were subject to the draft, of which, according to historical trends, between 3 and 5 percent could be considered to have evaded the draft. Kamali estimated that this makes about 500,000 subject to the new amnesty (*Hamshahri*, September 14, 2003).

16. Again, there are no official figures that specify the ratio between volunteers and draftees but the official figures regarding casualties perhaps offer a clue. According to Hadi Qalamnevis, director-general of the Statistics and Information Department at the Martyrs Foundation (*Bonyad-i Shahid*), 188,015 Iranians lost their lives during the war (172,056

at the front and 15,959 in air raids and missile attacks on residential areas, with an additional 8,000 still classified as missing in action), and 43 percent of the casualties were Basijis. He added that 21 percent were in the IRGC, 23 percent were in the Islamic Republic Army, 2.8 percent were in the Law Enforcement Forces, with the rest from other sectors of society (*Hamshahri,* September 23, 2003). I understand that the claim made about the essentially volunteer nature of the military mobilization is a controversial one. At the same time, at least the casualty figures, and the preponderance of Basij casualties, suggest that it is still the explanation that can be better supported. This explanation of course does not touch on the argument that the Basij forces were mobilized through massive and very intensive propaganda and use of cultural idioms and traditions that gave the volunteers the qualities of being "brainwashed." As mentioned above, war machines in all countries rely on such ideological mobilization. My point here is simply that a large portion of people that went to war at least initially did so by showing up at war mobilization centers and volunteering. What went in their minds is not the issue here.

17. Behzad Nabavi, spokesperson for the government, in *Jomhuri-ye Eslami,* 30 Azar 1359/ December 21, 1980. Quoted in Morad Saghafi, "Crossing the Desert: Iranian Intellectuals after the Islamic Revolution," in *Intellectual Change and the New Generation of Iranian Intellectuals,* edited by Haleh Esfandiari, Andrea Bertone, and Farideh Farhi (Washington, D. C.: Woodrow Wilson International Center for Scholars, October 2000).

18. The fact that the IRGC was organized in a haphazard manner to fight against domestic opposition is confirmed by the IRGC itself in its books about the Iran–Iraq War. See e.g., *Risheh-ha-ye Tahajom* (Roots of Aggression), the first in a two-volume set of books on the analysis of the war published by the IRGC's Center for War Studies and Research in 1378/1999. The same source identifies the number of IRGC forces at the beginning of the war as a mere 30,000 (Abolhasan Bani-Sadr, in his *My Turn to Speak: Iran, the Revolution and Secret Deals with the U.S.,* trans. William Ford (Washington: Brassey's, 1991) gives the number of 20,000). Interestingly, it also argues that for the first two years after the revolution, there was hardly any mention of the IRGC as an institution in the newspapers of the day. "Despite their decisive role in ending conflicts, they were merely identified as 'elements from defenders of revolution,' a title that was repeated even in the first years of the war." Ibid., p. 99.

19. Mohammad Dorudian, *Jang: Bazyabi-ye Sobat* (War: Regaining Stability) published by the Center for War Studies and Research, IRGC, Winter 1378/1999, p. 138.

20. For a comprehensive analysis of Iran's changing and debated war strategies, refer to a six-volume series of books entitled *Seyri dar Jang-e Iran va Araq (A Review of the Iran–Iraq War)* by Mohammad Dorudian published by IRGC's Center for War Studies and Research. The last volume entitled *Aghaz ta Payan* (Beginning to End) is a summary of the war while the other five volumes focus more on details of specific operations discussed chronologically.

21. One field commander offered an interesting view about the contrast between the front and the cities even during the war. He noticed, for instance, that when soldiers were given release time to visit their families, many of them ended up coming back sooner than their allotted time. The language used to describe the experience in the cities was one of being *gharib* (a combination of being alien and lonely). Part of this feeling had to do with the changed atmosphere but also with the fact that many in the cities could not understand and even ridiculed the commitment the volunteers had to the war. The kind of constant attention that was being given to the religious and spiritual experience of these young volunteers may have given the impression to others outside the front that these volunteers had something missing in their heads.

22. Alireza Kamari of the Bureau for the Literature and Art of Resistance suggested to me that so far between 2,500 to 3,000 books have been published about the war, including

memoirs, wills, poetry, and fiction. He also pointed out that governmental publishing houses and not private publishers have published almost all the material produced on the war so far. The Bureau for the Literature and Art of Resistance has published about 500 books, mostly memoirs. However, Kamari noted that it is important to understand that this literature began as a spontaneous move by people who believed in their cause and as such has a very strong emotive content. Recently more systematic efforts have been made to study this literature. The Bureau for the Literature and Art of Resistance along with the French Embassy's Iranology association in Iran and Tehran University's social science department held a roundtable in Azar 1378/December 1999 on the comparative analysis of the literature of war in relation to Iran's veterans and French veterans after World War I.

23. Not all confrontations between opposing forces are violent. Nevertheless, the logic of the confrontation between "those who are defending the war values" and their designated opponents is the same. Listen to Haji Bakhshi, a war veteran who was also instrumental in mobilizing many others to go to war. The following words were spoken at a rally held in July 2001 to commemorate the second year anniversary of the attack of some vigilante groups against some University of Tehran students. When asked why he was demonstrating against the rally, Bakhshi said: "As long as there is blood in our veins not only us but also our wives and children will be present for revolution, independence and the Islamic Republic of Iran. If they are telling the truth, why don't they commemorate the anniversary of Marsad and Kheybar? [The names of two of Iran's military operations against Iraq, the latter in early 1984, the former involving the entry of opposition Mojahedin into Iran at the end of the war] [They commemorate] this English plan. Don't destroy [the image of] students. Students are dear and honorable to us. But don't become instruments of others. A group of spies shouldn't be able to mess up everything." (Reported in *Iran* and *Nowrouz* on 19 Tir 2001/ July 10, 2001.)

24. Sa'id Tajik's book begins with his attempts to go to war as soon as it started at the age of thirteen. He is unable to do so initially but ultimately manages to do so by 1983. The book is interesting because Tajik recounts his repeated encounters at the front from 1983 until the end of the war. It is also notable because of the author's very accessible style of writing, sense of humor, and ability to portray the grave as well as the lighter moments of the most difficult circumstances.

25. Sa'id Tajik, *Jang Dust-dashtani Ast* (*War is Lovable*) (Tehran: Daftar-e Adabiyat va Honar-e Moqavemat, 1378/1999), pp. 585–86.

26. In terms of overarching concerns, there is also a third major question, which relates to the origins of the war and whether or not it was avoidable from the beginning. Ayatollah Hosein 'Ali Montazeri raises the possibility of the war being avoidable most eloquently in his memoirs. He argues that Ayatollah Khomeini was not at all interested in dealing with governments and did not think Saddam Hussein would dare to attack Iran and this inhibited preventive measures on the part of the Iranian government. (*Khaterat-e Ayatollah Montazeri*) (The Diaries of Ayatollah Montazeri) (Los Angeles: Ketab Corp, 2001, p. 315.) The question about the continuation of the war may be considered as part of an intra-regime dispute that later shows itself in the reformist critique of the war. The opposition inside Iran, such as the Freedom Movement, has also questioned the rationality of the strategy pursued after Khorramshahr. The question relating to the abrupt ending of the war and acceptance of Resolution 598 is a burning issue for the committed.

27. *Fakkeh*, Tir 1378/ June–July 1999, p. 10.

28. As Kashi points out, the reduction of the achievement of the war to not allowing the loss of any territory was itself a major retreat insofar as the "sacred defense" of values was concerned.

29. A fascinating series of books in this process of legend making was produced by the children and youth division of the Bureau for Literature and Art of Resistance. It is centered

on the life and war experiences of war commanders, including Mostafa Chamran, Medi Bakeri, Hosein Kharrazi, Mohammad Borujerdi, Abbas Baba'i, and Ebrahim Hemmat. In these very selective biographies, definite character traits, including lack of attention to material things, brotherly commitment to the welfare of others, piety and so on, are traced from the day these commanders were born until they died. It is important to note that while the overwhelming majority of these legendary figures are men, women have also been able to enter the discussion through their devotion not to their sacrificing husbands and fathers but to the cause and God. See for instance, *Nameh-ha-ye Fahimeh* (Fahimeh's Letters), edited by Alireza Kamari and published by the Bureau for the Literature and Art of Resistance (1379/2001, Fifth print). Fahimeh Baba'ianpur, who was married to Gholamreza Sadeqzadeh and remarried his brother Alireza after the former was killed in the war, is offered by Kamari as an exemplar in the "great test of life" offered by the war.

30. For instance, the person in charge of reconstruction headquarters of Abadan was arrested in 1994 for embezzlement (*Kayhan*, 21 Ordibehesht 1373/ May 11, 1994 as reported in Mehrangiz Kar, *Nakhl-ha-ye Sukhteh* (Scorched Palm Trees) (Tehran: Roshangaran, 1379/2000).) Kar's book is a collection of reports of her postwar trips to the country's southern border areas, concisely describing the devastation as well as lack of attention.

31. For instance, according to Reza Yusefian, the deputy from Shiraz who was himself a POW, *Setad-e Azadegan* (Headquarters for the Freed POWs), has created many economic firms that operate independently and it is not clear which organ supervises them. Neither is it clear who constitute the shareholders or board of directors for these firms. As reported in *Nourouz,* "Moshkelat-e Azadegan Hamchonan Baqist" (The Problems of Freed POWs Continue), 25 Mordad 1380/August 16, 2001, p. 9.

32. Personal interview, June 2001.

33. According to the Federation of American Scientists' analysis of the Iran–Iraq War, approximately 200,000 "ideology committed troops" were sent to the war front by November 1980, less than two months after the full-fledged Iraqi incursion into Iran. See http://www.fas.org/man/dod-101/ops/war/iran-iraq.htm.

34. The best treatment of the war opportunists can be seen in the movie *Leyli ba man ast* (Leyli is With Me) directed by Kamal Tabrizi. This light-hearted and very funny movie is arguably one of the best about the variety of people who volunteered for the war. It follows the life of a photographer who volunteers to go to the war in order to get a loan but keeps moving closer and closer to the front despite all efforts to stay away from it. In the process, he encounters all sorts of people with various motivations. In the advertisement for the movie, Kamal Tabrizi is quoted as saying, "I personally believe that this war, though violent and destructive, revealed traces of the greatness of the human spirit in extraordinary circumstances."

35. Akbar Ganji echoes this sentiment: "The problem of violence is not generated from lack of proof for being a good Muslim or with the reformists not being present at the war fronts. The problem began during the war." See "Goftogu ba Yek Sardar-e Nezami," in *Fath,* 7 Farvardin 1379/March 27, 2000, reprinted in Akbar Ganji, *Eslahgari-ye Me 'maraneh* (Constructive Reformation) (Tehran: Tarh-e Now 1379/2000). Pp. 27–30.

36. "*Ma ba jang ru-dar bayesti peyda kardeh budim,*" were the very interesting words of one field commander. It is difficult to translate this sentence but by it he meant something like "we had developed an embarrassed relationship with the war and could not fully express what we felt because so many friends were lost at the front and criticizing the war felt like abandoning friends."

37. Mohammad Kazemi, "Loqmanian Kist?" (Who is Loqmanian?) *Nourouz,* 20 Dey 1380/ January 10, 2002.

38. Masud Dehnamaki, interview with *Mellat,* 5 Sharivar 1380/August 27, 2001.

39. "Tarikh-negari-ye Jang" (The Historiography of the War) *Goftogu* 23 (Bahar 1378/ Spring 1999), pp. 19–33. This issue of *Goftogu* is devoted to the Iran–Iraq War.
40. Ibid. p. 20.
41. Ibid. p. 26.
42. Reported in *Nourouz*, 6 Mordad 1380/ July 28, 2001. Hatami Kia, the director of several important war-related movies including *Azhans-e Shisheh'i* (Glassed Agency), talked about this in the press conference for his new film *Mowj-e Mordeh* (Dead Wave), which has yet to be released despite the fact that it was produced by Ravayat-e Fath Foundation. In fact, reportedly the producer prevented the movie, which is about a military commander obsessed with attacking an American warship who also has problems with his son, from being screened. A very high quality video of this movie was however widely and illegally distributed.
43. Interview with Reza Borji, *Sorush*, 16 Tir 1380/ July 7, 2001, p. 27.
44. M. Zare'in, "Natarsid Az Siasat" (Don't Be Afraid of Politics), *Fakkeh*, Ordibehesht and Khordad 1380/ April–June 2001, p. 25.

Chapter 5

The War Generation in Iraq: A Case of Failed Etatist Nationalism

Faleh A. Jabar

As we strive to achieve our main slogan, "Win the youth over, win the future," we should also do our best to cut off these sources of strength and growth from our rivals.

—Saddam Hussein, February 15, 1976

Introduction

This chapter examines the factors that molded and mutated the social and political expectations and attitude of the war generation in Iraq during the period 1980–91. While international and regional factors as well as a multitude of domestic social, economic, and cultural factors have been constantly at work, these will be conceived in the framework of nation building. The major, but not exclusive theme in this examination is the role played by nationalism seen here as both an official creed and popular sentiment. The very logic of war requires the full-scale vitalization of nationalism as a space unifying divergent social groups and interests in one monolithic national community. This is all the more important since we are examining a multiethnic, multireligious, and multicultural society, in which Iraq has been a state in search of nationhood, rather than a nation in search of statehood. The Iran–Iraq War was initiated in September 1980 as a part of nation-building endeavors inasmuch as it aimed at enhancing regime security. War was sought as a means to further construct and enhance etatist nationalism, and this attempt, although challenged, was relatively successful during much of the Iran–Iraq War.

Central to this analysis is the complex nature of nationalism itself, resting on a major distinction between etatist nationalism and popular patriotism. Etatist nationalism is an official Arabist ideology, which, in the case of the Baath regime, has an authoritarian cast (liberal or authoritarian being beside the point). Popular patriotism, in contrast, is a sense of belonging to a national (here, Iraqi) community stemming from inclusive mechanisms, economic, political, and cultural. Etatist nationalism may lead to a peaceful cohabitation with popular patriotism, or may clash with it. The latter gradually diverged from the former, developing sundry, conflicting trends. The seeds of this divorce were latent in the interval between the two wars, but they ripened in the runup to, and during, the 1991 Gulf War. It overwhelmed the bulk of the war generation and revealed various forms of apathy, abstention, or conformism. In the end, the majority of them took up arms against their own government in March 1991. Much of the story of the war generation, who lost their sense of identity and belonging, lies therein.

What is a Generation?

The question "what is a generation?" is not irrelevant. As a concept, the very term "generation" is embedded in conceptual and empirical ambiguity. Empirically, difficulties arise from the meager field, sociological, or anthropological studies of Iraqi society before, during, or after the period under consideration.[1] Conceptually, sociological categories like class, stratum, group, or community are no less fraught with ambiguity than the category "generation." Nevertheless, these terms are empirically used with some approximation, or they are specifically defined in different senses in each study. A class may be defined on the basis of economic criteria, the Weberian "situation in the market," or the Marxian, property relations (the haves and the have-nots), or even differentiated on the basis of mere income, or on any other statistical criterion. A stratum may be defined in similar economic or extra-economic manner, a community in cultural terms within well-defined temporal–spatial demarcations.

As an informal social group, "generation" seems generally, but not exclusively, a temporally delimited category. Its borders are drawn by specific time limits in two ways: on the one hand, the objective, homogeneous, physical, empty time, universally organized by the calendar, and the biological duration of the subject itself or age. Both temporal limits, however, may be spatially bordered by definite modern communities—nations, otherwise they are globalized.

As a rule, social groups are conceived as being smaller than strata or classes, less informal, more mercurial and varied. They derive their compactness, so to speak, from cohesive factors external to them; in other words, their cohesion as a group is peripheral, feeble, and temporary, rather than intrinsic. What applies to social groups at substrata or subclass, or even subcommunity, levels also pertains to supra-class, supra-strata groups like generations.

The indistinct nature of any given generation comes into bold relief the moment the differentiating factors of class, ethnicity, culture, gender, and education are introduced. But the compactness of such oversized social groups may also come forward when modern national systems are brought to bear. Educational systems, bureaucracies, armed forces, and electronic media create common spaces and collective memories, bringing together various segments of definite age groups. Mass media as vehicles of cultural spaces create collective memories.

Some of these systems are formal organizations with powers of discipline and surveillance over their constituent members. Such systems tend to be coercive agents of socialization. Soldiers develop their own clannish solidarity, as do students or football and music fans, or smaller groups of office staff. Yet, each segment of which any generation is inevitably composed may well retain other links with their primordial networks, ethnic groups, or communal congregations. Rural residents have their villages, nomads their tribes, and city dwellers their neighborhoods, inasmuch as indoctrinated members keep their separate and often sundry ideological preferences. With these margins in mind, we use the term generation. But what are the boundaries that mark the "war generation" in Iraq? Which age groups are included and why?

Unlike in Iran, the generation who fought the eight-year Iran–Iraq War had to fight two more devastating wars in 1991 and 2003. We shall consider those age groups that did their first military service before they could start their postgraduate career, or their own new, usually marital, active, and productive life. During the war years several age groups were drawn into the war zone. Those who were at the age of four in 1977 were fit for recruitment in 1991. The age of compulsory conscription in Iraq is 18; only students are temporarily exempted until they complete their higher, secondary, or university study, provided they did not fail for two successive years. Unlike students, workers, peasants, and artisans (usually the self-employed or even the unemployed), have to join the army at 18. Sooner rather than later, graduates have to follow suit.

Hence we use the term "the generation of war" in two temporal senses: as young age groups across the national space, which developed under the impact of the Iran–Iraq War and those who were recruited before they could enjoy the fruits of civilian life in adulthood. These include various, successive age groups that we will define in greater detail below.

While some other age groups shared this experience, the war generation had the misfortune of confronting it while on the verge of beginning what other age groups had already achieved: self-realization, education, career-building, family-building, and so on. The *differentia specifica*, which sets this specific generation apart from the other groups, is that war became an obstacle to the normal development of careers at the very beginning of active life.

The Boundaries of the War Generation

As has been noted, those born between 1949 and 1968 were successively recruited to form the backbone of the armed forces, which grew massively to a force of one million men.[2] All age groups over the 24-years margin have been excluded. This may seem arbitrary, but the benchmark of differentiation set earlier demands such exclusion.

The war generation, thus defined, could be estimated on the basis of the 1977 official census to include around 5.5 million males and females in urban and rural settings.[3] According to the official population census, those whose ages ranged between 7 and 24 years were classified into four age groups. They are:

1- Group A, 5–9 years;
2- Group B, 10–14 years;
3- Group C, 15–19 years;
4- Group D, 20–24 years.

The size of these age groups, counted as the war generation, is around 5.5 million out of a nation of 12 million. This is roughly half of the nation on the eve of the war. The ratio of the male segment of the war generation to the total population stands at 25 percent.[4] These figures reveal the intensiveness and extensiveness that marked the role of this generational group in the war effort when we further add the growth and the size of the armed forces before, during, and after the war.[5]

The three million male segment of the war generation in question was the major fighting force, which had to bear the toll of the war. With the universal mobilization, other, older age groups were also drawn into the battlefield, but they formed a smaller section compared to the war generation in the sense we have defined. Of course the very experience of war was not shared evenly among the various segments: rural peasants as compared to educated urban dwellers, or Kurds, the bulk of whom were exempted from active military service, compared to Arabs. Other ethnic, communal, or even ideological divides were also instrumental in such variations.

Empirical Limitations and Conceptual Problems

This study relies heavily on extensive interviews with random groups of young Iraqi soldiers, deserters, POWs, and war veterans at various points from 1982 (in Iran), down to 1990–91 in Western Europe, and farther afield during 1994–98.

In Iran, a series of videotaped interviews were conducted with Iraqi POWs, who were Christians of various denominations (including Chaldeans and Assyrians), at a military compound in Tehran. Another set of interviews was also made with mostly young Shi'i deserters, who fled the country to join their forcibly deported families in Tehran and Karaj.[6]

The most extensive set of interviews was conducted in 1990–91 for the analysis of the 1991 uprisings and the role of the war generation in them.[7] This was a more diversified group in terms of ethnicity, religion, region, culture, education, and political orientation. To this was added in later years sporadic interviews made in Western Europe, the United States and Jordan, among some exiled or migrant Iraqis. Most interviewees belonged to the war generation as defined earlier.

The random, even accidental sample of military and civilian individuals ranged between 24 and 42 years of age (with 1991 as the base year). Some people were thoroughly and extensively interviewed, while others were less thoroughly scrutinized. Certain interviews were limited in scope and nature and may fall into the category of "conversation." The purpose was to pinpoint the attitude toward war, explore the factors behind such an attitude, and seek to build a sociological profile.

Another limitation is that the interviewees were, generally speaking, educated males descended from urban middle- and lower-middle strata, a limitation that may impede a sounder representation of the rural areas. Those of rural origins were few, and these individuals' numbers did not match their real weight in the war generation or, for that matter, in the armed forces.[8] While the group included a number of committed militants, leftists, nationalist Kurds, Islamists and, for the major part, members of the ruling Baath party, the number of non-committed individuals was small indeed. When scrutinized against the realities of the late seventies in Iraq, it would appear normal to have such a small number of "uncommitted" persons. The Baathization crusade was at its peak, and the Baath party expanded its ranks in gigantic strides, mostly among the young and educated, whose very social mobility depended on the party.[9]

The interviewees were, alas, an exclusively male group. Hence, the reference to the war generation in this chapter actually refers to the male segment of a male fighting force, in a male-run affair (the war) of a male-dominated society.[10]

The War

In one decade, Iraq waged two massive wars in which a whole generation was trapped. Both wars and the uprisings that followed in 1991 wreaked unprecedented havoc and left Iraq a destitute, torn, isolated nation. The war generation paid a heavy price. It bore the brunt of casualties at the war front, suffered the perils of the uprisings, and was entangled in the violence of the rebellion on both sides of the national divide.

The question of why these wars were waged deserves further debate. The general assumption is that they were launched because of regional ambitions on the part of Iraq's ruling elite. The first war was motivated, it is presumed, by the desire to destroy a regional threat (the Iranian Islamic revolution) and, in consequence, emerge as the champion of the Arab world, to fill the vacuum left by the demise of Gamal Abdel Nasser of Egypt.[11] In the second war, the aim was to remedy the negative effects resulting from the first war. Iraq emerged from the Iran–Iraq War a formidable military power, with the fourth largest army in the world, in terms of the size of its military machine and the volume of military hardware (but never in qualitative terms). Kuwait—King Solomon's treasure—was sought to create an economic power to match Iraq's military might.

We conceive the two wars fought by Iraq as the outcome of a mixture of domestic, regional, and international phenomena, the most important of which are Iraqi internal dynamics.[12] Regional factors notwithstanding, Iraqi internal dynamics were the hotbed from which such grand, regional ambitions emerged: war was not only a means to outward expansion but also a cohesive instrument of nation-building and regime security.[13] No phenomenon can ever make or break legitimacy of the state more than war, in its capacity as a ruling system and representative of a national community, or nurture or disturb the fervor of nationalism both as an ideology and social movement.

The Baath ruling party opted for a unique authoritarian model that may be regarded as totalitarian. It was anchored in a populist-etatist form of nationalist socialism with its command economy, etatist rentierism, and single party system. Backed by growing oil revenues, such a hegemonic system could, on the one hand, co-opt the consent of vast sections of the population through the expansion of free social services (such as education and national health care), or redistribution of national income favoring the upward mobility of the largest social class, the middle- and lower-middle strata. It could, on the other hand, enforce control through formidable security apparatuses. The "new" totalitarian, single-party system succeeded in promoting a state-run industrial sector, modernizing and developing social services, reducing unemployment and providing better chances for the rising middle classes, which grew from 34 percent of urban population in 1968 to more than 50 percent in 1980.[14] General prosperity and progress in social and economic development were palpable indeed.

By its very nature, the totalitarian regime tended to monopolize the political field and impose a monist ideology, which is incompatible with a multiethnic, multicultural society. Such monism has given rise to political exclusion and disfranchisement, unbalanced economic participation of regions and social segments, ethnic assimilation, cultural domination and coercive etatist measures to hegemonize each and every autonomous space of cultural and social action. This hegemonic coercion disturbed national integration processes and triggered adverse trends.[15]

Before the outbreak of the Iran–Iraq War in 1980, Iraq seemed economically sound and militarily powerful, on the one hand, although on the other hand political stability looked shaky and insecure. True, between 1975 and 1979 the security services managed to eliminate active nationalist Kurdish or communist networks and organizations, but it now met with a new challenge: Shi'i political Islam, which had been very active since 1970, long before the name of Khomeini was ever in circulation. With the latter's victorious return to Tehran in February 1979, a massive, anti-Baath, Shi'i movement emerged. At this juncture, a fierce schism plagued the Baath leadership. A changing of the guard followed, with the replacement of the ailing president, Ahmad Hassan al-Bakr, by a new one, Saddam Hussein, who consolidated his power base by purging 21 leading Baath figures. Iraq now shifted from rapprochement with Syria to antagonism with Iran.[16] A massive onslaught against Shi'i activists destroyed the networks of the Da'wa and other Shi'i groups. The grand ayatollah Muhammad Baqir al-Sadr was executed and war with Iran was imminent. Embroiled in turmoil, Iran seemed an easy prey, and the war promised to be another classical example of a successful blitzkrieg.

Iraq launched the war with general aims that combined Iraqi and Arab territorial and political claims: regaining control over the Shatt al-Arab waterway and other territories, and removal of Iran's occupation of the three Gulf islands, Greater and Lesser Tunb and Abu Musa.[17] Meant to be a blitzkrieg, the war dragged on for eight years. In the first phase, Iraq scored success in occupying Iranian territory and proved superior to the Iranian armed forces. The prolongation of the war made it imperative to call on reserves and mobilize wider sections of the younger generation. The majority, who gave their allegiance to the Baath regime and ideology, together with vast sections of Arabs, showed unmistakable signs of support and pride in Iraq's military power (interviews).

As the battles on Iranian soil continued endlessly, enthusiasm among the war generation weakened, and was gradually displaced by a sense of frustration. Voluntary surrender to the enemy increased alarmingly. Iraqi POWs interviewed in 1982 confirmed that this trend of deliberate capitulation was increasing daily during the second year of the war, and reports by political commissars, that is, party operatives in the army, attributed this tendency to "the plots of traitors," a term usually used to allude to Shi'i Islamist and communist influence (interviews). When defeat loomed on the horizon and the Iranians dislodged the Iraqi armed forces from various areas and recaptured Khorramshahr in May 1982, the passivity of the Iraqi units fighting on Iranian soil may have reached its peak (interviews). On June 20, 1982, Iraq officially announced withdrawal from the Iranian territories.[18]

During the second phase of the war, which covered more than six years, from May 1982 to July 1988, Iraq's war effort remained mainly defensive, whether during the ground war on the Basra, Amarah, and Marshes fronts, the Tanker War, or the so-called War of the Cities. This shift changed the nature of the war. So did, at least officially, the international and regional attitudes toward Iraq. Both the United States and the USSR supported Iraq. So did Western Europe, the Gulf States, and even radical Arab countries, with the exception of Syria.

The legitimacy of the war was enhanced in the eyes of the soldiery, who felt great relief at withdrawal from the Iranian territories, and for whom peace seemed a realistic hope, even if not imminent (interviews). Steadily, but gradually, the war against Iran was projected in the minds of the bulk of the soldiery as an Iranian aggression, a war driven by religious fanaticism, aimed at the installation of a theocracy in Iraq à la the Iranian model (interviews). The nature of the Iranian offensive, the blatant Iranian intention to "export" its version of Shi'i radical Islam, and the internal trend inside Iran toward an authoritarian hierocracy, eroded the earlier popular sympathy with the Iranian revolution as an antidote to the pro-Western, despotic regime of the shah. And the greater this threat seemed to be, the more Iraqi patriotism came closer to etatist nationalism. The previous trend of capitulation among the soldiery now waned, and cracks within the opposition groups developed (interviews). A similar sense of national threat was manifestly dividing dissident groups in exile and in the mountains.[19]

It would, of course, be a neat, oversimplified picture, to depict the sentiments of the war generation as developing from initial enthusiasm to frustration and back to solid patriotism. In all phases, there was a constant flow of the antithesis. The trickle of desertion, for example, never stopped in all phases, nor did active or passive opposition to the war effort. Mixed feelings even among some staunch enthusiasts never failed to bewilder the mind and soul (interviews).

To cite a few examples: the number of deserters hiding in the marshes or the remote rural areas was never estimated at less than 40–50,000; another segment (mostly Christians, Kurds, Shi'is, and leftists) running into tens of thousands managed to flee the country into exile; the number of Shi'i dissidents fighting in the Iran-sponsored Badr Brigade was estimated at more than 10,000 and the communist guerrilla force fighting in the mountains was no less than 4,000 partisans, while the Kurdish nationalist fighters were even more numerous, with some 20–30,000 under arms.[20] And these were mainly from the same generation of the youth fighting on the front. A similar trend was also observable in Iran: the Mojahedin-e Khalq was fighting on the other side of the front line, and tens of thousands of Iranian youth of every social and ideological strand sought asylum in the west.

In retrospect, divided loyalties were the order of the day in all phases, but the fine line that separates these cleavages was shifting and, sometimes, overlapping. The only induction to be added is that the patriotic trend among the war generation was dominant during the early phase as well as during the second part of the Iran–Iraq War; albeit it was inundated with a mix of great expectations for peace and prosperity and misgivings and fears of loss and mayhem.

Art, Literature, and the War

During the war, the ongoing effort to create a unifying cultural space for diverse ethnic, religious, and cultural groups was intensified. Along with the abstract concept of the Arab nation, an Iraqi form of nationalism was tailored in the mid-seventies to better conform to Iraqi realities. The new Iraqi nationalism was constructed out of diverse pre-Islamic, Islamic, and modern elements. Historical symbols and myths from the ancient Sumerian, Akkadian, and Babylonian past were deployed.[21] Muslim symbols like Shi'i Imams or Kurdish Muslim leaders, for example, Saladin, were incorporated into the fabric of Iraqi nationalism. All was meant to convey a sense of national unity and lend the modern Iraqi nation-state a sense of historical depth overriding the ethnic and religious divide. The need to recruit the Kurds on the war front, or to deter any communal unity, imagined or possible, between Iraqi and Persian Shi'is, further enhanced this drive.

The war itself was conferred with the title of Qadisiyya, named after first campaign the Muslim invaders fought against the Sasanian, that is, Persian, empire, in the seventh century on the soil of what in the twentieth century became Iraq.[22] Dramas, novels, paintings, and sculpture were used to indoctrinate these ideas. The shift from pure Arabism (*qawmiyya*) to Iraqi patriotism (*wataniyya*) was projected by these literary and artistic artifacts. The Iraqi stride forward was now the motto.[23]

Arab folk poetry and folkloric songs were directed at the rural peasantry, whose illiteracy and distaste for modern productions alienated them from other, more refined forms of art and literature now put in the service of the battle. Annual prizes were generously paid and festivals for war fiction and war poetry lavishly celebrated. Folkloric poets, once disdained for using local dialects rather than refined classical Arab idiom, were now summoned to convene endless festivals, use the *husa* meters (a tribal cry of war and challenge), or publish and broadcast their works. The president, personally, decorated many of them with medals. In addition to cash benefits, folkloric poets were rewarded with handguns, a symbol of both traditional tribal manhood and modern military honor.[24]

Shi'ism long has been an integral part of Iranian national self-consciousness, and Iranian war propaganda was anchored in Shi'i Islamic symbols. The use of nationalist and Shi'i symbols was therefore a matter of course. It depicted the Baath regime in religious language, with Saddam as Yazid, the Sunni usurper of the Imamate and the assassin of Imam Hussein, or as an atheist secular rule, hostile to Islam. Imam Hussein's image as a martyr and legitimate symbol of a true, divinely ordained leader was enlisted in the battle. By contrast, Iraqi propaganda focused on Iraqism in its various pre-Islamic, Islamic, and modern aspects, since it aimed to defame the Iranian enemy on religious–ethnic grounds, as being Persian/Magus, that is, non-Muslim Persians. While Iranian propaganda meant to win over Shi'i coreligionists in Iraq, the media in the latter focused efforts on delinking any possible inter-Shi'i liaisons and sympathies and creating a broad cultural space unifying diverse ethnic and religious groups. An ethnic divide did exist between Iraqi and Iranian Shi'is;[25] the cleavage was now further accentuated thanks to something old, rather than something new—Arab tribalism of the greater part of the Shi'i south.

The Great Cleavage

The delicate and fragile nature of Iraqi popular patriotism stands in bold contrast to the almost monolithic nature of etatist nationalism of a totalitarian regime. Nationalism is not simply an intellectual construction, an ideology, or mere social movement, but a cultural space in which history, religion, culture, and socioeconomic aspects play crucial parts. Far from being fixed, this is a complex space that is fluid and unstable.[26]

If the strong union of etatist nationalism and popular patriotism during much of the Iran–Iraq War was evident, their clash during and after the 1990–91 Gulf War was glaringly manifest. How and why did they diverge and, in the end, clash? Molded in the ideology of nationalist socialism and enthused by prospects of rapid upward social mobility, the young war generation pinned their hopes on the oil boom in the mid-1970s and sought to secure their share of state employment and free services. Large sections of this generation joined the Baath party ranks, which rapidly swelled from a few hundred in 1968 to 1.8 million members and candidates in the 1980s.[27] Their macabre experiences on the war front left deep scars in the minds and souls of the war generation. In the last year of the war, the negative pressures stemming from the prolongation of hostilities seemed to have, at least partly, encroached upon the sense of national threat motivating the young generation (interviews). If the war had continued longer, it would have had dire consequences, damaging troops' motivation and fighting spirit (interviews). As soon as Ayatollah Khomeini had to "drink the cup of poison" and accept UN resolution 598, the universal jubilation in Iraq revealed the depth of peace sentiment and war apathy not only among the young soldiers, but also across the board nationally. Despite strict instructions from higher authorities to keep discipline, soldiers and armed civilians kept shooting in the air to express their ecstasy at the prospect of peace.

On August 20, 1988, the date the ceasefire was declared, Iraq ushered in a new, precarious era. The eight beleaguered years resulted in many contradictions, which proved chronic and fatal. Iraq had emerged a mighty military power (the fourth in the world in the quantitative terms of equipment and manpower), but it was economically strained and socially overstretched. War expenditure, estimated at $130 billion, was greater than the gross domestic product during the war years. The economic toll of the war was indeed too great to absorb. It had not only consumed between $38–40 billion or so of prewar reserves, but the economy was now plunged into deep indebtedness, estimated between $50–80 billion, roughly half of it to the Gulf countries.[28] The nation had also to pay $63 billion for reconstruction projects. Decline of industrial and agricultural production augmented the negative impact of inflation. With oil revenues dwindling, both GDP and per capita income severely plunged, well below prewar levels.[29]

In 1980, soldiers had to pay 5 Iraqi Dinars (ID) (roughly $15.50, at $3.10 per ID), for a cab from Basra to Baghdad to spend their short vacations (3 days every 10 weeks); in 1981 the cost rose to 10 ID ($31); and in 1982 it increased to 15 ID ($46.50) (interviews). Prices of cigarettes, meat, and other essentials rose beyond the means of the bulk of soldiers. The lavish compensation paid by the government to the troops if they were injured, or to their families if they fell in battle, was stopped in 1982. Earlier, a wounded soldier would receive 300 ID ($930) for privates and 500 ID ($1550) for officers. The families of those killed in action got bigger rewards: a Toyota vehicle and a plot of land for housing (privates and noncommissioned officers); a Canadian Chevrolet car and a larger piece of residential land (officers) (interviews).

Another source of discontent and apathy was the level of casualties: more than 300,000 troops lost their lives on the battlefronts, and a greater number was maimed or injured. Some 15,000 fell captive and had to spend between 16 and 18 years (almost a life sentence) as POWs, notably for those captured in 1980 and released in 1996–98.[30] During hostilities, the latter were envied by their mates as the "lucky ones," "winning the lottery of survival" (interviews). Indeed, some Iraqi POWs in Iran were released by a special pardon and given leave to remain as free civilians. Captives turned into guests were Shi'i soldiers and noncommissioned officers who had either relatives deported to Iran, or had some family and other connections with the Tehran-based Shi'i Islamist groups. Pardoned captives were termed "*Tawabin*," that is, the repentant, for they were seen to have committed the sin of fighting the sacred Imam, that is, Khomeini. Those bereft of such connections had to spend between 2 and 18 years in POW camps. When the war ended, the image of those unlucky captives changed; now they were termed by their fighting mates as "the forgotten to rot" or "living dead," or "eternal captives" (interviews). The conscripts of beleaguered units regarded the level of casualties as unnecessarily high and attributed it to "inefficiency of leadership" and "disdain for loss of life" (interviews).

Another category must be added: the servicemen executed for retreat, desertion, disobedience, cowardice, or disloyalty. Their number is anybody's guess; still they form part of the horrendous experience of the war veterans, who have lost mates and/or next of kin, and were themselves under constant threat of being accused of collaboration, disloyalty, or treason. Such charges loomed even in cases of engine failure by tanks or armored vehicles (interviews). Worse still, disloyalty was not only punishable by death, but the wooden coffins of the victims were marked with the words "traitor" or "coward" and displayed before their mates in the unit and before the eyes of the local community where the victim lived. In such cases, a pension was denied and confiscation of property of "traitors" also followed (interviews).

The social fabric of a nation in the making was also overstretched by other policies; for instance, between 50,000 and 100,000 Shi'is were forcibly deported to Iran.[31] At least half a million Kurds suffered directly from forcible evacuation, resettlement, attacks by chemical gas or physical elimination en masse. The episode of

Halabja, where residents were gassed by chemicals in 1988, or the victims of the Anfal campaign, in which some 150,000–180,000, were massacred in the southern desert of Iraq,[32] are part of the grim reality that affected the nation and, by extension, the war generation. Although the flow of information and the very language of communication were controlled, anecdotes of deportation, resettlement, or physical elimination of ethnic, religious, or political groups were received by some soldiers with awe and pain and affected their attitudes (interviews).

Part of these oppressive episodes were not only felt but also echoed by the soldiery through family connections, community bonds, or tribal networks. Certain experiences, however limited, reflected the dual nature of fear stemming from this double threat from the enemy without and the enemy within (interviews).

The ceasefire period, a welcome development in itself, was problematic. It involved great expectations on the part of the soldiers, but greater concern on the part of the regime. For the regime's security, the biggest problem in this period of no-war, no-peace, was not opposition or dissidence at large, but the nation's own guardian: the army of one million men—how to feed it and how to keep it busy.[33] Documented evidence testifies to the existence of two equally valid arguments within the higher echelons of the ruling civilian and military elite: one argument stressed the dangers of continued mobilization while the other emphasized the hazards of demobilization.

In the first case, tensions within the army were feared. The Baathization of the armed forces, that is the indoctrination of the army and keeping it under the control of the ruling party, was successfully achieved in the seventies. For the first time in Iraq's modern history, the military were brought back to the barracks under civilian control.[34] Now with general mobilization, the nature of the army mutated in terms of tight party control; the new recruits reduced the proportionate weight of Baathists in the armed forces and weakened the party's grip. The war itself elevated several military commanders to the level of national heroes, competing with the civilian leaders in prestige and popularity. Under such conditions, the army was liable to go out of control.[35]

In the second case, tensions in society were feared. Those who had borne the burdens and horrors of the war had already gained the moral right to decent employment for those in good physical shape, and decent social care for those wounded, maimed, or disfigured. Yet, resources were too strained to meet such demands. This was a double-edged dilemma that resulted in aggravating the problem.

Thirsty for the comforts and safety of civilian life, the war generation had great expectations of rapid demobilization of the army and a greater share of the fruits of the nation's wealth (interviews). For eight years they had been told they were Saddam's heroes, the saviors of the nation. Those who had lost their lives were bestowed with the honor of martyrdom, and the martyrs were declared to be "the noblest of us all" as one official motto went.

Although a sense of relief that the macabre mayhem had ended overtook the war veterans, their frustration was exacerbated by the delayed demobilization promises, and the growth of a nouveau riche class of war "fat cats," who ostentatiously displayed their wealth and clout (interviews). Partial deregulation and dismantling of the command economy favored these rising, wealthy classes, much to the dismay of the impatient soldiers (interviews). As an experiment, 50,000 or so recruits (roughly

5 percent of men under arms) were demobilized, but the conscripts found little opportunity upon their return to civilian walks of life and their restiveness and violent behavior proved uncontrollable (interviews).

Civilians described the behavior of soldiers as wild, violent—even intolerable. More often than not, soldiers showed strong signs of clannish spirit among themselves. A street quarrel would erupt if and when any soldier, even in civilian outfit (recognized from his short haircut, or scars of battle) received what was regarded as "bad" or "inappropriate" treatment by other civilians, state functionaries, or the police. To some extent, these acts were looked upon by the community at large with tolerance, forgiveness, or even sympathy (interviews). Thus the young conscripts were not only adamant in their demands but also violent in their methods. And the commanders who advocated demobilization received a heavy blow.[36] During the interval between the two wars, a sense of social apathy and alienation gradually took hold of the intolerant soldiers, hungry for literally everything, deprived of their greatest hopes and denied their basic demands (interviews). In this period, the cracks in the union of popular patriotism and etatist nationalism may have deepened, rumbling beneath the surface, and exploding in sound and fury only sporadically.

A Fatal Blow

In the interim period, 1988–90, the nation teetered on the verge of two options: reform and rehabilitation, or another military adventure. A host of international and regional developments made it imperative to seek a way out of the dilemma. Transformations in Eastern Europe took the ruling elite by surprise and triggered deep concern. The Soviet totalitarian model, from whose arsenal much of the Baath dogma was drawn, collapsed. It dealt a fatal blow to the ideological pillars of Baath rule: the command economy, single-party system, and self-tailored legitimacy. The bloody street uprisings in neighboring Jordan and Algeria in 1989 ushered democratic reform into the two Arab countries. The Iraqi president offered a similar package of reforms: economic liberalization, a new constitution (which envisaged political pluralism), free press, and other democratic freedoms. An offer of genuine peace was made to the Iranian president, Ali-Akbar Hashimi-Rafsanjani. Both the reform package and the conciliatory move toward Iran were an endeavor to ease domestic and regional tensions, as a precondition to expand and exploit the Majnun oil fields (in the southern Amara province, bordering Iran). Another option was to seek quick and easy resources. The reform package was never delivered, and the invasion of Kuwait followed. Paradoxically, the invasion and annexation of Kuwait aimed, among other things, to secure enough oil wealth to relieve economic burdens, rekindle the flames of popular patriotism so as to go hand in glove with etatist nationalism, and, last but not least, win the allegiance of the war generation. The outcome, as is well known, is the direct antithesis of this miscalculated adventure.

Successive twists and turns bewildered and infuriated the bulk of the war veterans and ripped apart the mainstream official, nationalist creed and policy. The first frustrating turn was the prospect of fighting yet another war, while still licking the wounds of the first. Promises voiced by Prime Minister Sa'dun Hammadi to augment Iraq's oil wealth to $40 billion, were received with mixed feelings of hope and misgiving. The impact of these statements, aired several times in November 1990 by the Iraqi television network, faded with the buildup of U.S.-led allied forces in Saudi Arabia and the Gulf (interviews). With the new general mobilization, all dreams of taking off the military uniform dissolved into thin air (interviews). Another source of concern was the nature of the enemy. This time it was not the Third-World Iran with its "inferior" war-machine, but the most technologically advanced country on earth they had to face (interviews). Another turn of policy produced bewilderment and confusion. Out of pragmatic calculations, the Iraqi government extended an apology to Iran and even pointed to U.S. machinations behind the prolonged war between the two countries, much to the dismay of the war "heroes." But neither the goodwill of Iran nor the support of the conscripts was won. What this conciliatory gesture toward Iran meant to many of them was that their sacrifices, their blood, their agonies, and their much-celebrated heroism had all been in vain (interviews). It ran counter to the very logic of the Iran–Iraq War itself as a nationalist stand against aggression.

In the runup to the Gulf war, a sense of anxiety and *angst* took hold of a majority of the war generation, now veterans in the strict sense of the word. All attempts by the ruling elite to imbue this generation with Arab and Third-World pro-Saddam enthusiasm were fruitless. Such sentiments of anxiety and angst, which appear in military jargon as "low morale," could easily lead to passivity, which in turn may result in abstention or inaction. But passivity and inaction could develop into antigovernment action if the final break with an etatist, jingoistic form of nationalism occurred.

Such a break was in the end brought about by the combined effect of defeat, disorganized retreat and destruction in January–February 1991. As a result of the massive U.S.-led air campaign and ground war, early estimates put the number of human casualties at a horrendous level: perhaps 120,000–150,000 military and 10,000–15,000 civilians were believed to have perished. (Other estimates made later were much lower.) In the uprisings more than 20,000 rebels lost their lives and 25–30,000 Kurdish civilians were killed during and in the aftermath of the uprising.[37] The horrific nature of these figures may be appreciated when their intensity is measured. In the eight years of the Iran–Iraq War, an average of 300 fatalities was sustained a day; in the Gulf War the average surpassed 4,000 a day. The extensive nature of the first war was surpassed by the intensive nature of the second. The previous three trends within the war generation, namely, support, passivity, and challenge, now materialized in the open. The Iraqi armed forces split along these lines. The military exhibited different trends: first, mutiny in the south (i.e., the Kuwaiti theater); second, passive desertion, mainly in the north (Kurdistan); and third, disciplined cohesive pro-regime fighting (in the middle).[38]

This differentiation in the attitudes of various sections of the Iraqi military results from a number of factors, such as the level of destruction wreaked upon each formation (with a varying sense of proud security or bitter defeat), the existence or disruption of centralized chain of command, and, lastly, the density (thick or thin) of loyal party and kinship networks in these units. In the southern sector all negative factors were at work, in the northern sector, some of them, and in the middle sector, none. Indeed, the conduct of the troops, notably in the Kuwaiti theater, proved the point. They voted with their feet and did not put up much of a fight. Of the quarter of a million soldiers in this theater, around 150,000 raised white flags and surrendered within hours of the ground war's beginning in February 1991. The survivors took up arms against their own government. In fact, it was the retreating soldiers from the Kuwaiti theater who triggered the uprising in Basra.[39] Spontaneous and organized civilians in a host of major towns and cities echoed their anger and rebelled. Among the insurgents were a large number of Baath party members. They were soon to be joined by Islamists from exile in Iran. The uprising was the doing of the radical section of the war generation, be they in military or civilian outfits. The average age of the rebels was around 24, their major affiliation in the southern districts was Baath party with Islamists connected later, while in the north, Kurdish nationalists and communists formed the core of the movement.[40]

A General Profile

War demands unity of the nation, rebellion reflects its discord. The logic of war, if prevailing, buries all schisms under a thick, even monolithic layer of union of purpose and action and channels energies outwards. The logic of revolt hoists aloft the principle of dissent and directs fury inwards. The war generation were drained of their sense of loyalty to the "state," in the sense defined by their ruling class, and took to arms. They longed for peace but ended up in a beleaguered cul-de-sac.

During the second Gulf War, the nature of the enemy, together with symbols of mobilization and rallying points, changed beyond recognition. Official ideology shifted from Arabism to Iraqism; propagated cultural norms altered from secularism to religious symbols; political ideology moved away from notions of progress, vanguard-party, and socialism, to tradition and tribe; nationalist socialism changed direction from command economy, state-guaranteed employment, and free social services, to deregulation, commercialization, and pauperism. The middle classes to which most of the young war generation belonged or yearned to join, and which were the backbone of the Baath regime, now plunged into the abyss.[41]

Of the outstanding generational traits, values of violence and social apathy stand in bold relief. In the period before the overthrow of Saddam Hussein, the rates of violent crime were doubling by seasons rather than years. The violent nature of antigovernment opposition was another indication. Nowhere had the level of arms distribution among civilians or the level of military training reached such massive proportions. Backed by the revival of tribal norms of retaliation and self-justice, this violent trend assumed an almost general character. Worse still was the collapse of already corrupt law enforcement agencies and the judicial system. In light of the reality of a violent generation, prospects of a peaceful change seem fragile.

Another quality is the disintegration of ideological orientation, as it were, of the mind. Modern holistic solidarities, observed earlier among this generation, such as

solidarity of class or nation, have been displaced by primordial, segmentary loyalties, of the clan, the tribe, the family, or local community. As a result, a state of
hyper-segmentation now exists, cutting across regions, communities, social classes
and groups. Re-making the Iraqi "nation" seems an arduous task. Local forms of traditionalism may well have increased the chances for the growth of primordially
organized Islamist trends, both Sunni and Shi'i. Wahhabism, à la the Taliban, has
been gathering pace among Sunni youth since 1992, whereas among the Shi'i primordially embedded, communal or fundamentalist trends have also been flourish-
ing. If this trend continues, Islamist ideologies might ironically break the
de-ideologizing process.

Work ethics, once solid and renowned among the youth, have degenerated into
patron–client ethics. This has been fostered by a rentier economy and the politics of
patronage. With the collapse of oil rentierism, the salaried middle strata lost middle-class
status, but not the longing for it. Impoverished and humiliated, they form an insurgent,
educated "marginalized proletariat," from which violence rather than conformism may
emerge. Lacking social peace, rational private business may prove difficult. With no
solid institutions to protect property and the legality of contracts, business will retreat
into primordial confines, reinforcing social fragmentation and traditionalism.

All in all, violence, de-ideologization, and segmentation of this generation are coupled with relapse into various forms of supra-natural beliefs: religious piety or fundamentalism, self-insulated mysticism, magic, and sorcery. These are manifestations of
a sense of alienation from the state as a national community. Leaving this national
space has become the strongest of inclinations: indeed, seeking asylum in the West has
become the ideal prospect. Sociologists maintain that migration is a statement of
protest. Nowhere is this true more than the case of the war generation.

Notes and Tables

Notes

1. Marion Farouk-Sluglett and Peter Sluglett, "The Historiography of Modern Iraq," in *The American Historical Review*, vol. 96, no. 5 (December 1991), pp. 1408–21.
2. See table 5.3.
3. See tables 5.1 and 5.2.
4. Ibid.
5. See table 5.3.
6. In the spring of 1982, I conducted research on Iraqis exiled in Iran, including Tehran, Karaj, Qom, and other places. Whereas Shi'is and Kurds represented militant Islamism and Kurdish nationalism, Christian POWs in Tehran revealed part of the episode of the war generation. Dr. Hikmat Dawod, an Iraqi film director, helped document these inter-views on videotape.
7. Consult my contribution, "Why the Intifada Failed," in *Iraq Since the Gulf War: Prospects for Democracy*, ed. Fran Hazelton (London: Zed, 1994), pp. 97–117.
8. See table 5.2.
9. See table 5.5.

10. A notorious difficulty, which sets limits on any extensive survey, is the complex nature of Iraqi society, renowned for the intersection of vertical and horizontal solidarities, and the intertwining of modern ideologies and traditional culture. These factors cut through various generational groups, affecting their identities, and, by extension, their choices and responses. Another problem emanates from two facts. On the one hand, Iraq is the most understudied society in the Middle East. The poverty of anthropological or sociological studies, let alone surveys, is too apparent to dwell on at length. On the other hand, the free flow of information was notoriously absent under the authoritarian grip of a regime obsessed with secrecy. Perhaps the only counterbalance is the mass exodus of large segments of the war generation, together with groups of ex-military and ex-officials, who provide some information, albeit limited and in some cases anecdotal, of certain experiences of the war. An archive of about 10 million documents was confiscated from government security and other agencies in Kurdistan by the rebels during the 1991 uprising and transferred to the United States. There it was processed by a private company and is now available on compact disk. The prominent Iraqi author and scholar, Kanan Makiya, played a vital role in the project. Supervised by the Iraq Foundation in Washington, D.C., a score of researchers have been working on the archive and trying to rearrange the jigsaw pattern. It will take some years to realize the end product.

11. The available literature on the Iran–Iraq War suggests various reasons for its causes. The official literature focuses on the Iranian threat to national security, whereas critical literature takes account of internal and regional dynamics. See for example: Hanns Maull and Otto Pick, eds., *The Gulf War: Regional and International Dimensions* (London: Pinter, 1989); Edgar O'Balance, *The Gulf War* (London: Brassey's, 1988); Anthony H. Cordesman and Abraham R. Wagner, *The Lessons of Modern War*, vol. 2, *The Iran-Iraq War* (London: Mansell, 1990); Tareq Aziz, *Iran-Iraq Conflict: Questions and Discussions*, trans. Naji Al-Hadithi (London: Third World Centre, 1981); Baath Party, *The Central Report for the Ninth Regional Party Congress-June 1982* (Baghdad: Al-Dar al-'Arabiya, January 1983); Committee Against Repression and for Democratic Rights in Iraq (CARDRI), *Saddam's Iraq: Revolution or Reaction?* (London: Zed, 1989).

12. On the internal dynamics see Jabar Muhsin, "Iraq in the Gulf War," in CARDRI, *Saddam's Iraq*, pp. 229–40. See also my contribution, "Roots of an Adventure," in *The Gulf Between Us: The Gulf War and Beyond*, ed. Victoria Brittain (London: Verago, 1991), pp. 27–42.

13. Perhaps the best analysis of the problems of nation-building and regime security involved in the war effort can be found in Mohammad-Mahmoud Mohamedou, *Iraq and the Second Gulf War: State Building and Regime Security* (San Fransisco: Austin and Winfield, 1998).

14. On the size and steady growth of salaried and propertied middle classes in Iraq, see Hanna Batatu, *The Old Social Classes and the Revolutionary Movements of Iraq* (Princeton: Princeton University Press, 1978), p. 1126. Batatu's figures cover the period 1950–68. Further calculations of these classes in the eighties and nineties are provided in chapter 5 of my study of socioeconomic formations in Iraq, *State and Civil Society in Iraq 1980–1992 (Al-Dawla wa'l mujtama' al-madani wa'l tatawur al-demoqrati fi-l 'Iraq)* (Cairo: Ibn Khaldoun Centre, 1995), table 1, p. 233 and table 14, p. 234.

15. Jabar, *State and Civil Society in Iraq*, chapter 7.

16. On the Iraqi–Syrian Baath conflict see Eberhard Kienle, *Ba'th Versus Ba'th: The Conflict Between Syria and Iraq, 1968–1989* (London: Kegan Paul International, 1987; republished by I.B. Taurus, 1990), p. 135 and passim; Marion Farouk-Sluglett and Peter Sluglett, *Iraq Since 1958: From Revolution to Dictatorship* (London: I.B.Tauris, 1990), pp. 200–05.

17. CARDRI, *Saddam's Iraq*, p. 229 and passim.

18. Dilip Hiro, *The Longest War: The Iran-Iraq Military Conflict* (New York: Routledge, 1991), p. 64.

19. Hazelton, *Iraq Since the Gulf War*, p. 99 and passim.

20. Faleh A. Jabar, *The Shi'ite Movement in Iraq* (London: Saqi Books, 2003).

21. On the restructuring of Iraqi nationalism under the Baath, see Amatzia Baram, *Culture, History, and Ideology in the Formation of of Ba'thist Iraq, 1968–89* (New York: St. Martin's Press, 1991); and "Mesopotamian Identity in Ba'thi Iraq," in *Middle Eastern Studies*, vol. 19, no. 4 (October 1983), pp. 246–55.

22. On the role of Islam in the first and second Gulf wars, see my essay, "The Double Edged Sword of Islam," in *The Gulf War and the New World Order*, ed. Haim Bresheeth and Nira Yuval-Davis (London: ZED, 1991), pp. 211–18.

23. The role of high and low cultures in war propaganda and mobilization during this period has been the subject of limited research. In this narrow area, however, two Iraqi writers stand in bold relief: the literary critic, Dr. Fatima al-Mohsen and the writer, Zuhair al-Jazairi. On various occasions, they analyzed and followed the so-called "war literature" in Iraq. In my assessment I have relied heavily on their observations.

24. With regard to the folkloric poets and the role they played, and the rewards they received, I am indebted to the London-based Dr. Hashim 'Iqabi, himself a folkloric poet who has firsthand information.

25. Understanding the cultural differentiation between Iraqi and Iranian Shi'ism is owed primarily to the Iraqi sociologist, 'Ali al-Wardi, in his seven volumes titled *Lamahat ijtima'iya min tarikh al-'Iraq al-hadith* (Social Aspects of Iraq's Modern History) (Baghdad: Matba'at al-Ma'arif, 1966–78). The "bedouin" nature of Iraqi Shi'ism that al-Wardi emphasized was fruitfully reiterated by the historian, Yitzhak Nakash, in *The Shi'is of Iraq* (Princeton: Princeton University Press, 1994).

26. On the nature of nationalism, there are two major contrary theoretical approaches: Benedict Anderson stresses the cultural homogeneity of nationalism, whereas Eric Hobsbawm stresses its political and cultural complexities. In both approaches, nationalism figures as a complex space in itself, where history, religion, language, and race overlap. See Benedict Anderson, *Imagined Communities: Reflections on the Origin and Spread of Nationalism* (London: Verso, 1983) and E.J. Hobsbawm, *Nations and Nationalism Since 1780: Programme, Myth, Reality* (Cambridge: Cambridge University Press, 1992).

27. See table 5.7 below.

28. Estimates vary to a considerable degree. See my *State and Civil Society in Iraq*, chapter 6, para iii.

29. Abbas Alnasrawi, *The Economy of Iraq: Oil, Wars, Destruction of Development and Prospects, 1950–2010* (Westport, Conn.: Greenwood Press, 1994), p. 92 and passim. On war economic losses, see also a paper by Alnasrawi, "Economic Sanctions: Theory, Effectiveness and Application to Iraq" (Vermont, USA, n.d.).

30. *State and Civil Society in Iraq*, chapter 7.

31. Ali Babakhan, "The Deportation of Shi'is During the Iran-Iraq War: Causes and Consequences," in *Ayatollahs, Sufis and Ideologues: State, Religion and Social Movements in Iraq*, ed. Faleh Abdul-Jabar (London: Saqi Books, 2002), pp. 183–210.

32. On the Anfal campaign see Kanan Makiya, *Cruelty and Silence: War, Tyranny, Uprising and the Arab World* (London: Jonathan Cape, 1993), pp. 24, 152, and 177–99.

33. In his two well-documented books on the Iran–Iraq War and the invasion of Kuwait, Saad Bazzaz, an ex-Ba'thist figure in the media world, reveals staggering facts about the volatile state of the Iraqi army. To keep the soldiery "busy" was, in his opinion, among the catalysts for the invasion of Kuwait. The books referred to above are: *Harb talidu 'ukhra: al-tarikh al-sirri li-harb al-Khalij* (A War is Born from Another: The Secret History of the Gulf War) (*Amman: al-Ahliyah li-l Nashr wa al-Tawzi'*, 1993) and *Al-Jiniralat akhir*

man ya'lam (The Generals Are the Last to Know) (London: Dar al-Hikmah, 1996). His firsthand information is vital for an assessment of the state of mind of the war generation.

34. Majid Khadduri, *Socialist Iraq: A Study in Iraqi Politics since 1968* (Washington, D.C.: Middle East Institute, 1978); May Chartouni-Dubarry, "The Development of Internal Politics in Iraq from 1958 to the Present Day," in *Iraq: Power and Society*, ed. Derek Hopwood et al. (Reading, U.K.: Ithaca Press for St Anthony's College, Oxford, 1993), pp. 30–33.

35. Many academic scholars and the majority of high military commanders who took refuge in western countries during the 1990s share this view.

36. I am indebted to Saad Bazzaz for this information.

37. Again estimates vary. Oxford Analytica, for example, gave similar figures, whereas Middle East Watch had different estimates. See e.g., Eric Goldstein and Andrew Whitley, *Endless Torment: The 1991 Uprising in Iraq And Its Aftermath* (New York: Middle East Watch, 1992). See also Faleh Abd al-Jabbar, "Why the Uprisings Failed," in *Middle East Report* (*MERIP*), no. 176 (May–June 1992), pp. 2–14.

38. On the responses of the Iraqi army in February–March 1991, see *Le Monde Diplomatique*, Mars 1998, pp. 14–15; see also my chapter, "State, Society, Clan, Party and Army in Iraq," in IDE Spot Survey, *From Storm to Thunder, The Unfinished Showdown Between Iraq and the US* (Tokyo: Institute of Developing Economics, March 1998), pp. 1–28.

39. There is general agreement that the uprising was triggered by the retreating soldiers in Basra, the most devastated city in the Gulf wars. Prominent high-ranking officers confirmed this was the case. This had already been supported by the world media coverage in March 1991. See for example, General Najib al-Salihi, *Al-Zilzal: madha hadatha fi-l 'Iraq ba'd al-insihab min al-Kuwayt? Khafaya al-ayya, al-damiyah!!* (The Earthquake: What Happened in the Aftermath of Withdrawal from Kuwait) (London: Al-Rafid, 1998).

40. Abd al-Jabbar, "Why the Uprisings Failed," in *Middle East Report*.

41. General Jabar Muhsin, a veteran Baathist of Shi'i and rural origin, lamented the "middle classes which we have lost" in the Baghdad-based *Babil* daily, December 20, 1994. Muhsin was in charge of the Directorate of Morale Mobilization in the Ministry of Defense, and his opinion reflects the state of mind of the ruling, military and civilian, elite.

Tables

Table 5.1 The four age groups of the war generation divided according to gender and rural–urban origin, for the year 1977

Age group	a. Urban		b. Rural		Aggregate a + b
	Males	*Females*	*Males*	*Females*	
5–9	635,915	600,350	427,657	181,037	1,844,959
10–14	524,839	474,242	289,365	251,513	1,539,959
15–19	368,338	353,270	119,968	168,685	1,010,261
20–24	410,593	333,182	191,769	180,832	1,116,376
Total	1,939,685	1,761,044	1,028,759	782,067	5,511,555

Source: Republic of Iraq, Ministry of Planning, *Annual Abstract of Statistics*, 1992, p. 39.

Table 5.2 Ratios of the male war generation to total urban, rural, and overall population in 1977

Category	Size	%*
a. Male urban war generation	1,939,685	
b. Total urban male population	3,979,549	a : b. 48.7
c. Total urban population	7,646,054	a : c 25.3
a. Male rural war generation	1,028,759	
b. Total rural male population	2,203,349	a : b 46.4
c. Total rural population	4,354,443	a : c 23.4
a. Total male war generation	2,968,444	a : c 25
b. Total war generation(m + f)	5,511,555	b : c 48.4
c. Total population	12,000,497	

Note: *All percentages are rounded up.

Source: Republic of Iraq, Ministry of Planning, *Annual Abstract of Statistics*, 1992, p. 39.

Table 5.3 The size of the armed forces, labor force, and their ratios to population (in millions), 1970–88

Year	Labor force	Armed forces	Ratio of L to A	Population	Ratio of armed forces per 1,000 of pop.
1970	2.4	0.062	2.9	9.4	6.6
1975	2.8	0.082	2.9	11.1	7.4
1980	3.2	0.430	13.4	13.2	32.6
1985	4.2	0.788	18	15.5*	51
1988	4.7	1.000	21.3	17.6	57

Sources: Abbas Alnasrawi, *The Economy of Iraq: Oil, Wars, Destruction of Development and Prospects, 1950–2010* (Westport, Conn.: Greenwood Press, 1994), tables 5.2, p. 92 and 8.1, p. 152. The table is derived from Iraq, *Annual Abstract of Statistics*, p. 35.

Table 5.4 Gross GDP and GDP per capita in constant 1980 prices, 1970–93

Year	GDP (billion $)	Per capita GDP ($)
1950	3.4	654
1960	8.7	1,085
1970	16.4	1,754
1975	30.0	2,703
1980	53.9	4,083
1982	42.8	3,035
1984	35.1	2,279
1986	29.1	1,764
1988	30.9	1,756
1990	16.4	868
1992	11.1	555
1993	10.0	485

Source: Alnasrawi, *The Economy of Iraq*, p. 152.

Table 5.5 The growth of urban propertied and salaried middle strata, 1958–87

Year	% of middle strata to urban population
1958	28
1968	34
1987	48

Table 5.6 Estimated ratios of middle, working, and marginal strata and classes to urban population (1987)

Group	% of urban population
Middle strata	48
Working classes	33
Marginal groups	8.4

Table 5.7 The Growth of Baath Party membership, 1968–80

Year	Full membership	Candidates and grassroots*
1968	100–200**	?
1976	10,000	500,000
1981	25,000	1,500,000
1988	?	1,800,000***

Notes
* This category is divided into three categories or ranks: second militant, first militant, and candidate to membership. Actually, these three categories could be termed as "new members," as is the case in other political organizations.
** Some estimates put the figure at 400–500 full members and candidates.
*** This is the total figure of both categories of party affiliates cited by Taha Yassin Ramadan in 1988.

Chapter 6

Iraqi Shi'i Politics

Laith Kubba

Iraq's 14 million Shi'is, who make up over 60 percent of its population and more than 80 percent of its Arabs, hold the key to its future. Once Iraq resolves its Kurdish demand for an autonomous federal northern region, it will be left with a tiny minority of Arab Sunnis, and an increased majority of Shi'is, who will certainly demand wider participation in the decision-making process. Consequently, Shi'i political attitudes are crucial to Iraq's stability. Although analyzing Iraq from an ethnic-confessional standpoint does not offer the best insight into its political dynamics, nevertheless it has become necessary in contemporary political analysis of Iraq to do so. This chapter is an attempt to introduce Shi'i political attitudes and actors and identify their commonly perceived issues and sentiments.

Ethno-Religious Polarization of Iraqi Shi'is

The past three decades of Baath rule have dramatically altered Iraq's political landscape. The two Gulf wars, the UN sanctions, and the ruthlessness of Saddam Hussein's regime have all polarized Iraq's main communities—the Shi'is, the tribal Arab Sunnis, and the Kurds—along ethnic and confessional lines. The effects of this polarization are deep, irreversible, and will probably reshape both the roles of the state vis-à-vis these communities and the country's intercommunity relationships. Saddam Hussein's domestic policies, coupled with the decade-long sanctions regime, have weakened Iraq's national unity and identity, revived ethnic and religious sentiments, raised communal tensions, and undermined the role of the state. Communal divisions became evident in the aftermath of the recent war that deposed Saddam. Despite their call for an Iraqi sovereign government, Kurds, Shi'is, and Sunnis have pursued their own limited communal interests at the cost of a shared national interest. Today, Iraqi politics have been transformed, from that of traditional competing ideologies to ones that emphasize ethnic-tribal expediency. An entire generation of Iraqis no longer relates to traditional political parties and is influenced by foreign forces, communal rather than national interests, and narrow perspectives. New players have now emerged in response to new challenges and sentiments among Iraq's communities.

Fragmentation of National Politics and the Emergence of "the Shi'i" Opposition

Up until 1980, the Iraqi polity was not dominated by ethnic or confessional concerns. The political discourse was national and reflected the main political trends in the region, which were liberal, leftist, nationalist, and/or Islamist. These diverse political trends spread throughout Iraq and among all communities, and the Arab Shi'is were not an exception. Some ethnic and marginalized communities leaned more toward national and secular political trends that held broad appeal, while others sought radical reforms to improve their intrinsic socioeconomic deprivation. Indeed, these variations in political tendencies were complex, and could not be reduced to mere ethnicity or religious confession. The socioeconomic conditions of the Shi'i have been more relevant to political discourse than communal identities. For example, the Marsh Arabs, known also as the Maadan in the south, and Shi'is in the poorer Baghdad districts were attracted to radical leftists, as well as to Islamic movements. Kurds were attracted to nationalist, tribal, communist, and Islamic movements. Even the Islamic and Kurdish movements, which seemed to be confessional and ethnic, respectively, are better understood in the context of ideological and national struggle. For many decades Iraqi political discourse remained national and provided a framework for the emergence of a national identity and the integration of its diverse communities. The Iran–Iraq War was a test case for Iraqi nationalism. Despite religious appeals from Iran's leaders, Iraqi Shi'is fought against Iran and the eight-year war did not shake the foundation of Iraq's national polity.

In the past decade, however, Iraqi politics has been reshaped by the emergence of ethnic and religious sub-identities and tribal loyalties, which have overridden the traditional national discourse. The most serious erosion is evident in the absence of a national Iraqi movement, the failure to agree on a national leadership and the fragmentation of its main political groups along ethnic lines. Despite claims to the contrary, the meeting of these groups in London in December 2002, under the umbrella of five main opposition groups, amply illustrated the lack of this national discourse. Speakers from the ethnically diverse groups expressed general aspirations for peace and respect for human and community rights, but did not engage in serious discourse to address future issues or develop a realistic post-Saddam national agenda. More importantly, the politics of these exile groups indicated that there has been a clear surge in ethnic sentiments, communal loyalties, and regional agendas. To some extent, the assertion of ethnic and communal identities may be understood as a backlash against three decades of a state policy that sought to promote a uniform identity, and enforce a state version of sub-identities. Expressions of strong ethnic sentiments may also be understood by fear of communities being left out in a post-Saddam Iraq as the state is restructured and reformed. It may also be argued that the trends among the ethnic exile groups are not indicative of the real communal aspirations inside the country. Nevertheless, the narrow sectarian agendas of these self-proclaimed and exiled political groups cannot be dismissed. Their failure to provide an alternative national framework, as well as their active participation in the promotion of ethnic-confessional political options, will surely further undermine Iraq's national identity.

Similarly, political attitudes of the Arab Shiʻis have changed beyond recognition and metamorphosed. In the first three decades following the creation of the Iraqi state in 1920, the majority of Shiʻis were passive participants in Iraqi politics. With the advent of urbanization and education, the new generation of Shiʻis were drawn into national politics for the following three decades. Unlike the case in Lebanon, Iraqi politics did not produce groups advocating an explicit Shiʻi agenda, be it secular or religious. However, in the past 15 years, a new brand of Shiʻi political actor emerged and became vocal and explicit about Shiʻi interests. Shiʻi demands surfaced recently within the context of a national political discourse. One clear example is an attempt by a small group of Iraqi Shiʻi exiles who rallied fellow Shiʻis to form an exclusive Shiʻi political platform around a "Shiʻi Declaration of Principles" for a post-Saddam Iraq. The declaration, which was signed by more than one hundred Shiʻi intellectuals and dignitaries, called for an explicit recognition of Shiʻis in an Iraqi polity. Although many Iraq Shiʻi exiles sympathized with the spirit behind the declaration, by and large they rejected its explicit nature. Moreover, in the months that followed Saddam's downfall, exiles pushed for an ethnic and sectarian allocation of cabinet and governor seats, whereas self-proclaimed Shiʻi representatives claimed a simple majority. Hence the question: Is there a future for an emerging Shiʻi political movement with an explicit Shiʻi political agenda or is there simply a surge for Shiʻi participation in Iraq's national politics? More importantly, who are the Shiʻi constituents and who are their leaders?

The Battle for Shiʻi Constituents

The end of Saddam's regime set off a contest for the minds and hearts of Iraqi Shiʻi. Secular and religious groups now competed to win Shiʻi political allegiance. Conservative and radical ulema are also in an open race to control the seminary at the holy city of Najaf. The tragic assassination of Sayyed Abdel Majid al-Khoei in April 2003 is a case in point.

By the Summer of 2004, the most radical clergy were followers of Moqtada al-Sadr, while the most conservative were the followers of Ayatollah Sistani. Nearly all political attempts to win the Shiʻi overlook their reality. Shiʻis constitute the poorest and most deprived citizens. They form neither a homogenous religious community nor a mass-based society. The majority are tribal Arabs, mostly urbanized and mainly concentrated in southern Iraq. Baghdad has influential Shiʻi families, a highly urbanized Shiʻi population, and more than half of its inhabitants are of tribal Shiʻi origin. Non-Arab Shiʻi are better understood as ethnic communities in clearly defined districts. This includes the Fayli Kurds in the northeastern province of

Diyala, Turkomans in the provinces of Kirkuk and Mosul, and Iraqis of Persian origin in the holy cities of Najaf, Karbala, and Kazimayn (Khadmiya). Most of the latter are concentrated in specific districts and their attitudes and interests differ from the majority tribal Arab Shi'is. Overall, the three most influential Shi'i communities are those in Baghdad, the Arab tribes in southern Iraq, and the religious communities in the holy cities of Najaf, Karbala, and Kazimayn.

Although Shi'i constituents have sub-identities based on class, ethnic, and tribal lines, they are still bonded through shared beliefs, initiation rituals during the month of Moharram, and through the leadership of the ulama and the Marja'iyyat. Shi'i adhesion to religious institutions is deeply rooted in their communal traditions. The impressive religious march to Karbala by one million people a few days following Saddam's overthrow is a case in point. These religious bonds, however, are not sufficient to make them a distinctive bloc like tribal Sunnis, Assyrians, or other minorities. Their religious affiliation plays little role in defining their daily interests but acquires great significance during national crises.

The impact of Saddam Hussein's era on Iraq's Shi'is varied among the communities. In the 1980s, Fayli Kurds and Iraqis of Persian origin, for example, were prime victims of the regime. Following the March 1991 uprising, the main victims were the Arab tribes in southern Iraq and those in Najaf and Karbala. Shi'is in Baghdad suffered too, because of state neglect of their neighborhoods, but they were not otherwise targeted by the government. Baghdadi Shi'is suffered from a serious breakdown in their social fabric, unlike those in southern Iraq, because most lost their religious linkages with the South. The March 1991 uprising further illustrated that the Shi'is rallied around the traditional Marja'iyya and other ulama in Najaf. They formed local communities to reflect parochial interests but could not lead or perform on a national level, because their capacity to organize and form effective structures was weak.

Who are the Shi'i Political Actors?

The political vacuum that followed the demise of Saddam encouraged new groups to emerge and cooperate with local leaders, smaller groups, and social dignitaries. Clergy, tribal leaders, businessmen, and community leaders all over Iraq now provide a new tier of political players who aspire to national politics through broader alliances. Following the end of Saddam's regime, leaders of Iraqi tribes are also reconfiguring to exercise influence and play an increasing role in Shi'i politics.

By and large, Shi'i political actors fall into two categories: religious and secular. Within each, the political trends and actors are as broad as the national spectrum. Variations in political trends reflect class, communal, and educational pressures, as well as exposure to outside influences, the capacity of various players to accommodate regional demands, and overall conditions within the region. The oldest secular group and most rooted among Shi'i constituents is the Iraqi Communist Party (ICP), whose members remain active. On the religious side, the oldest fundamentalist Islamic (Shi'i) group is the Islamic Da'wa Party (IDP), which has roots in secular communities throughout Baghdad. Despite their long history, the absence of the

IDP and the ICP from Iraq over the past decades has led to their fragmentation and, consequently, to the emergence of new leaders and alliances among the Shi'i. The ex-state run Baath party also had a large Shi'i membership. Despite their fragmentation, these three parties are still rooted in Shi'i communities and have the capacity to re-organize and reenter the political fray in new configurations as serious contenders for power.

New Old Actors

In addition to the three main political parties, ICP, IDP and the ex-Baath, Shi'i are influenced by networks of politicized clergy, of which the most influential were that of Muhammad Bakr al-Hakim, the head of the Supreme Council for the Islamic Revolution in Iraq (SCIRI) (killed in August 2003), and Moqtada al-Sadr, the son of the late Muhammad Sadiq al-Sadr. Influential religious families with a long history in Iraqi politics, such as the Bahr al-'Ulum and Al-Khalisi, are also important. In addition, there are new actors who are controlled by or dependent on outside support, the most important of which is the emerging Iraqi Hizbullah, who believe in *wilayat al-faqih* and are supported by some factions in Iran. Also, there are new Shi'i actors and groups of diverse conviction who are supported by the United States. Following the demise of Saddam and the return of hundreds of ulema to Iraq from Qom, more independent and influential ulema will continue to emerge and it may take a few years for the Iraqi Shi'i religious polity to be clearly defined. More importantly, Najaf will regain its historical and influential religious role and provide an alternative to the concept of *wilayat al-faqih*. Iran's ruling theocracy will likely be challenged by Najaf's religious rulings on public and political issues. Ayatollah Khomeini's grandson, Ayatollah Seyed Hassan Khomeini, chose to take refuge in Iraq and made a public critique of Iran's theocracy in Najaf.

The Role of Shi'i Clergy in Politics

Iraq's Shi'i seminary, the Hawza led by Ayatollah Ali Sistani, remains popular and apolitical, which is in line with his predecessors, Abu'l-Qasim Al-Khoei and Muhsin Al-Hakim. Although the seminary of the late Muhammad Sadiq al-Sadr has a network throughout Iraq of hundreds of young ulema with effective social networks in poor districts, it has no political program or leadership. Moqtada al-Sadr, who inherited thousands of his father's devout followers, emerged as a leader by default. He is the only outspoken Shi'i who opposed the occupation. Despite his incendiary speeches and popularity among poor and deprived Shi'is, he lacks the political agenda and long-term vision to enable him to lead. In this respect, it is critical to note that there are two important factors in defining the role of the clergy in Iraqi politics. First is ethnic origin, defined by the Arab-Persian element of the leadership. The religious hierarchy in Najaf has taken on a serious theological leadership role vis-à-vis Qom. However, Najaf has increased its Iraqi identity and enhanced its leadership among Iraqi Shiʿis. Ayatollah Sistani, for example, a non-Arab marjaʿ, commands influence among Shiʿis outside, rather than inside, Iraq. The late Sayyed Muhammad Sadiq al-Sadr was a rising leader, and his assassination in 1999 left a political vacuum. In Iraq's current communal crisis, Iraqi Shiʿis may well be galvanized by an Arab Shiʿi marjaʿ from one of the established religious families, such as members of the al-Hakim family in Najaf.

The second factor is the political outlook of the grand marjaʿ who emerges as the most senior among the few marjaʿ. As the highest religious authority in Najaf, the grand marjaʿ stays out of politics, unless there is a national or religious crisis as there was in the spring of 2004. In such times, Shiʿis throughout Iraq tend to bypass their political and local leaders and abide by the direction of the marjaʿ. This trend is neither rooted in religion nor in politics but rather culture and is likely to continue. It is unlikely that the marjaʿ of the Najaf school of thought will push for a political role, and if he did, Shiʿi Iraqis would not necessarily accept his extended political leadership. Moreover, the grand marjaʿ may or may not be an Iraqi citizen, as is the case with the current and the previous grand marjaʿs in Iraq. The attitude of the current grand marjaʿ, Sayyed Ali Sistani, on Iraq's recent turmoil is a case in point. He has neither endorsed the American-led war nor opposed it but has issued a fatwa branding any constitution drafted without real representation from Iraq's constituents as invalid. Less senior marjaʿ and clergymen are likely to seek a political role in conjunction with parties and alliances and this too bodes ill for the future.

Political Culture

Shiʿi political actors are responding to a combination of issues including: (a) strong Shiʿi feelings and sentiments on a wide range of issues such as victimization, self-reassertion, marginalization, and unfair treatment; (b) the need for leadership and cohesiveness; and (c) pressures to compromise, reconcile, and balance national interest with specific Shiʿi interests. However, having experienced extreme authoritarianism over the past two decades, Iraq's Shiʿi will not passively endorse or tolerate another authoritarian regime in a post-Saddam Iraq. Given that the majority of Iraqi Shiʿi are of tribal origin, with leaders who acknowledge the need for consultation and consensus building (but with no democratic tradition of elections), accountability or participation are not impossible to fathom. Moreover, diversity within Iraq's Shiʿi as well as diversity in Iraq's other communities necessitates consensus building. Under the circumstances, in the short term few should anticipate an agenda that aspires for democracy, or an open society.

There are as many political views among the Shiʿis as there are political groupings and it is difficult to simplify the attitudes of Iraqi Shiʿis on these matters. Over a year after Saddam's downfall, there are no signs yet of meaningful dialogue or setting a working agenda for political discourse among the Shiʿi and in Iraq at large. Iraq's various communities have not yet had the chance to exchange views and compromise their differences on the future. So far, the most inclusive and transparent debates have taken place among Iraqi exile groups, some under the auspices of foreign powers, namely Iran, Syria, and the United States, and hence lack credibility. At present, there are some points of consensus, but efforts to define an agenda or agree on a new constitution are in their infancy. The confusion among the 13 Shi'i members of the Governing Council over signing the Transitional Administrative Law is a case in point.

In a rare 1993 meeting hosted by the Al-Khoei Foundation in London, more than 150 Shi'i intellectuals of different political affiliations met and expressed their views on a number of issues. The proceedings of these meetings included a Shi'i perspective on the political crisis in Iraq, political trends among the clergy, Shi'i attitudes toward other communities, and those towards the state, Iran, and various Arab countries. Naturally, Iraqi Shi'i share with others aspirations and ideals for a peaceful country, but they lack leaders, political parties, and mechanisms to proceed on a number of key issues. These debates, as well as statements of independent political groups, highlight the need to develop consensus on a number of critical issues. In 2002, a group of Shi'i intellectuals who participated in an Al-Khoei Foundation meeting articulated political demands in an open declaration on behalf of Iraqi Shi'is. At the same time, the Al-Khoei Foundation with other senior Iraqi Shi'i dignitaries formed an Iraqi Shi'i Council, similar to the Supreme Islamic Shi'i Council of Lebanon. Iraqi Shi'i institutions and leaders have yet to realize their regional and historical potential beyond short-term political gains and articulate a strategic vision of the future of Shi'is and Shi'ism.

Specific Issues

Despite lack of consensus among Iraqi Shi'is on current and future political challenges, their intellectuals and politicians have constantly expressed the following points of views:

First, Kurdish demands for a federal state. Although Arab nationalists, both Shi'i and Sunni, endorse the need for self-rule and an autonomous status in "Kurdistan," they do not share with the Kurds an agenda for an ethnically divided federal state. Shi'i Islamists do not have clearly-cut views on the future of the Kurds. During the INC meeting in November 1992, ten different views were expressed by the Islamists. While Shi'i liberals and leftists see the need for a federal system for Iraq and do not object to it, confusion became evident in March 2004 when Shi'i members of the Governing Council could not agree on a position on one article that gave the Kurds veto power over Iraq's constitution.

Second, the role of the army. The Shi'i will seek to limit the role of the military in politics and broaden its middle ranks and leadership to become inclusive of all of Iraq's communities. They argue that the Iraqi army should be a national institution meant for the defense of the country and reject its previous composition where the majority of officers are of tribal Arab Sunni origin.

Third, the state structure. While the Kurds clearly favor decentralization, there is no consensus among the Shi'i on necessary reform of the state structure. Nationalists—Shi'i and Sunni—advocate a reformed centralized government buttressed by national reconciliation in defense of a strong united Iraq. Liberals pragmatically argue that the administration of the country, from a central government in Baghdad, led to the marginalization of the regions and to fierce competition by Iraq's main communities; hence they advocate a temporal democratic system with a decentralized government.

Fourth, numerous foreign influences. While there is consensus among the Kurds on the need for foreign support, including foreign assurances of rights and agreements, the Arabs, both Shi'i and Sunni, are against increasing foreign influence in Iraq. Still, some Shi'i communities have been exposed to foreign influence and called for foreign assistance in their struggle to end Saddam's regime. Three cases of foreign influence are of interest:

(a) *Iran*: Shi'i communities, especially those in the holy cities, resented the war with Iran on religious grounds. Some clergy and Islamic groups openly opposed the war, sympathized with Ayatollah Khomeini and sided with Iran. The SCIRI continues to represent that trend. Today nearly all of the clergy inside Iraq and many of the Islamic groups in exile see Iran as a state that manipulates Iraqi Shi'i in pursuit of its own interest. Shi'i members of the Baath party and the ICP are more hostile to Iran and cynical of its attempts to influence Shi'i religious affairs. Iraqi Shi'i who took refugee in or were deported to Iran are bitter over their treatment and struggle to leave it.

(b) *The United States*: Shi'i have been cynical, resentful, and extremely critical of its policy on Iraq, from the 1991 uprising up until now for a combination of reasons: prolonged sanctions, harshness toward Iraq, and inconclusive measures against Saddam. This has been most evident among the followers of Moqtada al-Sadr. Some Islamic radical groups may seek to incite anti-Americanism and radicalize public opinion. However, these feelings have not yet evolved into broad political positions and the majority will seek positive future relations with the United States.

(c) *On Arab unity and identity*: All Shi'i constituents are affected by Iraq's affiliation with Arab causes and concerns but differ in the extent to which they favor such affiliation. Arab nationalists pursue Arab unity, Islamists pursue Muslim unity and closer ties to Iran whereas liberal and leftist groups focus on a purely Iraqi identity. Some Shi'i exiles, both religious and secular, played on sectarian sentiments and wanted to distance Iraq from the Arab Sunni world. A few went beyond that and called for federating Iraq along Shi'i, Sunni, and Kurdish lines. So far, such anti-Arab and anti-Sunni calls have had little influence on mainstream Shi'is, who remain strongly Arab and Iraqi nationalists.

Fifth, on power sharing and civil liberties. Although the majority of Shi'i are adamant in their demands for future political participation, they still need to agree on an agenda concerning the principles of participation, governance, and accountability at the local, regional, and central level. Although there may be agreement on a regional level, there are profound differences on how to proceed with respect to the central administration. All political groups among the Shi'i agree on the need for broad political participation and protection of basic civil rights. Islamic groups call for an elected government based on an Islamic referendum and seek an alliance with Sunnis and Kurds. Liberal, secular, and leftist groups advocate a secular democratic system with a decentralized government. Arab nationalists and ex-Baathists see the need for a reformed strong centralized government backed with national reconciliation. Shi'i and other actors have committed themselves to the principles of human and civil rights, minority status, freedom of expression and association, and other related issues, but the extent to which these rights will be observed and protected by international laws and agreements is questionable.

Sixth, developing the economy. Iraq's future economy, the allocation of resources, and the role of the state in providing welfare services will be critical to Iraqi Shi'i. Still, this crucial issue has not been subject to discussions and Shi'i actors have not given it sufficient consideration.

Seventh, on their relationships with the Sunnis. In general, Shi'i–Sunni religious-confessional differences are of minor importance compared to their disparity in wealth and power. Baghdad in particular has had widespread inter-marriages between the two communities over the past few decades. Shi'i bitterness is focused against those who held and abused power and see their problem as one with Saddam's regime and not with the Sunni community. Though it may not be realistic, Shi'i still wish and dream of good relations with the Sunnis in the future. Still, the Shi'i will not substitute goodwill for solid assurances against future power abuse.

The Political Future of the Shi'is

Iraqi Shi'i face tough political choices that will have lasting consequences. They define themselves by a strong sense of victimization, poverty, and confessional sentiment. Moreover, Shi'i communities are vulnerable and exposed to a wide range of influences. Iraqi Shi'i will attempt to fully participate in reconstructing the country under a new constitution, and restructuring its many institutions. Immediate Shi'i concerns may well be limited by the pressing need for security and welfare, rather than their long-term aspirations for democracy, development, or prosperity. However, much of what will occur depends on the kind of government that succeeds the Coalition Provisional Authority (CPA). No future government can lead by force alone, or implement lasting reforms without the consent and and cooperation of Shi'i political actors. Shi'i leaders will challenge the new government if it tries to use the pretext of necessity, security, political stability, law and order, and Iraq's unity to extend the term of its authority.

Conclusion

Iraqi Shi'i have neither developed a political agenda nor have clear leadership. The most likely scenario is that they will go through a political crisis at a national level where the traditional religious leadership will lead for a short period followed by a weak political leadership or a period of confusion. The marja' will only in the short term be in a position to lead the community and offer a sense of direction. Extreme and radical politics will flourish among the Shi'i during the transition period, especially in Baghdad. Political parties that are rooted among Shi'i, such as the ICP and the IDP, will not take power but can either be partners with others or be disruptive to them. Tribal leaders will partially fill the power vacuum during a transition period in the south and will be critical in building bridges with the Sunni tribes. In the long term, the Shi'is will find that, out of necessity, it is in their best interest to reform the state and work within it rather than to oppose it. The political prospects of Iraqi Shi'i are mixed but many actors may well be prodded by their constituents to compromise and chart a new direction for the country.

Chapter 7

Outsiders as Enablers: Consequences and Lessons from International Silence on Iraq's Use of Chemical Weapons during the Iran–Iraq War*

Joost R. Hiltermann

In a book published in 2001, Stephen Pelletière, a former U.S. intelligence analyst responsible for monitoring the Iran–Iraq War, reiterated a claim he first made publicly in 1990 and, presumably, within the intelligence community shortly after the events in question: that in the chemical attack on the Iraqi town of Halabja in March 1988 in which thousands of Kurdish civilians perished, *both* Iran and Iraq had used gas, and that, "in all likelihood, Iranian gas killed the Kurds."[1]

Pelletière does not deny that Iraq used chemical weapons (CW) in its war with Iran, but denies the occurrence of certain specific incidences, generally plays down the impact of CW use on the course of the war, and accuses Iran of also having carried out chemical attacks. In this, Pelletière was not at all an exception inside the American intelligence establishment; it is just that he gained visibility through his many publications on the subject. Moreover, he has stubbornly held on to his convictions in the face of persuasive evidence, brought forward in the 1990s, that Iraq used CW systematically and repeatedly from 1983 to 1988, including in Halabja, the Faw Peninsula, and Badinan in the war's final year, and the continuing absence of persuasive evidence that Iran ever used CW.

Today, the claims of Stephen Pelletière and the constituency he represents may sound unbelievable. But in the final years of the Iran–Iraq War they played a role it would be dangerous to underestimate. The Iraqi chemical attack on Halabja, whose gruesome results were shown to the world within days, posed a potentially great embarrassment to the Reagan administration, which had displayed a marked tilt toward Iraq during the war (except for the Iran-Contra hiccup) and was at the time concerned that Iran's human wave assaults would overwhelm Iraqi defenses around Basra and bring down the regime. The allegation that Iran might have been responsible for most deaths in Halabja helped mute and diffuse criticism of Iraq's use of CW there, giving the Iraqi military a free hand to use massive amounts, and increasingly lethal types, of CW against the human wave assaults just at a time when Iran was launching its desperate final offensives.

In this chapter I argue that the absence of a strong and unequivocal international condemnation of Iraq for its use of CW in the war, and the Western tilt toward Iraq generally, had at least five important consequences: It gave a signal to Iraq that it could continue, and even escalate, the use of CW—and Iraq did; it enabled the genocide of rural Kurds during the Anfal campaign of February–September 1988, as tactical use of gas succeeded in flushing terrified villagers out of the rural areas; it gave the impetus for Iranian programs of weapons of mass destruction; it may have misled Saddam Hussein, who had just gotten away with mass murder, into believing that he would also get away with the invasion of Kuwait; and it undermined international law (the prohibition on the use of poison gas) and institutions (the perceived impartiality of the United Nations).

Why the focus on CW use in a war in which many atrocities were committed? Arguably, the use of gas is the most serious of the war crimes committed during the war. And arguably, the use of gas was the war's only feature over which the international community, on the one hand, had a moral and possibly legal obligation to intervene, and in which, on the other hand and at the same time, it had an active security interest because of the threat of proliferation. In other words, this is an issue on which the international community could and might well have intervened, yet failed to do so.

This chapter seeks to reexamine the record and implications of the Iran–Iraq War, using a human rights analysis. It forms the basis for a book on the same subject, currently in progress.

The Use of Gas

Starting in 1983, Iraq used CW with growing frequency and intensity as the war wore on, expanding its target set from Iranian soldiers to Iranian civilians, Iraqi Kurdish guerrillas, and finally Iraqi Kurdish civilians. The chemical attack on Halabja still stands today as the first and only major chemical attack on a population center in history, with a civilian toll in the thousands.

CW are generally not considered to be effective killers (primarily because they cannot be delivered efficiently), and the early agents used by Iraq, like blister agents (mustard gas), are not even particularly lethal. Rather, CW are primarily instruments of terror, and as such can be enormously powerful. Iraq consistently used CW to sow terror in the ranks of its enemies—with sensational results. Poison gas was the only weapon that proved capable of breaking up the Iranian human wave assaults, dispersing and demoralizing the curious mix of zealots and forcibly inducted foot soldiers. And it was also the only weapon able to utterly defeat the Kurdish insurgency, flushing Kurds hardened to years of artillery and air bombardments out of the countryside in a matter of hours.

While the record of Iraqi CW use is not complete (most incidents remain under-or undocumented in the West, especially those involving Iranian troops), the basic facts are not in dispute. Evidence is contained in the reports of eight successive investigations by CW experts contracted by the United Nations (see below), public admissions by Iraqi officials (and captured pilots), Iraqi secret police documents,[2] numerous eyewitness accounts,[3] forensic evidence (soil samples),[4] and last but not least, U.S. intelligence documents obtained under the Freedom of Information Act (FOIA). There is also no doubt about Iraqi acquisition and production programs; these were comprehensively exposed by the UN Special Commission (UNSCOM) in the early 1990s.[5]

Iraq may have experimented with tear gas as early as 1982, but the first credible reports of the use of mustard gas surfaced in the second half of 1983, first in the battle over Haj Omran in August, then in battles in the southern marshes in the fall. Nerve gases may have been introduced as early as February or March 1984.[6] Iraq used CW repeatedly to break up Iranian offensives later in 1984, and until the end of the war in August 1988. But it wasn't until the spring of 1987 that Iraq turned its poison weapons on its own Kurdish citizens. After the appointment of Saddam's cousin Ali Hassan al-Majid as head of the Baath party's Northern Bureau in late March, Iraqi forces ratcheted up their campaign to defeat the Kurdish insurgency. The rebellion had simmered for decades but in the 1980s started posing a serious threat to Iraqi control of the north, benefiting from the space provided by the war, specifically Iraq's preoccupation with very dangerous Iranian attacks in the south, and from material Iranian support as part of the latter's war effort.[7]

Three weeks after his appointment, al-Majid gave orders to use CW against the headquarters of the two largest Kurdish parties, the Patriotic Union of Kurdistan (PUK) and Kurdistan Democratic Party (KDP), and subsequently against the PUK's regional command centers as well. In the middle of April, many Kurdish civilians were killed and injured in a chemical attack on several villages in a PUK stronghold.[8] Other attacks followed but the main offensive came after the melting of the first snows in 1988, initially against the PUK's headquarters in the Jafati valley, then against Halabja, and finally on the first day of every stage of the Anfal campaign, including the final stage that started days after the ceasefire in the Iran–Iraq War.

When publicly confronted with accusations that their forces had used CW, the Iraqi leadership issued routine denials. At the initial height of these accusations, however, in March 1984, a senior Iraqi commander blithely referred to Iraq's right to use "insecticide" to "exterminate" this "swarm of mosquitoes."[9] And in 1988, when Iraq's CW use had entered the realm of conventional wisdom, Iraqi Foreign Minister Tariq Aziz openly admitted CW use against Iranian troops, justifying Iraq's resort to CW by referring to the alleged prior use of CW by Iran.[10] But Iraq never publicly and explicitly admitted to having gassed its own citizens.[11]

The literature on the Iran–Iraq War reflects a number of allegations of CW use by Iran, but these are marred by a lack of specificity as to time and place, and the failure to provide any sort of evidence. They appear to be mere assertions that gained in public credibility as they were repeated, over and over, by a growing circle of commentators in academia, the media, and policy institutes. The U.S. government, prone to excoriating Iran for all manner of atrocities and nominally concerned about proliferation in the region, not once made a specific accusation against Iran for its purported CW use, except in the case of Halabja (see below). If it did accuse Iran, it was often done through a UN Security Council resolution condemning *both* Iran and Iraq, usually in the wake of credible allegations of CW use by Iraq. The Iranian leadership was on record as opposing the use of CW as constituting a violation of Islamic principles.[12] Yet, by 1987, Iran began making noises, in the face of international failure to stop Iraqi CW use and growing domestic opposition to the war, that it might be left with no choice but to also resort to CW.[13] It is generally accepted that Iran did initiate a CW development program during the war, and while it is quite conceivable that Iran would have started using CW in the war as well, there is no strong evidence I have seen that it had actually done so by the time the war ended.[14]

The International Response

The international community was quite well informed about Iraq's CW use, as it was about other atrocities committed during the war by both Iraq and Iran: the air and missile attacks on major population centers, the targeting of civilian shipping in the Gulf, Iran's use of child soldiers (including in mine clearing operations), and so on. After an initial lack of interest in the war as long as Iraqi forces occupied Iranian territory, the United Nations became actively engaged in the war once Iran succeeded in expelling those forces in 1982 and launched its own (chronically unsuccessful) counter-invasion of Iraq. U.S. intelligence, of course, was following the war closely, concerned about the threat it might pose to the stability of its allies in the region and its impact on the price of oil. Other governments were similarly engaged: Russia, the United Kingdom, and France foremost among members of the Security Council with substantial interests in the region, and Israel and the Arab states.

The first serious public reports of Iraqi CW use started to surface in early 1984, and the U.S. government was among the first to issue a public condemnation.[15] This was at a time when the Reagan administration was involved in sensitive negotiations with Iraq about reestablishing diplomatic relations. It was also an election year: perceived missteps could be expected to cost the administration dearly. Moreover, this was at an early stage of the U.S. tilt toward Iraq, when criticism of Iraq may have been less unacceptable than it would soon become. Not only did the administration condemn the use of CW publicly, it also imposed export restrictions on chemical precursors and urged its allies to do the same.[16]

These actions could be read as a strong message to Iraq that the United States did not condone Iraq's CW use. In reality the signals were quite weak. While some U.S. officials proudly refer to the administration's record on this episode,[17] the public condemnation was not repeated; the démarches made in meetings appear to have been little more than asides or minor agenda items, so much so that one senior Iraqi diplomat could not even recall that the subject had ever been broached;[18] and the U.S. export restrictions were ineffective in that the primary exporters were West German companies and the Iraqi CW program was increasingly becoming self-reliant. Much-touted U.S. démarches to the West German government do not seem to have had a tangible effect. In any case, Iraq did not end its use of CW, but indeed escalated it once Iran's new spring offensives got underway in 1985 and following years.

UN Secretary-General Javier Pérez de Cuéllar authorized a total of nine investigations of possible war crimes during the war, mostly in response to Iranian allegations of Iraqi wrongdoing. Of those investigations, only the first one, in 1983, did not concern CW, and the other eight were exclusively focused on CW use. The first CW investigation took place in March 1984, when a team of experts traveled to Tehran and border areas. While producing proof of CW use (affected Iranian soldiers had undoubtedly been exposed to chemical agents), the experts were unable to positively identify the perpetrator. A second investigation, in 1985, equally unambiguous in its conclusions, was limited to visits to Iranian casualties who had been transported to hospitals in Europe for treatment. The third investigation, in 1986, included a visit to the Iranian side of the battlefront in an area where recent chemical attacks had reportedly taken place, and produced conclusive evidence that Iraq had carried out the attacks. This finding led to a "note" by the president of the UN Security Council, acknowledging Iraq's use of CW and condemning it as a violation of the 1925 Geneva Protocol.[19]

Not to be caught out again, Iraq made sure to invite the UN delegation the next time an investigation was planned, in the spring of 1987. The results of this investigation, which took place in both Iran and Iraq, are of critical importance. True to their scientific training, the experts took care not to stretch their findings. In Iran, they once again found Iranian CW casualties—both soldiers and civilians—and were able to conclude definitively that these were victims of Iraqi CW use. In Iraq, they were shown Iraqi chemical warfare casualties. In their report they did not, however, identify the perpetrator of the attack that had produced the Iraqi casualties, leaving the reader to speculate whether Iran was to blame or, possibly, Iraqi "friendly fire."[20] A casual reader, or one driven by a political agenda, might be led to conclude that the United Nations had found evidence of CW use by Iran.

This is certainly an interpretation that soon surfaced. In October 1987, U.S. Secretary of State George Shultz for the first time (for a U.S. official) referred to CW use by *both* Iran and Iraq.[21] He offered neither evidence nor source for the allegation, leading one to suspect that he (or rather his staff) had seen the 1987 UN report and was either misinterpreting or misrepresenting it. But from this time on, the claim of Iranian CW use became part of the mainstream discourse, repeated like a mantra. It may have encouraged Iraq to further escalate its CW use, and proved very useful when Iraq committed what is by any definition a war crime and crime against humanity at Halabja the next spring.

The precise nature of events at Halabja in March 1988 is deserving of thorough study, not only because of what happened but also because of what is said to have happened, and the impact of the resulting confusion. What matters for the purposes of this chapter is that a seemingly straightforward episode—the massive chemical bombardment of a major Kurdish town by Iraqi aircraft, as reported by victims—became the source of great controversy once Iran started exploiting the event for its own propaganda purposes by ferrying Western reporters to the area, which was under the control of its forces. Initial condemnations of Iraq by the U.S. State Department were replaced by the end of the month by assertions that not only Iraq but also Iran was to blame for the attack, and that in fact Iran might have been responsible for the majority of casualties. The known facts of the matter were diluted and challenged by shrouding them in the "fog of war" argument. No persuasive evidence of the claim that Iran was the primary culprit was ever presented; photographs of the Kurdish victims suggested precisely the opposite of what they were purported to show, and the nature and content of communication intercepts that the United States claimed to have—a reliable fall-back for the intelligence community—have not been disclosed. When the UN Security Council finally got around to dealing with the attack on May ninth, almost two months after the event, it condemned the use of CW in the war without specifying the perpetrator and called on both parties to refrain from future use.[22]

A sharp U.S. condemnation did follow Iraqi CW attacks during the final stage of Anfal (*Khitamat al-Anfal*) in August 1988, after a ceasefire in the Iran–Iraq War had gone into effect. The U.S. action—in early September—triggered a commitment by Iraq to refrain from further CW attacks, but by then the counter-insurgency campaign had been completed—a smashing success by any measure—obviating the need for continued resort to CW. The Iraqi promise was therefore arguably cost-free at the time.

Consequences

Escalating CW Use

Neglect of the CW issue in the Gulf had a number of serious consequences. In the first place, the absence of a strong and unambiguous early condemnation of Iraq for its use of CW is likely to have given a signal to the Iraqi leadership that its conduct was being condoned and that it could therefore continue to use gas against Iranian human wave attacks with impunity. In 1984, when in many ways Iraq was still testing the waters, the United States could have issued a more meaningful and effective condemnation of Iraq's CW use, unilaterally or via the UN Security Council. It certainly had leverage: Iraq was quite eager to reestablish diplomatic relations now that the tables had been turned in the war. But animus against Iran was strong in the West, especially in the United States, in the wake of the fall of the shah, America's guardian in the Gulf, and the hostage crisis that followed it. The 1982 battlefield reversal and related fear of Iranian hegemony in the Gulf—with the progressive takeover of repressive regimes by Shi' majorities—and its implications for the West's access to cheap oil was an even stronger factor in the calculus of those who decided to afford Iraq a free pass, however implausible the scenario of an Iranian-led domino effect in the Gulf appeared at the time to some experts on the region.[23] Lack of access to the war zones (Iran and Iraq both being repressive states with closed societies), combined with Iran's unpopularity in the West, militated against an effective exposure of the horrifying events on the battlefield.

In short, Iraq experimented with gas, then faced no real opposition as the international community realized it was able to ignore it, and this in turn gave further impetus to Iraq to escalate its use of gas to defeat the enemy or at least reverse its thrust into Iraqi territory. In fact, Iraq developed more lethal gases—nerve agents like tabun and sarin, and even VX—and displayed increasingly less restraint in its resort to these weapons.

This worked as long as the victims were mostly Iranian troops—and even Iranian civilians, as long as these events were accorded no publicity by Iran, which kept a tight lid on information in an apparent effort to prevent mass panic. But once Iraq started targeting its own citizens, this opened up the potential for public embarrassment over the U.S.'s posture of tolerance with respect to CW attacks. Of course, the Kurdish guerrillas (*peshmerga*) were seen as Iranian proxies, and therefore as outlaws who had it coming to them. But almost from the beginning of Iraqi attacks on peshmerga command centers, civilians were affected by the chemicals as well, and once information to this effect started to come out—shortly after the first such attacks in April 1987—a new approach emerged: diffusing Iraqi responsibility by playing up the possibility of Iranian CW attacks. The refusal to single out Iraq as the perpetrator may have given the Iraqi leadership renewed confidence that its impunity had not been harmed. The attack on Halabja followed, on March 16, 1988.

A Green Light for Genocide

Then, as a second major consequence of international neglect of the issue, further public prevarication on the precise responsibility for the Halabja attack is likely to have given the Iraqi leadership the signal that targeting its Kurdish population was being condoned and even that Iraq, quite literally, could get away with mass murder.[24] The Iraqi leaders also benefited from the fact that they kept a tight control on information, especially in the northern governorates. The Anfal campaign had already started three weeks earlier with an assault on the PUK's headquarters in Jafati valley on February 22–23. The chemical attack on Halabja led to the collapse of Kurdish morale; the PUK's headquarters, defended successfully from a continuous chemical barrage for four weeks, fell within days of the Halabja disaster, on March 18.[25] The second stage of Anfal was launched four days later, and when it was completed, the next stage followed, and so on until the "general and comprehensive amnesty for Iraqi Kurds from any legal prosecution for any action punishable under the law committed prior to this statement, be they outside or inside Iraq" (with the exception of PUK leader Jalal Talabani) on September sixth, 1988.[26]

On the first day of every stage of the Anfal campaign following the Halabja attack, Iraq used CW selectively against a small number of villages in the targeted area, apparently to create a demonstration effect. These attacks killed relatively few people—a few score here, a handful there, depending on the location of the target, the direction of the wind, and other factors. This was sufficient, however, to trigger a mass panic among the rural population—and the peshmerga interspersed with it—who were fully cognizant (through word of mouth as well as peshmerga communications) of what had happened in Halabja. Invariably they ran, to the border if they thought the distance was manageable, or to relatives in the nearest towns and resettlement camps.

In most cases, they first had to cross a main (paved) road. Here the Iraqi military, helped by pro-government Kurdish militias, was waiting. It gathered up the fleeing villagers with all their belongings and handed them over to the secret police. The Kurds were then taken to a transit center in Kirkuk where men roughly in the age range 15–70 were separated from women and children (a second group) and those over 70 (a third group). After some time the three groups were sent off to their separate fates: to their deaths in the case of the men; either to their deaths or, depending on their region of origin, to detention camps in the case of the women and children; and to a prison in the desert west of the southern Iraqi town of Samawa in the case of the old folks. Those who survived their detention were released in the September amnesty and dumped into designated areas near Kurdish towns, becoming the inhabitants of a new generation of resettlement camps that were erected shortly thereafter.[27]

The meticulously organized and executed, systematic mass murder of tens of thousands of rural Kurds—men, women, and children—in the span of six months was made possible by the tactical use of poison gas as a weapon of terror. Villagers who had learned to cope with intermittent air and artillery attacks for years, often preferring caves over their homes for shelter while working their lands during the day, had no resistance to the fear of gas attacks. Their response was spontaneous, even when the casualties in their midst from CW attacks were low and even when they only heard rumors of a CW attack somewhere in their region, not even necessarily in their immediate vicinity. The Iraqi army arguably could not have succeeded as swiftly and successfully in its sweep of the Kurdish countryside if it had not been able to use CW—first at the massive Halabja "demonstration," and subsequently, in mini-reminders, at the outset of each stage of the Anfal campaign.

In short, tens of thousands of innocent lives might have been saved had Iraq been unable to deploy its weapon of terror against a population whose only crime was to be living in their ancestral homes during a war in which their loyalty was questioned. International silence and then prevarication over responsibility for the Halabja attack diffused pressure for a condemnation of the perpetrator, Iraq, and made the continued use of gas by Iraq during the Anfal campaign possible. The trauma visited on Iraqi Kurds, in addition to the destruction it caused to lives and psyches, also had a direct impact on their actions when they felt threatened again, in March 1991, after Iraqi forces crushed the Kurdish uprising in the wake of Iraq's defeat in the second Gulf War. If everybody spontaneously and massively ran from their homes in towns and resettlement camps to the nearest border as Iraqi forces advanced and helicopters strafed the roads, it was because they remembered—could not help but remember—the poison gas attacks and the disappearance of tens of thousands of Kurds in the Anfal campaign only three years earlier.

Proliferation of Weapons of Mass Destruction

A third consequence of the relative international silence on Iraq's use of CW was the decision by Iran to launch its own CW program, as well as, probably, programs to develop biological and nuclear weapons.[28] Clearly resisting the temptation in the face of escalating Iraqi CW attacks, Iran ultimately suggested that what it perceived as double standards on the part of the UN Security Council offered it no choice but to follow Iraq's path in developing a CW capability as its sole remaining means of self-defense (this, of course, at a time when Iran continued to pursue the war on Iraqi territory). The Iranian CW program is thus a direct result of the Iraqi CW program, Iraq's repeated CW use in the war, and the failure of the international community to put an end to it, or even give it the serious and sustained attention it was due. If Iran has active, or even dormant, programs in weapons of mass destruction (WMD) today (something denied by Iran), this would therefore be an undisputable legacy of this failure.[29] Moreover, the world's ability to address Iran on any programs it may have today is reduced dramatically by the Iranian perception, based on its jarring sense of having been abandoned during the war with Iraq, that it has no one to protect it from Iraq's WMD but its own WMD deterrent.

Iraq as a Regional Threat

A fourth consequence of international neglect of Iraq's CW use must be seen in the larger context of the Western tilt toward Iraq during the war. Significantly and remarkably, Iraq was able to count on the support of at least four of the five permanent members of the Security Council for most of the war (China opting to remain largely neutral)—even though Cold War polarization marked almost all other international conflicts at the time. The United States, the United Kingdom, and France, despite occasional dalliances with Iran (hoping to free their nationals held as hostages in Lebanon), provided significant military, financial, and diplomatic support to Iraq.[30] Their main interest was in maintaining the balance of power in the Gulf and protecting their access to cheap oil. The Khomeini revolution, seen as expansionist (especially after the 1982 battlefield reversal), was assessed to be a superior threat to these interests than Saddam Hussein's admittedly ruthless but reassuringly secular rule. In fact, the regime's brutality was directed inward (never mind its invasion of Iran in September 1980) and thereby guaranteed the regional stability and predictability that Western nations craved. For years, the preferred outcome of the war was a stalemate—and, arguably, this is how the war ended—or even an Iraqi victory, but under no circumstance an Iranian victory. Hence the consistent efforts to shore up the regime in Baghdad after 1982 in the face of perennial Iranian military assaults aimed at breaching Iraqi defenses and delivering the regime its coup de grâce.

As part of this support, Western states time and again chose to close their eyes to Iraqi atrocities, and even to Iraqi attacks on their own assets.[31] Iraq repeatedly received signals that the ends justified the means, and it is highly likely—subject to further investigation—that the regime read these signals as a tacit endorsement of its aspiration to regional superpower status in the Gulf as a successor to the shah's Iran. This being the case, it could be argued that Saddam Hussein's ill-fated move into Kuwait for pressing economic reasons was guided by the same mindset, cultivated throughout the 1980s, that the West would not oppose such a crass landgrab.[32] After all, the thinking may have been, Iraq could be relied upon, no less than Kuwait, to be a responsible partner in OPEC, keeping the oil price at a level acceptable to the consumer states. In an era in which there appeared to be no red lines that Iraq could cross, the red line of Kuwait must therefore have come as a rude awakening to the regime.

Add to this the awareness that Iraq possessed CW and, given its past use, might use these against the Gulf War allies and/or Israel. The U.S. military displayed a great preoccupation with the potential CW threat that it saw as emanating from Iraq as it built toward war in the fall of 1990. Iraq's capabilities helped to ratchet up the tension and led to suggestions, not too subtly communicated by U.S. Secretary of State James A. Baker III to Iraqi Foreign Minister Tareq Aziz, that the United States would retaliate with superior force (read: with nuclear weapons?) should Iraq resort to its chemical arsenal.

In other words, by banking on Iraq to contain the perceived threat posed by Iran, the United States and others helped unleash the Iraqi genie, which, through its invasion of Kuwait, ended up posing a very serious threat to Western interests in the Gulf, arguably a more serious threat than Iran ever posed. In the aftermath of the second Gulf War, the international approach toward Iraq switched to active containment and a dismantling of its WMD programs. The lack of closure on the Iraq issue led to renewed war in the region in 2003, as the Bush administration sought to settle once and for all the business left unfinished in 1991.

International Law and Institutions Tarnished

In their sustained support of Iraq during its war with Iran—and this is the fifth consequence of international neglect of the CW issue and the tilt toward Iraq generally—the Western states helped to undermine and erode customary norms of state behavior and the credibility of international institutions such as the United Nations. First of all, the failure to condemn Iraq's repeated and escalating CW use did tremendous damage to the customary norm against the use of CW in warfare, enshrined in the 1925 Protocol,[33] which itself arose from the horrendous experience of chemical warfare in World War I. It is one of the ironies of the Iran–Iraq War that Iran, which has much to account for in terms of its own war crimes, repeatedly and with increasing sophistication reminded the UN Security Council of its obligation to uphold international humanitarian law (in this case, the 1925 Protocol).[34] The Iranian position, whether or not it was inspired by a genuine concern for the international rule of law, was correct: If the very institution responsible for protecting and promoting international norms allows these to be violated, deliberately and repeatedly, in front of the world's eyes, then the inevitable consequence is that these norms depreciate in value and in the end may become as worthless as the paper on which they are written.

At least, this story has a happy ending, not for the victims of Iraq's CW attacks but for those who, in future armed conflict, might otherwise be exposed to chemical warfare: After the Iran–Iraq War ended, realization dawned about the damage that had been done to the 1925 Protocol. Although no mention was made of the Iraqi record in particular, the Paris Conference of January 1989, convened to discuss the proliferation of CW, was emblematic of the emergence of this new consciousness. Negotiations for a comprehensive ban on CW accelerated, and these resulted in the signing of the Chemical Weapons Convention in 1993.[35]

Second, the credibility of the United Nations, especially the authority of the Security Council, as an impartial arbiter of world affairs, suffered a direct hit.

The tilt toward Iraq displayed by the Security Council's most powerful members was extended to the Council itself. A survey of Security Council resolutions issued during the Iran–Iraq War reveals a pattern of consistent bias toward Iraq. Following the Iraqi invasion of Iran and as long as Iraqi forces remained on Iranian territory, the Security Council adopted a pose of studied neglect. Rather than urging Iraq to withdraw—a normal reaction in the face of a sustained breach of international borders, for example, in the case of Iraq's invasion of Kuwait ten years later—the Security Council called on both parties "to refrain immediately from any further use of force," a call that suggests shared responsibility and comparable action by both parties.[36] Once Iran turned the tables on its neighbor in 1982, the Security Council swung into action, immediately calling for a ceasefire and the "withdrawal of forces to internationally recognized boundaries."[37] For the next six years, the Security Council displayed a consistent bias toward Iraq, commending it for its expressed willingness to heed the Council's call for a ceasefire while calling on *both* sides to abide by the 1925 Geneva Protocol even when the evidence presented by UN investigators clearly implicated only Iraq in the use of poison gas.

Of course, the Iran–Iraq War is not the only instance in which the Security Council has exhibited its clear preferences while maintaining the pretense of impartiality. But it is a particularly revealing case. In fact, it is the repeated call on *both* Iraq and Iran to refrain from such and such that was particularly insidious when the actions that were being criticized were often Iraq's alone, especially the use of CW. Iran's growing desperation, as the war wore on and Iraq escalated its use of poison gas, over the fact that it lacked an impartial institutional resort for its legitimate grievances—being the victim of the internationally prohibited use of gas—is evident in its refusal to defend its own actions in the Security Council, its repeated rejection of Security Council resolutions (until July 1988), and its ultimate near-rejection of the United Nations as an institution holding moral authority. If Iran was eventually brought to its knees, it was because of popular exhaustion at home in the absence of major breakthroughs on the battlefield, Iraq's growing military strength based on massive resupplies from the West and access to U.S. satellite intelligence, the very real fear that Iraq might put chemical warheads on the missiles it was launching at Tehran in the spring of 1988, and the effective mobilization of the United Nations, or at least the Security Council, by Western states in pursuit of their own interests in the Gulf.[38]

Lessons

A student taking a strict international relations approach toward the Iran–Iraq War might conclude that, on balance, the United States and its Western allies, operating at the tail end of the Cold War and facing two equally distasteful parties, made the right choice in throwing their support behind Iraq. Yes, Iraq proceeded from its victory over Iran to invade Kuwait, but this can also be attributed, as critics like Stephen Pelletière have argued, to the alleged abandonment of Iraq by the Reagan administration after the ceasefire in the Iran–Iraq War went into effect. They cite, for example, Secretary of State George Shultz's September 1988 reprimand of the Iraqis for gassing Kurds after the end of the war as Exhibit A in their contention that anti-Iraq factions in the Reagan administration had prevailed and were able to go public once the war was over and the immediate threat of Iranian expansionism had receded.[39] And yes, U.S. support of Iraq may have encouraged the WMD programs of both Iraq and Iran, but the United States was able to contain both Iran and Iraq in the 1990s, bringing to the Gulf the desired stability. In that view, an Iranian victory over Iraq would have been a lot more unpredictable and dangerous for Western interests than the situation as it actually unfolded in the 1990s.

And perhaps this is a sound conclusion. But the truth is that, as described above, the Iraq tilt had a number of adverse consequences, many of which clearly could not have been intended. A human rights analysis, focusing on war crimes, genocide, the development and use of WMD, and international complicity in these events, would yield an entirely different set of lessons from the Iran–Iraq War. By stressing the active condoning of what clearly constitute serious violations of international humanitarian law, including war crimes, for the sake of protecting immediate geostrategic interests, such an analysis would show that the failure to condemn human rights crimes helps create a culture of impunity in which worse crimes may be committed and further actions are condoned that in the long term may lead to precisely the sort of insecurity and instability that the silence in the face of those crimes was meant to prevent. This, in turn, suggests that it may be a strategic failure to exclude human rights considerations from calculations of interest.[40] This would constitute a victory of the idealist over the realist approach to foreign policy, or— better put—of the idea that the realist approach, to be successful in promoting long-term interests, must fully incorporate the key principles of the idealist approach and make them its own.

Because outside states, especially superpowers, play such an inordinately large role in the conflicts between lesser states (particularly from the latter's perspective, of course), an impunity-based analysis would have to start with the actions carried out by the enabling outside actors as these may magnify the existing conflicts in a given region and turn human rights violations into human rights crimes. The specific linking of a superpower's actions to its human rights consequences could help in formulating moral arguments that might then be made to mesh with arguments of national and international security. The deployment of such arguments could in turn be used to "disable" the enabler's role, or at least some of its worst aspects, for example the active condoning of CW use in the case of Iraq during the Iran–Iraq War.[41]

The need to consider human rights as an integral part of strategic decision-making may be given an important boost by the increasing attention to the question of legal culpability for complicity in war crimes, crimes against humanity, and genocide in the wake of the signing of the Rome Statute in 1998.[42] At this point, it is unlikely that any senior U.S. government official who had a clear understanding of the human rights consequences of U.S. material support for Iraq will ever be held accountable for complicity in the crimes that were committed during the Iran–Iraq War. For example, it could be argued that culpability rests on the shoulders of those who shared satellite imagery of Iranian troop formations on the Faw peninsula with Iraq in April 1988, knowing that Iraq was then likely to use CW to dislodge Iranian troops dug in there—as it did, committing a clear violation of international humanitarian law. But international humanitarian law, which has taken huge strides forward since the end of the Cold War, remained relatively undeveloped on this score at the time these atrocities occurred; for example, the question whether CW use against enemy combatants constituted a war crime is controversial.[43] Today, however, those same officials would have to think twice about offering unquestioned support to notorious human rights offenders, knowing that they might be held to account, not only in the eyes of history, but before a court of law and with direct consequences for their own liberty.

Notes

*   I could not have written this essay without the invaluable research assistance, in 1999-2000, of Ranya Ghuma, then a superb graduate student at the Center for Contemporary Arab Studies of Georgetown University. The brief discussion below of the role of the United Nations in the war relies on research done by another graduate student at CCAS, Julienne Gherardi, who enthusiastically took on a slice of my research project in 2000 and ran with it. I am very much indebted to both. Research for this essay was supported in part by a 1999 grant from the Individual Project Fellowships Program of the Open Society Institute in New York.

1. Stephen C. Pelletière, *Iraq and the International Oil System* (Westport, Conn: Praeger Publishers, 2001), p. 206. For the earlier, even more explicit, claim, see Stephen C. Pelletière, Douglas V. Johnson, and Leif Rosenberger, *Iraqi Power and U.S. Security in the Middle East* (Carlisle Barracks, Pa.: U.S. Army War College, Strategic Studies Institute, 1990), p. 52; Stephen C. Pelletière and Douglas V. Johnson, *Lessons Learned: The Iran–Iraq War*, Volume I (Quantico, Va.: U.S. Marine Corps, 1990), p. 100; and Stephen Pelletière, *The Iran-Iraq War: Chaos in a Vacuum* (New York: Praeger Publishers, 1992), pp. 136–37.

2. In two separate shipments in 1992 and 1993, Iraqi secret police documents seized by Kurdish rebel parties during the short-lived uprising of March–April 1991 were brought to the United States for safekeeping and analysis. They were housed in a facility of the U.S. National Archives under supervision of the U.S. Senate Foreign Relations Committee. The nongovernmental organization Human Rights Watch was given exclusive access to the documents in 1992–94 to sift for evidence of human rights crimes by the Iraqi regime. I supervised this project for Human Rights Watch during this period. The principal results are contained in two publications by Human Rights Watch: *Iraq's Crime of Genocide: The Anfal Campaign Against the Kurds* (New Haven, Conn: Yale University Press, 1995), and *Bureaucracy of Repression: The Iraqi Government in Its Own Words* (New York: Human Rights Watch, 1994). The documents have since become available on CD-ROM. The original documents are stored in the archives of the University of Colorado in Boulder. The Iraq Research and Documentation Project at Harvard University, one of several institutions that possess a full set of the CD-ROMs, has received U.S. government funding, via the Iraq Foundation in Washington, to index and translate the documents, and make them available online (available at http://fas-www.harvard.edu/~irdp/).

3. Iranian victims were interviewed by UN investigators in 1984–88 (see below). Kurdish victims and other eyewitnesses were interviewed by Human Rights Watch in 1992–93. See *Iraq's Crime of Genocide*. I conducted additional interviews in Iran and northern Iraq in May–June 2002.

4. Physicians for Human Rights and Human Rights Watch, "Scientific First: Soil Samples Taken from Bomb Craters in Northern Iraq Reveal Nerve Gas—Even Four Years Later." Press statement, April 29, 1993, located at: http://www.hrw.org/reports/1993/iraqgas/.

5. Available at http://www.IraqWatch.org/un/index.html.

6. For an independent assessment, see, "Report of the Specialists Appointed by the Secretary-General to Investigate Allegations by the Islamic Republic of Iran Concerning the Use of Chemical Weapons," United Nations Security Council, S/16433 (March 26, 1984), p. 9; and for an assessment by U.S. officials, see Seymour M. Hersh, "U.S. Aides Say Iraqis Made Use of a Nerve Gas," *New York Times*, March 30, 1984.

7. *Iraq's Crime of Genocide*, chapters 1 and 2.

8. Ibid., pp. 39–49.

9. *Time*, March 19, 1984.

10. Aziz was quoted as saying, referring to CW: "Sometimes such weapons were used in the bloody war, by both sides. It was a very complicated, bloody conflict. It has to be judged within the circumstances and the facts." Serge Schmemann, "Iraq Acknowledges Its Use of Gas But Says Iran Introduced It in War," *New York Times*, July 2, 1988.

11. Of course, captured Iraqi secret police documents have proven to be highly self-incriminating; they obviously were never intended for public release. See *Iraq's Crime of Genocide*, pp. 241–42.

12. For example, Iranian Foreign Minister Ali-Akbar Velayati declared in a letter to the UN secretary-general in 1987 that Iran had "the power, whenever it decides, to use its similar and even more advanced capabilities to retaliate," but that "respect for humanity, Islamic principles and international law have so far prevented us from retaliating." In "Letter from the Minister for Foreign Affairs of the Islamic Republic of Iran addressed to the Secretary-General," S/19193 (Annex), October 9, 1987.

13. There are repeated statements to this effect in letters from the Iranian Permanent Representative in New York to the UN secretary-general in 1987 and 1988.

14. Following its ratification, in 1997, of the 1993 Chemical Weapons Convention, Iran complied with its treaty obligation to make a public declaration that it possessed a chemical warfare program. There is, however, no requirement under the treaty to publicly declare the types of chemicals present in one's arsenal. Iranian officials claim that Iran declared possession of a single chemical agent, mustard gas, to the international agency overseeing implementation of the CWC, the Organization for the Prohibition of Chemical Weapons (OPCW) in The Hague. Interview with Foreign Ministry officials, Tehran, May 21, 2002.

15. On March 5, 1984, the Reagan administration formally accused Iraq of using "lethal chemical weapons." George P. Shultz, *Turmoil and Triumph: My Years as Secretary of State* (New York: Charles Scribner's Sons, 1993), p. 239.

16. Ibid.

17. Ibid., pp. 238–41, and interviews with U.S. State Department officials, 2000.

18. Interview with Ismat Kittani, former Iraqi Permanent Representative to the United Nations, Geneva, November 13, 2000.

19. "Note by the President of the Security Council," S/17932, March 21, 1986. Such a "note" from the president of the Security Council is obviously of lesser import than a resolution passed by all Security Council members.

20. The relevant passage reads: "The specialists' findings that chemical weapons were again used against Iranian forces by Iraqi forces, also causing injuries to civilians in the Islamic Republic of Iran *and that now also Iraqi forces have sustained injuries from chemical warfare* must add new urgency to the grave concern of the international community." "Report of the Mission Dispatched by the Secretary-General to Investigate Allegations of

the Use of Chemical Weapons in the Conflict between the Islamic Republic of Iran and Iraq," S/18852 (May 26, 1987), p. 2 (emphasis added). There are repeated, credible reports of Iraqi "friendly fire" involving chemical weapons, including in the UN experts' reports. Iqbal Riza, the UN official who accompanied the investigators on their mission in 1987, has said that at the time the evidence presented by Iraq of Iranian CW use "was clearly fabricated," and that "the experts said that," even if that assessment did not end up in their report. Interview, New York, July 12, 2000.

21. "Chemical Weapons," *Reuters*, October 19, 1987.

22. UN Security Council, Resolution 612 (May 9, 1988). The resolution was based on yet another official UN investigation (in both Iran and Iraq), this time by a single medical specialist whose product reflects a lack of time and resources and a consequent lack of thoroughness in the investigation. The report fails to identify the perpetrators, but does identify the victims. "Report of the Mission Dispatched by the Secretary-General to Investigate Allegations of the Use of Chemical Weapons in the Conflict between the Islamic Republic of Iran and Iraq," S/19823 (April 25, 1988).

23. Interview with Jean-François Seznec, an adjunct professor at Columbia University with expertise on the Gulf, Washington, D.C., June 12, 2001.

24. In another disquieting precedent, the "disappearance" of several thousand members of the Barzani clan in 1983 had also met with a thunderous international silence. None ever returned. See Human Rights Watch, *Iraq's Crime of Genocide*, pp. 26–27. Saddam Hussein, in a speech on September 12, 1983, explicitly stated that the men had "gone to hell." *Al-'Iraq*, September 13, 1983.

25. In a joint operation with the Iranian military, Pasdaran, Basij, as well as other Iraqi opposition groups—Kurds and Arabs—the PUK had fought their way into Halabja on March 15, apparently as a feint to divert the Iraqi armed forces from their assault on its headquarters in the Jafati valley. The capture of a major town by the Kurds, assisted by the foreign enemy, evidently so enraged the Iraqi leadership that it retaliated with a massive chemical strike. See *Iraq's Crime of Genocide*, pp. 68–73.

26. Decision of the Revolutionary Command Council, September 6, 1988, read on the radio that day and printed in all the major Iraqi dailies, e.g. *Al-Jumhuriyeh*, *Al-'Iraq*, and *Al-Thawra*, the next. For the English translation, see FBIS-NES88–174 (September 8, 1988), pp. 38–39.

27. *Iraq's Crime of Genocide*, passim.

28. See, e.g. W. Seth Carus, "Iran and Weapons of Mass Destruction," published by The American Jewish Committee, December 18, 2000.

29. International Crisis Group, *Iran: The Struggle for the Revolution's Soul* (Brussels: 2002), pp. 27–28.

30. This aspect of the war has been particularly well documented. Useful sources include: Alan Friedman, *Spider's Web: The Secret History of How the White House Illegally Armed Iraq* (New York: Bantam Books, 1993); Bruce Jentleson, *With Friends Like These: Reagan, Bush and Saddam, 1982–1990* (New York: W.W. Norton, 1994); and Mark Phythian, *Arming Iraq: How the U.S. and Britain Secretly Built Saddam's War Machine* (Boston: Northeastern University Press, 1997).

31. For example, the Iraqi attack on the USS Stark on May 17, 1987. See Anthony H. Cordesman and Abraham R. Wagner, *The Lessons of Modern War*, vol. 2, *The Iran-Iraq War* (Boulder: Westview Press, 1990), pp. 549–58.

32. The Glaspie episode in July 1990 would have reinforced this perception in the Iraqi leadership, whatever Ambassador Glaspie intended to convey.

33. Its full name is the Geneva Protocol for the Prohibition of the Use in War of Asphyxiating, Poisonous or Other Gases, and of Bacteriological Methods of Warfare

(1925). For a useful commentary, see Adam Roberts and Richard Guelff, eds., *Documents on the Laws of War* (Oxford: Oxford University Press, 2000), pp. 155–67.

34. This point was made repeatedly in letters from the Iranian Permanent Representative in New York to the UN secretary-general.

35. The Chemical Weapons Convention (CWC) entered into force in 1997. Iran has ratified the CWC and is a prominent member of the CWC's oversight agency, the Organization for the Prohibition of Chemical Weapons (OPCW) in The Hague. According to Julian P. Perry Robinson, the 1989 Paris Conference was "an attempt [by the international community] to make amends. Iraq wasn't mentioned but everybody knew." Then, the negotiations over the draft Chemical Weapons Convention accelerated because of "the knowledge that Iraq was getting its stuff *not* from the USSR but from private Western companies. Chemical weapons proliferation was now seen as an entirely different problem, and Halabja gave it the final push: the public saw that that stuff was actually being used. Yet Halabja didn't play in the actual negotiations; the focus was on proliferation, not on use." Interview, New York, October 21, 2001.

36. UN Security Council Resolution 479 of September 28, 1980.

37. UN Security Council Resolution 514 of July 12, 1982. Three months later, the Security Council reiterated this call but went further by declaring it "welcome[d] the fact that one of the parties [i.e., Iraq] has already expressed its readiness to co-operate in the implementation of resolution 514 (1982) and calls upon the other to do likewise." UN Security Council Resolution 522 of October 4, 1982.

38. The rift that existed between the Security Council and the office of the secretary-general on the issue of the Iran–Iraq War merits an essay by itself. See Giandomenico Picco, *Man Without a Gun* (New York: Times Books, 1999), p. 61. See also Javier Pérez de Cuéllar, *Pilgrimage for Peace* (New York: St. Martin's Press, 1997), and Cameron R. Hume, *The United Nations, Iran, and Iraq: How Peacemaking Changed* (Bloomington, Ind: Indiana University Press, 1994).

39. Pelletière, *Iraq and the International Oil System*, pp. 206–14.

40. A previous example of this is U.S. support of the shah, especially the close alliance with SAVAK, his secret police, and its sordid record of political oppression and torture.

41. To do so, however, credible information is required about the nature of actions and their consequences. In a war between two closed societies, access to reliable information by independent agencies can be prohibitively difficult to obtain; this certainly was the case in the Iran–Iraq War. This calls for a greater role by independent human rights monitors, as it was independent agencies like the International Committee of the Red Cross and Amnesty International that made public information during the war that was largely accurate and that might have led to a modification of policy if these organizations had enjoyed greater influence at the time.

42. For an argument about legal complicity in war crimes and crimes against humanity under the Rome Statute and other instruments of international humanitarian law, see William A. Schabas, "Enforcing International Humanitarian Law: Catching the Accomplices," in *International Review of the Red Cross*, vol. 83, no. 842 (June 2001), pp. 439–59.

43. See, e.g. Steven R. Ratner and Jason S. Abrams, *Accountability for Human Rights Atrocities in International Law: Beyond the Nuremberg Legacy*, 2nd ed. (Oxford: Oxford University Press, 2001), pp. 102–03 and 106. By comparison, there is absolutely no question that the use of chemical weapons against civilians, as indeed any direct attack targeting noncombatants, constitutes a war crime and a crime against humanity.

Chapter 8

The Gulf States and the Iran–Iraq War: Pattern Shifts and Continuities

Gerd Nonneman

Overview

The Iran–Iraq War can be seen both as a symptom of longer-term dynamics in Gulf regional politics, and as a source of subsequent dynamics and events. Looking back from the post–Iraq War ("third Gulf war") vantage point, and taking account of the "second Gulf war" over Kuwait, a number of patterns can be identified in relations between the conservative Arab Gulf states on the one hand and Iran and Iraq on the other. These reveal both continuities and shifts, and cannot be fully understood without examining their roots in years prior to 1980. An examination of trends in relations during the Iran–Iraq War itself is an essential part of any attempt to understand post-1988 patterns, from the ceasefire through to the 2003 Iraq conflict and its aftermath. This chapter surveys and analyzes relations during the war itself, while also attempting to draw out those longer-term continuities and shifts, and their implications for regional politics.

For the six conservative Arab states of the Gulf, the Iran–Iraq War represented a host of conflicting threats and opportunities. The ways in which these combined and contrasted, moreover, was anything but uniform: they varied both across time and between the states themselves—and indeed, in the case of the United Arab Emirates (UAE), even between the member emirates. All six were vulnerable and shared some aspects of their political makeup and outlook—including a basically pro-Western foreign policy and security stance. At the same time, different dynamics were imparted by different geographical location, economic links, and size. It should be no surprise, then, that the policies of the Six toward the conflict and the combatants showed divergence as well as convergence,[1] evolved through a number of phases, and featured complex attempts to balance various threats in ways that avoided burning any bridges if at all possible.

Six main *common features* may be identified:

(1) An initial leaning toward Iraq, explained by fear of the direction the Iranian revolution was taking.
(2) The defensive reaction of gathering in a new sub-regional grouping, the Gulf Cooperation Council (GCC), the creation of which was not only driven by the threats posed by the new regional environment, but was also made possible by

the war's effect of taking the two main opponents of such a grouping out of the equation.

(3) A common desire, once it was clear that it was going to last longer than the blitz-krieg Saddam had envisaged, to see the war end, while avoiding an Iraqi defeat.

(4) Strenuous efforts, once the initial phase of the war was over, to create or respond to Iranian openings for improved relations, while searching for ways to avoid Iranian threats, and exploring possible peace initiatives.

(5) The use of different channels and platforms to send differing messages to different audiences. This featured divergences between individual state policies and statements on the one hand, and policy and statements in the context of the GCC on the other; between governmental policy and the permitted expression of alternative views in the media; and between declaratory policy and actual measures taken.

(6) A continued and, eventually, strengthened reliance on Western defense cooperation—even if done very cautiously and combined with gestures and declaratory policies to counteract domestic and Iranian criticism of such reliance.

The main *divergences*, which emerged gradually, were those between Saudi Arabia and Kuwait on the one hand—giving the most explicit support to Iraq and criticizing Iran most forcefully—and the states of the lower Gulf on the other, retreating into actual or semi-neutrality although remaining part of the declaratory GCC line (itself the result of compromises between the two tendencies). Bahrain hovered in between—eventually coming closer to the Kuwaiti–Saudi end of the spectrum—while the UAE featured two camps: a clearly neutral group led by Dubai, including Sharjah and Umm al-Qaiwain, and a more pro-Iraqi group including Abu Dhabi and Ras al-Khaimah (along with Ajman and Fujairah), although the UAE as a whole, too, became effectively neutral.

Viewed from the perspective of the post-1990 era (of which the 2003 Iraq War was the culmination), these patterns find a striking if paradoxical reflection in the changed circumstances after Iraq's 1991 defeat and the establishment of UN sanctions. Iraq continued to depend to a significant extent on the GCC states, and continued to employ persuasion, charm, and threats to obtain their support for Iraq's reintegration into the regional and international system. So, too, it was able to count on a division emerging among these states, with those most directly affected—Saudi Arabia and Kuwait—maintaining the hardest position, while the southern Gulf states, driven by vulnerability as well as pragmatic interest, took on a role that was a mirror image of their earlier cautious pragmatism and bilateral neutrality. Even Saudi Arabia, moreover, wanted to explore ways of possible peaceful settlement and the lifting of sanctions on Iraq—mirroring the willingness of all GCC states during the Iran–Iraq War to explore avenues for dialogue with Iran. The GCC as an organization once again functioned as an alternative policy channel and instrument, to compensate bilateral positions and send alternative signals in declaratory foreign policy, and in part to paper over divisions between the members. By the same token, just as Iran found there were limits to the extent to which such divisions could be exploited before its acceptance of the UN Security Council's ceasefire resolution in 1988, so, too, did Iraq find that it was unable to undo GCC unity in applying UN sanctions, to overcome the Saudi–Kuwaiti veto over how far the collective GCC position could evolve, or to get much more than declaratory support in its attempt to avert the military intervention of 2003.[2] The epitome of this phenomenon was Qatar, which, although probably the most vociferous in arguing publicly for lifting sanctions and reintegrating Iraq into the region, nevertheless provided the main base for the Coalition assault on Iraq in March 2003. Kuwait apart, all the other member states' policies featured less extreme versions of the same position. This tells us much about the imperatives and constraints of foreign policy-making in the GCC states, and about the multilevel uses of the GCC itself as an instrument.

Determinants of Policy

The policies of the Six in the Iran–Iraq War, including their attitudes toward the two combatants, must be seen against the background of a number of determinants, of which the war itself provided only one set. Some of these stretch back to well before the war, so it is instructive also to consider the longer-term policy patterns: indeed, the shift in policy toward Iraq in particular—erstwhile a radical republican threat— while highlighted and intensified by the outbreak of the war, did not begin there, and can be traced back even to before the Iranian Revolution. The determinants in question comprise, at a general level (1) these states' vulnerability in the face of a range of external threats; (2) the consequent need for external protection; (3) the conflict of the latter with domestic legitimacy needs, and the consequent need to tread carefully in obtaining and clothing such protection; (4) domestic political dynamics more generally; (5) location; (6) the interests to be served by trade and economic relations regionally (Iran, Iraq) and globally (oil exports and vital imports); and (7) the changing environment. The latter, more specifically, included the political and foreign policy evolution evident in Iraq since the mid-1970s; the Iranian revolution and the implicit and explicit threats emanating from it; the Soviet invasion of Afghanistan; the outbreak of the war and its subsequent evolution; and the evolution of Iranian attitudes. The first three determinants above do not need further elaboration here, but some comments may be in order on the remaining ones.

Certainly, the very vulnerability of these states is a common factor; nor can any of them escape the significance that their location in and around the vital oil and shipping region of the Gulf has for bigger powers. Yet individual stances can diverge due to various combinations of factors. One illustration comes in the form of the contrasting positions taken by Kuwait and Oman in the war. In Oman, virtually locked away from the rest of the Arab world until 1970, Arab nationalist ideology never had quite the same hold on popular opinion and the legitimacy question as elsewhere. Conscious of Western support, Sultan Qaboos has very much gone his own pragmatic way. Even so, such pragmatism still implied a need to maintain bridges with the moderate Arab majority and, at the same time, to give careful consideration to the vulnerabilities related to the geopolitics of the Strait of Hormuz and the towering presence of Iran. Kuwait, on the other hand, has long been characterized by its location next to Iraq, and by a population relatively more politically articulate. Both of these factors traditionally led its government to adopt a more distinctly Arab nationalist stance and a more genuinely non-aligned foreign policy. Kuwait's position was further complicated by its sizeable Shi'i population, partly of Persian ancestry, some of whom would oppose the government's support for Iraq.[3] The other emirates occupy a middle position in these terms. They could not (and still cannot) ignore either neighboring Iran, in part because of their sizeable Shi'i populations, or Iraq, partly because of the salience of Arab nationalism as a legitimizing factor. For Dubai, there are the additional factors of the significant section of the population that is of Iranian origin, and the longstanding lively trade relations with Iran. In the case of Sharjah and Umm al-Qaiwain in particular, an important factor was the joint management with Iran of the Mubarak oil field off Abu Musa island, from which a considerable proportion of their income derives. Bahrain and Qatar, too, have had significant trade with the Islamic Republic.

Saudi Arabia, while much larger and better armed, nevertheless suffers from high vulnerability given its exposed, difficult-to-protect oil facilities and the limited capability of its armed personnel fully to operate the military hardware available. Equally important has been the Al-Saud's need to take account of the effect of certain foreign and security policies on domestic legitimacy, with particular reference to the themes of Islamic probity and the Arab cause. William Quandt has observed that the effect of these factors has been that the Saudi leadership, "pushed and pulled in various directions, will try to find a middle ground, a consensus position that will minimize pressures and risks." This tendency has often been exacerbated by the nature of the foreign policy decision-making process, which, after King Faysal's death, became more diffuse—with several senior princes' voices being heard, each expressing views reflecting their somewhat differing backgrounds, ideas and sympathies. In this context, "decisions may be postponed or compromises forged to preserve the façade of consensus."[4]

Saudi Arabia's regional policy has been marked throughout by the pursuit of raison d'état, "omnibalancing"[5] between the various threats the regime has perceived, trying to forge or maintain consensus in the region even to the extent of a willingness to cooperate with the Arab "radicals" (especially once the latter's radicalism was waning, from the mid-1970s), using its wealth to smooth relations, and attempting to maintain reasonable relations even with revolutionary Iran, as an Islamic country (as well as a potential threat). Nevertheless, neither these consensus-seeking, conflict-avoiding instincts, nor the domestic decision-making factors referred to above, have meant that Saudi Arabia avoided more drastic policy choices in the few but momentous instances where the alternative appeared worse. Thus, after initial attempts to appease the young revolution in Iran, the conclusion that the Iranian regime had become a real threat to the region that would not be subdued by conciliatory gestures led the Saudi leadership to react assertively by extending strong support to Iraq in the war against Iran.

Iranian policy, indeed, was crucial in determining the policies of the Six toward Tehran and the war: all feared the impact of the revolution, all attempted to appease this new threat initially, and all then, albeit to varying degrees, veered toward Iraq in the face of explicit ideological threats issuing from leading figures in Tehran. Yet none was willing to ignore possibilities of improving relations with the Islamic Republic if there appeared a chance. Consequently, signs of Iranian rapprochement were eagerly responded to. The limitations of such responses, and at times renewed crises in the relationship especially with Saudi Arabia and Kuwait, must be explained essentially by Iran's policies themselves, and in particular the implacable determination to continue the war long after Iraq had sued for peace in 1981, the threats uttered against Gulf regimes, and, even when a policy of rapprochement appeared prevalent, the persistently mixed messages emanating from Tehran.[6]

By the same token, the changes in Iraq's own foreign policy stance since the mid-1970s were also of crucial importance. Until the early 1970s, the revolutionary and socialist strands of Baathi ideology had been predominant, but they lost in relative importance to the pan-Arab element after 1974, as Saddam Hussein increasingly came to control both ideology and policy. At the same time, non-alignment (rather than alliance with the Soviet Union) was emphasized. This was argued to be the best way to cope with the global system that was gradually changing from a bipolar to a multipolar one.[7] Underlying this double shift in ideology was an increasingly pragmatic approach to international relations, the main source of which was again Saddam Hussein, who argued that such a policy shift was necessary to allow Iraq to assume the more active and leading role in the Arab and Third Worlds that he saw as Iraq's logical task.[8] Indeed, actual policy development from the mid-1970s demonstrated that the regime did now want to normalize relations with the other Arab states of the region. This policy shift was both explicitly recognized and accentuated further in the report of the Ninth Regional Congress of the Baath Party, held in 1982, which also drew attention (if not in so many words) to the coinciding of this shift with the formal takeover of the reins of power by Saddam. The report stressed the strong development of Iraq's participation in Arab and Third World affairs since July 1979. Moreover, the fight against imperialism lost in relative ideological importance to the concern for assisting Third-World countries economically.[9]

The increasingly pragmatic (if strongly Arab nationalist) actual foreign policy behavior of the Iraqi state since the 1970s was not determined solely by the changes in the Baath Party's ideology. Saddam himself pointed out that the positions of Party and State can diverge: "the state has to adapt to changing circumstances and conduct day-to-day affairs; the party does not."[10] A further part of the explanation for the shift toward moderation and toward the West must be sought in a number of domestic motives. First, Iraq needed the West to obtain both the materials and technology for the speeded-up development spurt and, later, the import of consumer goods, that the jump in oil revenues was making possible. At the same time, this newfound wealth gave the leadership the financial independence to opt for the shift away from the Soviet Union. Second, improved domestic security after the Algiers agreement arguably made revolutionary ideology less important as a legitimizing tool. Third, both domestic and regional prestige could be derived more effectively from an enhanced regional and international role, as well as from increased economic prosperity. Finally, particularly from 1979 onwards, a policy of economic liberalization and a degree of privatization was introduced, which Robert Springborg has argued was at least in part a reflection of Saddam's intention to enhance his grip on power by weakening the hold of the Party over the economy and by paving the way for the emergence of a new social group that would support him.[11] It also ties in with a more general departure from Iraq's erstwhile socialism and thus confirmed the trend that saw ideology lose much of its effect as a complicating factor in Iraq's relations with the conservative Arab states and the West.

The revolution in Iran reinforced the sense in Baghdad of common threat with the Six as well as with the West. It increased both the need and the opportunity to draw closer to the rest of the Arab world (with the key exception of Syria), including the conservative Gulf states. Finally, the Soviet invasion of Afghanistan, which directly influenced the conservative Gulf states' view of regional security, also increased Iraq's coolness toward Moscow (in turn yet another factor in eliciting a rapprochement from the side of the Six).

The "National Charter for the Arab States," which Saddam proposed on February 8, 1980, confirmed the change Iraqi foreign policy had undergone.[12] The document stressed non-alignment, the peaceful resolution of problems between Arab states, Arab mutual defense, adherence to international law, and Arab economic integration. A very clear implication was the recognition of the existing Arab state system.

Iraqi policy toward the six conservative Arab Gulf states prior to the Iran–Iraq War emerged as part of the overall evolution of foreign policy. In addition, Iraq's behavior toward the Six was influenced also by these states' own orientation, as well as by the Iranian factor. There were several dimensions to this: (1) strategic, as Iranian control over the Shatt al-Arab, coupled with Kuwaiti control over Warba and Bubiyan, jeopardized Iraq's military capacity in the Gulf; (2) economic, since the Shatt and the Gulf comprised Iraq's most important outlet to the world; (3) ideological–nationalist, in that the influence of Iran (non-Arab and pro-Western, then revolutionary Islamist) in the Gulf had to be curbed; and (4) more broadly political, in the desire to strengthen Iraq's position and influence in the region. Clearly, then, there remained room for friction with the Six: regional rivalry with Saudi Arabia, the islands question with Kuwait, and foreign policy orientations toward Gulf security with all six, were among the main irritants. Yet these were now embedded in a broader Iraqi policy of rapprochement.

Prewar Trends

There was an obvious sharp change in relations between the Six and Iran in the aftermath of the Iranian Revolution, both because of the implicit threat posed to regional stability and domestic security, and because of a series of threatening statements aimed at the monarchical regimes of the Gulf from senior Iranian officials and clerics—among them Khomeini himself and President Bani-Sadr.[13] The early radicalization of the revolution only made this more acute: in the balancing game of Gulf relations, an alliance with Iran was clearly no longer an option from now on. It did not mean all contacts were given up; indeed, efforts continued to be made to build bridges, and Dubai in particular remained concerned to safeguard its trade with Iran. Yet undeniably Iran, for these states, had changed in a very short space of time from a warily observed but reassuringly Western-oriented regional policeman, to a potentially significant threat. By contrast, the Iraqi evolution sketched above meant that relations with Baghdad evolved in a positive sense over a period of at least five years before the war. The Iranian revolutionary threat, now experienced in similar ways by both sides, would reinforce this further. The outbreak of the Iran–Iraq War, and the instances of close Iraqi–Gulf cooperation that this occasioned, did not, therefore, signify a clear break so much as, at least for some among the Six, the reinforcement of an already existing trend.

The evidence of improved relations with Iraq prior to the war is found in economic as well as political spheres. Although it is easy to observe a legacy of distrust in the Gulf capitals' attitudes toward Baghdad during the second half of the 1970s, they were nevertheless ready to enter into economic cooperation with it.[14] In the Saudi case, a desire to respond to Iraq's overtures coincided with Saudi Arabia's own growing pragmatism under the influence of Crown Prince Fahd. Improved relations with Baghdad, for one thing, provided Riyadh with a counterweight against Tehran. The Islamic revolution across the Gulf waters strengthened this calculation for all of the Six, and, as already pointed out, soon put paid to any ideas of counting on Iran as an ally in the regional balancing game. Iraq's growing coolness toward the Soviet Union also influenced the Gulf monarchies' attitudes to Baghdad, while the invasion of Afghanistan led one Gulf official to comment that Iraq had now become the second line of defense for protecting the region's oil producing areas.[15]

It is no surprise, then, that the Iraqi opening up was mirrored in Gulf attitudes. A mutual security pact was signed between Riyadh and Baghdad in February 1979, and one year later the Iraqi information minister declared, "any attack on any of the Arab Gulf states is a direct aggression against Iraq."[16] All of the Gulf states except Oman quickly expressed support for Saddam's proposed "National Charter." In the period leading up to the war, especially after Iraqi–Iranian tension began to rise during April 1980, the position of the Gulf states shifted further as the Iranian threat of exporting the revolution became more clearly spelled out. On May 8, the information minister had announced that Iraq considered the Algiers agreement null and void.[17] From May onwards, diplomatic activity between Baghdad and the six Gulf capitals increased markedly, featuring a range of high-level visits in both directions (with the exception of Qatar, although this may mean the Qataris felt represented by the Saudis).[18] There was even a visit by one of Oman's most senior officials and confidantes of the Sultan, Qays al-Zawawi, who now also expressed support for the National Charter (although later claiming he wanted it clarified and that there was no radical change in Oman's policy). Oman, he said on arrival, wished to initiate cooperation with Iraq and to "remove any misunderstanding that might have arisen as a result of certain political opinions."[19] During visits to Baghdad, Bahrain's prime minister, Kuwait's crown prince, and Shaikh Saqr of Ras al-Khaimah all expressed strong support for Iraq, followed by much of the region's press, which was warning Iran not to venture too far. Renewed border demarcation discussions were agreed between Iraq and Kuwait in July.[20] And on August 5 came Saddam's much-commented-upon visit to Saudi Arabia. The resulting joint communiqué stressed agreement between the two countries on "the present situation . . . in the Islamic world"—code for relations with Iran—and on "Arab solidarity."[21]

As I have argued elsewhere,[22] it seems highly likely that Saudi Arabia, at least, was informed in advance of Iraq's plan to invade Iran, and that Riyadh had given the green light, probably on the occasion of the August 5 visit. Ras al-Khaimah's Shaikh Saqr later said that Saddam had informed him in advance of the decision to abrogate the Algiers treaty.[23] All six governments, it would seem, showed varying degrees of support for Iraq's initiative, having reluctantly come to the conclusion that there appeared to be no effective alternative, and believing that a short military operation could cut the revolutionary threat down to size.[24] In the UAE, Dubai and Sharjah were the main exceptions to this general stance.

It is worth briefly noting the expansion of economic relations between Iraq and the Gulf states from the mid-1970s, both at the governmental and private level. Iraq was a participant in a whole range of pan-Arab Gulf organizations, ministerial conferences, and joint projects. Nevertheless, trade remained on the whole low. Yet a fairly dramatic expansion of relations with Kuwait took place, especially from 1980. A number of major contracts were awarded to Kuwaiti companies, and projects involving the piping of water from the Shatt al-Arab and linking the two countries' electricity grids were revived. There was a major increase also in Kuwait's importance as a transit port, with special facilities for Iraq, because of congestion at Basra and Umm Qasr. UAE ports were increasingly used for transhipment as well. In oil policy, Iraq, which had in the course of the late 1970s already moved toward a more moderate position, in 1980 appears to have coordinated its pricing policy with the other Gulf states on several occasions.[25]

Relations during the Course of the War

The Iraqi Offensive: September 22–October 1980

As the war broke out, the Gulf monarchies were effectively on Iraq's side, with the neutral exceptions of the emirates of Dubai, Sharjah, and Umm al-Qaiwain. From the start, and for the reasons laid out earlier, these three insisted on, and succeeded in, keeping good relations with the Islamic Republic. By contrast, Ras al-Khaimah's ruler, Shaikh Saqr, is thought to have supported the idea of an Iraqi invasion of Abu Musa and the Tunbs as one of the early war aims put forward by Saddam (in an attempt to gain further Arab legitimacy and Gulf Arab support). Abu Dhabi was more cautious, and declined active cooperation in such an operation, although it is reported to have offered shelter to Iraqi planes and ships.[26] The extent of support and the ways in which it was expressed differed among the Six, with care still taken to a greater or lesser extent to avoid burning any bridges with Iran. However, that should not obscure the basic picture of political stances in this early phase of the war. Even Oman, long wary of an Iraq that had, until the 1970s, lent support to the Popular Front for the Liberation of Oman, appears to have initially been caught up, however cautiously, in the pro-Iraqi camp. Several reports indicate that Iraq was originally given permission to use bases in the country to reconquer Abu Musa and the Tunbs, a permission only withdrawn after pressure from the United States and Britain. All an Omani official would confirm was that two Iraqi transport planes had landed during the first days of the war, although one report claims Iraq had assembled a number of helicopters and troops in the Sultanate, prior to their discovery by British intelligence.[27] Saudi Arabia, where both local rumors and intelligence reports indicate that Iraqi planes were allowed to traverse Saudi air space and to land, still cloaked its support for Baghdad in neutral language about the conflict.[28] Kuwait, meanwhile, kept open the land link to Iraq for the transhipment of goods, which became especially vital when Iranian raids made the northern tip of the Gulf a no-go zone for Iraq.

This basic picture also did not change when the initial days' blitz failed to produce the expected quick win, although greater caution set in as Iran began to threaten the Gulf states for cooperating with Iraq. The Six now all hastened to express their official neutrality in the conflict—Saudi Arabia persuaded Iraq to drop the plan of the islands invasion and sent the Iraqi planes back once the U.S. AWACS had arrived. Yet the underlying support for Iraq remained; indeed, even the insistence by the leaderships on a peaceful resolution of the conflict was in line with Iraq's position from September 28, when it accepted a UN ceasefire appeal. Intriguingly, Sultan Qaboos convened a meeting of senior Gulf military officers, with the reported attendance of a senior Iraqi army officer.[29] The tone of most of the region's governments and media at this time also confirmed the pro-Iraqi leanings in the Six.

Stalemate Sets In: November 1980–Late September 1981

The changing fortunes of the war did begin to have a more significant impact on the attitudes of the Six, however, once the conflict clearly turned into a stalemate after November 1980 (Kuwait's northern area of Abdali, moreover, was hit twice by missiles on the 11th and 16th of that month). The need to avoid a long-drawn-out conflict, with its implications of economic drain, military spill-over and superpower involvement, became more important than anything that could be gained from further bleeding the two combatants. The main concern of the Six therefore became to end the war—a point on which they were very much in agreement with Iraq. The second imperative was becoming to prevent an Iranian victory—hence the very substantial active support given to Iraq. A third and related imperative now became to find a means to shore up their collective security: the decision to create the GCC in February 1981, and its inauguration in May that year, would be the expression of this concern (it appears not coincidental that the Saudi proposals sent to the other five states, and which would become the basis for the GCC, were sent in November 1980, when stalemate set in).

Saudi Arabia offered Iraq transhipment of military and civilian supplies, and gave $6 billion in direct financial aid by April 1981 and a further $4 billion during the remainder of 1981. Kuwait's first $2 billion loan was given in the autumn of 1980, followed by a further $2 billion in April 1981. The UAE (in essence Abu Dhabi) is thought to have contributed between $1–3 billion, and Qatar some $1 billion.[30] It was also in this period that Saudi Arabia agreed in principle to the construction of an oil pipeline to the Red Sea (Iraq Pipeline Trans Saudi Arabia, or IPSA) that would allow Iraqi oil to avoid the Gulf. Kuwait's role in transhipment to Iraq increased further: by 1981, seven berths in Shuaiba port were specially dedicated to Iraq-bound cargo (up from four in the period preceding the war), and road transport from Kuwait to Iraq tripled that year. Yet Kuwait's support did not extend to giving in to Iraq's demand for a 99-year lease on Bubiyan island; arguably, indeed, the emirate was in a strong enough position to refuse the Iraqi offer of a favorable border settlement in return, precisely because it knew itself to be a vital supporter of Iraq. The government also struggled, however, with increased resistance among some of the Shi'i population and Iranian immigrants against its pro-Iraqi policy. This, as Plotkin has shown, was the first clear sign that the regional conflict was having unsettling reverberations for Kuwait's domestic security, causing tension between the Shi'i and Sunni segments of the population and leading to a longer-term policy of increasing deportations of foreign nationals and closer tracking of immigration on the one hand, and a combination of containment and co-option for opposition by Kuwaiti nationals.[31]

For Oman, this phase of the war proved an important watershed, making the country retreat from its cautiously pro-Iraqi stance into one of neutrality. Following a naval accident in late 1980 that caused a near-clash between the Omani and Iranian navy, Sultan Qaboos worked out a *modus vivendi* with Iran in Gulf waters. Oman's stance from now on would be similar to that of the neutral emirates of the UAE.

Even for Iraq's supporters in the conflict, however, traditional concerns about Iraq had not disappeared altogether. In the security discussions that led up to the creation of the GCC, Iraq was never thought of as a potential partner—indeed the fact that Iraq was engaged in the war and increasingly dependent on Gulf assistance, and thus not in a position to object, is one of the key reasons the GCC could be formed at all. The council's creation confirmed the republic's status as an outsider—however much effort the member states put into avoiding the impression that the grouping actively excluded Iraq for political or security reasons.[32]

Iraq's growing dependence on its conservative allies was reflected in the gradually diminishing importance of ideology as an irritant in relations. Examples of this were its eventual, grudging, acceptance of the GCC, and the expulsion of the Baghdad representatives of the Popular Front for the Liberation of Oman. Yet a degree of friction with Kuwait over the question of Warba and Bubiyan remained.[33]

The Iranian Counteroffensive: September 28, 1981–June 1982

When Iranian forces broke the siege of Abadan, a new phase of the war had begun. Khorramshahr was recaptured and Saddam announced the withdrawal of Iraq's troops to the international border by the end of June 1982. In this phase, the "sensitive" attitude that Baghdad had begun to display toward the GCC states developed further. There was little overt criticism now of the cautious stance of some of the Six. The GCC, for its part, had now clearly established itself and Iraq acquiesced in the fact of its exclusion. The GCC's declarations remained studiously neutral, but this covered differing attitudes on the part of its members. Saudi relations with Iran had already worsened further by clashes with Iranian pilgrims in Mecca in October 1981. The Bahraini coup attempt in late 1981, which stimulated the organization's members to include security as a more explicit aim, was blamed squarely on Iran by the Bahraini and Saudi governments. Saudi Arabia's Interior Minister Prince Nayif, in particular, henceforth repeatedly stated the Kingdom's support for Iraq, urging other Arab states to follow the Saudi example. Always one of the more outspoken members of the Al-Saud in criticizing Iran, he was quoted several times as calling Iran "the terrorist of the Gulf." Against the background of these developments, the final border agreement between Saudi Arabia and Iraq was signed. The Kingdom supplied considerable further aid. So did Kuwait, with another $2 billion loan in December 1981. This followed Iranian missile attacks on Kuwaiti oil installations at the beginning of October, which also led Kuwait to recall its ambassador from Tehran. The press in both Saudi Arabia and Kuwait turned strongly against Iran—even if the Kuwaiti government worked hard at keeping up the front of official neutrality, including by seeking a mediating role; indeed, the Kuwaiti government approved a request from Iran and Iraq that it be one of the sites for family visits to prisoners of war.[34]

This effort to join support for Iraq with these alternative strategies followed directly from the realization of Kuwait's vulnerability. The three southernmost GCC member states in this period adopted a very low profile, similarly aware of their vulnerability, Iranian threats, and the interests referred to earlier. Yet there was one intriguing indication of a more proactive peace-making attempt on the part of the GCC states. At the end of May, after the Iranians had captured Khorramshahr and looked set to continue their march, the GCC's foreign ministers gathered in Riyadh. Their communiqué called on Iran to respond to peace initiatives and drew particular attention to the Islamic Conference Organisation's (ICO) mediation committee, which was convening in Jeddah a few days later. This, and the extensive consultations the Six were involved in with other Arab capitals, lends plausibility to speculations that they suggested secret proposals to Iraq in early July 1982 which would have included the Six paying up to $25 billion in war reparations to Iran and helping Iraq with reconstruction.[35]

Iran's Crossing of the Border, and Renewed Stalemate: July 12, 1982–February 1984

Iran during this phase carried the war into Iraq, capturing the Majnoon islands in the southern marshes and attacking Basra. Yet Iraq consolidated its defenses and a renewed stalemate of sorts ensued. Iraq proved highly conscious of its dependence on its Gulf supporters. The GCC's communiqués remained fairly bland, even if Iran was reprimanded for having crossed the border. As usual, this covered varying individual policies. The Saudi position, both declaratory and in substance, amounted to an effective alliance with Iraq. This included another $4 billion in loans in the course of 1982, and probably another $6 billion in the first half of 1983 (bringing the total Saudi non-oil aid to Iraq thus far to some $20 billion), as well as the start of a "war relief crude" arrangement (see below). This was reflected in Iraq's change of heart on the so-called Fahd plan on the Arab–Israeli conflict: having rejected the initial plan, Baghdad approved the marginally changed version at the Arab League summit in Fez in September 1982.

Kuwait for its part had cause to feel threatened by Iran's advances into southern Iraq. Hence the government on the one hand strengthened its official stance of neutrality (including via the GCC forum), while at the same time maintaining material support for Iraq. From 1982 onwards, Kuwait does not, however, appear to have given any more financial aid of the magnitude already disbursed (a total of $6 billion)—this would only resume in 1986 after the Iranian capture of Faw. Yet it does, in the intervening years, appear to have provided down payments of some 10 percent on the value of contracts of a number of companies supplying Iraq, as well as down payments to providers of long-term loans. Altogether this is unlikely to have reached $1 billion a year. Kuwait also, together with Saudi Arabia, started giving some 330,000 barrels per day (b/d) of crude oil for sale to Iraqi customers from February 1983 (200,000 b/d from Saudi Arabia, with Kuwait's contribution rising from 50,000 b/d in the first half of 1983 to 130,000 b/d from the second half onwards).[36] Nevertheless, Kuwait was determined to show it would not relinquish Bubiyan island, and indicated this by constructing a bridge in record time between the empty island and the equally empty mainland opposite.

Among the others, Abu Dhabi appears to have contributed another $1 billion or so to Iraq's coffers in 1982 (bringing its total contribution to $2–4 billion). Beyond this, into 1983, there was very little sign anymore of a clear pro-Iraqi bias on the part of Abu Dhabi. Qatar too, no longer appeared willing to follow the Saudi lead, as it had traditionally done in its foreign policy. Indeed, after the initial spike in concern over Iran's advances, Bahrain, Qatar, the UAE, and Oman all quickly reverted to their previous low profile and official neutrality.[37] The general drop-off in aid caused considerable concern and irritation in Baghdad, although this was expressed in a somewhat veiled way.[38]

Internationalizing the Conflict: The Tanker War, Spring 1984–January 1986

Iraq in this phase of the war intensified its strategy of internationalizing the conflict by targeting Kharg island and other Iranian oil outlets, leading to Iranian retaliation against Arab ships and tankers carrying Arab oil. The intention of bringing in external intervention would only be realized in 1987, however.[39] Meanwhile, Iran's repeated threats against Saudi Arabia and Kuwait for assisting Iraq, and indeed its attacks against Saudi and Kuwaiti shipping, led to a successful Saudi–Kuwaiti move to produce a GCC initiative explicitly criticizing Iran: the organization sponsored a UN resolution that condemned the Iranian attacks on international shipping. Iran's verbal assault on the Gulf states was also stepped up, in turn heightening Gulf antagonism. It is in the midst of this deteriorating situation that, on June 5, 1984, Saudi air force pilots shot down an Iranian F4 over Saudi territorial waters—the first such assertion of military force against Iran by Saudi Arabia.

By the same token, all, including Saudi Arabia and Kuwait, remained extremely concerned about the threatening turn events were taking and continued to look for ways of containing the fallout. In the case of Kuwait this was tied to an increasing obsession with security following an assassination attempt on the Emir and a number of bombings in 1985, and to concern over heightening tension between Shi'is and Sunnis, and between Kuwaiti nationals and foreigners.[40] Kuwait's foreign minister, Shaikh Sabah, had already called for international intervention to stop the war in March 1984, and when the Tanker War erupted in May of that year, he pointed out that, since the waters of the Gulf were an international waterway, it was the responsibility of the international community to assure its security. This theme in government thinking occasioned strong opposition from nationalist members of the National Assembly—arguably one of the contributory reasons why the Assembly would eventually be suspended in 1986.[41]

Saudi Arabia itself sought the good offices of the Islamic Conference Organisation, the non-aligned movement and the United Nations to help end the war, and although the pilots who had downed the Iranian plane were celebrated, the incident appears to have been one trigger for attempts by both sides to seek to bring relations back to a more normal plane.[42]

This coincided with a more general policy-rethink in Iran, evident in Khomeini's instruction to Iran's diplomats in October 1984 that a new approach was needed to end the country's isolation and expand relations with governments around the world. This was followed by Prime Minister Mir-Hosein Musavi's reassurance that Iran "[did] not want to export armed revolution to any country."[43] In Saudi–Iranian relations, Iran's very restrained reaction to the shooting down of the F-4 was followed up very quickly by diplomatic overtures from both sides. From the spring of 1985 an Iranian charm offensive toward the GCC states became very evident, and was violently denounced by Saddam Hussein who reminded these states that "had it not been for Iraq's steadfastness, black and greedy Khomeinism would have stormed through all the region's countries."[44] Nevertheless, Saudi Foreign Minister Prince Saud al-Faysal went to Tehran in May at the invitation of the Iranian leadership, a visit reciprocated at the end of the year by Iran's Foreign Minister Ali-Akbar Velayati. Riyadh did not give up its effective support of Iraq, however. Although the GCC's November 1985 communiqué was again more even-handed toward Iran and Iraq, it continued to insist on basing peace negotiations on the two relevant UN Security Council Resolutions, even though Iran had rejected them. Iran's own refusal to shift its position on the conduct and ending of the war would inevitably cause new tension. Indeed, accounts of occasional secret negotiations between the two sides from 1984 on reveal that while the Saudis were eager to reduce tension and were not wedded to Saddam's leadership, they were repeatedly riled by Tehran's demands and intransigence.[45] Meanwhile, though, Abir claims, "to win Tehran's goodwill and Washington's favour, Riyadh, through prince Bandar, . . . became involved in 1985/86 in Washington's attempt to improve relations with Tehran and to free the American hostages [in Lebanon] through a limited supply of arms to Iran. . . . Saudi Arabia not only facilitated the flying of American weapons to Iran but itself sold the latter badly needed refined oil products."[46] Saudi "facilitation" may have been no more than Saudi arms dealer Adnan Khashoggi's involvement in the U.S. arms-to-Iran deal, but it would appear the royal family had given its permission.[47] As to the sale of oil products (which took place mainly in the following phase), this was not officially government-sanctioned but could, presumably, have been prevented.

Kuwait too was amenable to Iranian overtures and welcomed Iran's apparent change of policy in 1985. Yet since the emirate did not reduce its support for Iraq, threats from Tehran soon resumed, in turn leading to explicit expressions of support for Iraq by members of the ruling family as well as the press and the National

Assembly. Friction with Baghdad over Warba and Bubiyan continued, however, and the islands became even more strategically important to the Iraqis than before. Although Saddam Hussein now reduced his demands by asking only for a 20-year lease on part of the islands, the Kuwaiti leadership did not budge, and rather pointedly transformed Bubiyan into a military island. The island and border issues thus remained a serious irritant in Iraqi–Kuwaiti relations.[48]

By the beginning of 1986, when the war relief crude arrangement was meant to come to an end, the value of three years' worth of supplies by Saudi Arabia and Kuwait on behalf of Iraq had amounted to a total of $9 billion. Together with the financial aid detailed earlier, this means that Gulf aid to Iraq by this point amounted to the equivalent of about $40 billion—all but $3–5 billion of which came from Saudi Arabia and Kuwait.[49]

The four southern Gulf states had by the end of this period come to accept that neutrality was their best option and might even help to create possibilities for peaceful resolution of the conflict. Even so, in the framework of the GCC they still collectively tilted toward Iraq. This is a good example of how different fora and avenues can be, and were, used in order to follow consciously "schizophrenic" policies serving conflicting interests and aimed at different constituencies, including domestic ones. At the same time, the collective vehicle of the GCC also allowed the more staunchly pro-Iraqi actors in Kuwait and Saudi Arabia to retain possible interlocutors with Iran.

The Capture of Faw and Its Aftermath:
February 9, 1986–June 1987

The capture of the Faw peninsula by Iranian forces transformed the shape of the Gulf War, not least for the GCC states and, in strategic terms, for Kuwait in particular. The other two features of the changing war scene were problematic for the Six, but were nevertheless probably at least partly the result of a conscious policy shared between Saudi Arabia and Kuwait on the one hand, and Iraq on the other. The plummeting of oil prices to below $10 per barrel affected all severely, but most of all Iran. It would appear that this was to a degree engineered as one way of putting pressure on Iran by undermining its economic capacity to continue the war. The second feature was the escalation of the tanker war by the Iraqi extension of its strikes on Iran's oil terminals to the southern Gulf. This too was meant to affect Iran's economic capacity, but at the same time, by bringing a general escalation, made international intervention to end the war more likely—as would indeed prove the case. Saudi Arabia and Kuwait, then, were both active participants in the developing regional scene, and clearly on Iraq's side.

The dramatic shift in the war also stimulated a striking departure from Kuwait's own traditional foreign security policy. On the one hand, Kuwait, after being the lone hold-out among the GCC members since 1981, finally joined the grouping's mutual defense pact in late 1986. On the other, the new situation, together with the escalating threat of Iranian attacks, was the context for the initiation of the emirate's plan to have its tanker fleet reflagged and thus protected. This was initiated with the strong support of Saudi Arabia. Bahrain's foreign minister, too, expressed his country's approval for the operation—which would inevitably bring a sizeable foreign naval presence into the Gulf—although rather feebly trying to reassure Tehran that this would not be aimed against it.[50] Although this was a visible change in Kuwait's policy stance, it did not come out of a vacuum: witness the 1984 calls by the government—then opposed by the nationalists in the National Assembly—for international intervention of some sort. Arguably, indeed, the execution of the reflagging plan only became possible after the suspension of the Assembly in 1986.

The Iranian conquest of Faw immediately elicited condemnation from each of the six GCC states. Saudi Arabia and Kuwait attacked Iran strongly and explicitly. But while Riyadh still showed a willingness to try diplomatic conciliation if possible, Kuwait from the start of this phase stands out by the unequivocally pro-Iraqi stance that was now adopted both by government and press. The Saudi and Kuwaiti foreign ministers traveled to Damascus to pressure Syria to restrain Iran but to little effect. Iran responded with further threats, which only succeeded, at least initially, in hardening Saudi and Kuwaiti feelings and, strikingly, in a collective condemnation by the GCC, in the strongly worded communiqué of its foreign ministers' meeting of March 1–3. Bilaterally, both governments and the press in the four southern GCC states also condemned the Iranian moves, but they remained more restrained.[51]

Iran now again attempted to divide the Six by combining pressure with conciliatory messages, and by explicitly singling out Saudi Arabia and Kuwait as its main sources of ire. Over time this worked—at least to the extent that the UAE, Qatar, and Oman were gradually again reduced to effective neutrality. Although the GCC umbrella continued to provide cover for the expression of more pro-Iraqi sentiments, these appeared by now to be little more than formulations urged upon them by Saudi Arabia and Kuwait. Bahrain, however, had shifted somewhat in the direction of the Saudi position—which may be explained by its own experience with Iranian-inspired protest, and the island's high degree of dependence on Saudi aid, oil supplies, and military protection. Kuwait and Saudi Arabia, for their part, are thought to have extended another $4 billion loan to Iraq in the second half of 1986, while Saudi Arabia is reported to have allowed Iraqi planes to land and refuel following strikes on Iranian oil facilities in the southern Gulf.[52] Between Kuwait and Iraq a mutually beneficial deal was concluded in the form of the agreement to supply Kuwait with 220 cubic feet per day of non-associated gas from Iraq; this came into effect in May 1986.

Yet the Saudi position was more nuanced than the "two camps" image would indicate. As in the previous period, Riyadh was still ready to respond to overtures from Tehran; the U.S. arms-to-Iran deal was ongoing; shipments of Saudi refined products were sold to Iran after mid-1986 (although there is no clear evidence that the authorities approved of this), and Riyadh became keen, as 1986 wore on and oil prices stayed dangerously low, to cooperate with Iran on oil issues. As indications of some of this penetrated Baghdad, they caused a significant rift. Saddam refused King Fahd's request to cooperate with OPEC efforts to firm up prices again, instead demanding a doubling of the war relief crude arrangement. Iraq also demanded that Saudi Arabia stop placing obstacles in the way of the free flow of Iraqi crude through the IPSA-1 pipeline, which had been completed in 1985. In response to Iraqi bullying, Riyadh reportedly reduced the flow even further by the end of 1986. It was not until a visit in February 1987 by a high-level Iraqi delegation that the Saudis grudgingly agreed to allow through 500,000 b/d (double the throughput of January and February).[53]

Yet in March 1987 serious Saudi efforts to find a face-saving formula to end the war finally proved fruitless, leaving the Saudi leadership (and Prince Saud al-Faysal in particular) exasperated with the Iranian policy establishment's inability to deliver due to its internal divisions.[54] From now on, Saudi–Kuwaiti solidarity in supporting Iraq and confronting Iranian threats was once more clearly established. Bombings in Kuwait in April, May, and June 1987 were blamed on Iran, bringing severe threats in return. In June, Iran also deployed Silkworm missiles on Faw, directly threatening Kuwait. This happened in a context in which Kuwait's reflagging deal with the United States had just (in May) been formally concluded. The GCC collectively approved the plan in early 1987 but the three neutrals appeared to make a point of not commending it individually.

Indeed, the UAE and Oman in particular made efforts in 1987 to be on friendly terms with Iran: Shaikh Zayed even stated in May that foreign protection was not needed for the UAE's ships. The Iranians capitalized on this mood by sending Foreign Minister Velayati on a tour of the three southern states, while an aide stood in for his originally planned visit to Bahrain.[55] Nevertheless, all six GCC states subscribed to the foreign ministers' communiqué of June 8, which supported peace moves but also condemned the "terrorist and sabotage acts" against Kuwait and supported the latter's measures to secure its economic and commercial interests. Although some of this language must be ascribed to heavy Saudi and Kuwaiti pressure, it does perhaps also indicate that there were limits to the extent to which Iran could divide the grouping.

From the Reflagging Operation and Resolution 598 to Renewed Attempts at a GCC–Iran Dialogue: July 1987–January 1988

July 1987 was a momentous month both for the Iran–Iraq conflict and for the triangular relations between the two protagonists and the GCC states. At a press conference on July 20, Kuwait's Crown Prince Shaikh Saad came out explicitly and strongly in support of Iraq, and the same day the UN Security Council issued Resolution 598, the strongest call yet for a ceasefire and for a step-by-step resolution of the conflict. The following day the reflagging operation began. Only ten days later, hundreds of pilgrims died in Mecca, in the chaos and violence that had erupted following political demonstrations by Iranians. This had itself followed seven weeks of Iranian threats and Saudi warnings about demonstrations during the Hajj.[56] Iraq accepted Resolution 598; Iran, while avoiding outright rejection, insisted on prior condemnation of Iraq as the aggressor and claimed that the resolution reflected the Iraqi formula for settling the conflict.[57] This, together with its continued attacks on Arab shipping and its perceived responsibility for the Mecca riots, further worsened relations with Kuwait and Saudi Arabia. A Saudi diplomat died in an attack on the Saudi embassy in Tehran and the speaker of the Iranian Parliament, Ali-Akbar

Hashemi-Rafsanjani, called for the Al-Saud to be uprooted from the region. The Saudi press was now for the first time given carte blanche to attack Iran, and at the Arab League foreign ministers' meeting in Tunis in August, Saud al-Faysal called the Iranians "terrorists." At the same time, Saudi Arabia is believed to have renewed attempts to draw Syria away from Iran by offers of generous financial aid.[58]

Kuwait, meanwhile, was specifically in Velayati's sights when he threatened that Iran would no longer exercise restraint in retaliating against countries supporting Iraq. This merely cemented Kuwait's enmity in return: the emirate positioned itself squarely behind Saudi Arabia over the Mecca tragedy. Bahrain, too, condemned Iran over the events at the Hajj. Yet Qatar remained almost completely silent, while Oman and the UAE continued to try to steer a neutral course. Oman received the Iranian foreign minister in August 1987 and labeled Iran a source of pride for the Gulf (even while supporting Kuwait's right to reflag). Baghdad's irritation with the two countries at this point flared up, the Baath party newspaper criticizing those who were receiving "enemies of the Arabs, . . . Islam . . . and humanity."[59] Oman and the UAE, indeed, were among those most forcefully arguing against a break between the Arab states and Iran at the Arab League foreign ministers' meeting in August. The meeting did, however, issue a stern warning to Iran that Resolution 598 should be accepted.

After an Iranian missile attack on Kuwait from Faw in September, Kuwait expelled five Iranian diplomats, while Bahrain once again openly condemned Iran, calling for international sanctions if Tehran failed to accept Resolution 598. The same month, Saudi Arabia and Iraq signed the contract for the second phase of the IPSA pipeline; on completion this would allow another 1.65 million b/d to be transported from Iraq to the Red Sea. Saudi Arabia and Kuwait are believed to have contributed more than $1 billion in aid during 1987 (one unconfirmed report has Riyadh alone giving another $2 billion grant). Bahrain was now classified by Iran itself as a member of the pro-Iraq camp: the commander of the Revolutionary Guards commented in October that as the island was "U.S.-occupied," it was fair game for attacks on the Americans. The three southern Gulf states persisted in their neutral posture, though. Oman, explicitly calling for even-handedness between Iran and Iraq, was clearly establishing itself as a go-between between Iran on the one hand and the pro-Iraqi camp and the West on the other.[60]

Another milestone was passed when two tankers—one U.S.-flagged—were hit in mid-October in Kuwaiti waters by Iranian missiles, and the United States retaliated by destroying two Iranian oil platforms used by the Revolutionary Guards. The U.S. action was justified by the press in both Kuwait and Saudi Arabia. Iran in turn hit a Kuwaiti oil terminal, which now also kindled Bahraini protest and appears to have been the last straw in the process of swinging large sections of public opinion in the Gulf against Iran. This still was not reflected in official policy in Qatar, the UAE, and Oman, even if they, too, subscribed to the strongly worded statement of the Arab summit in Amman in November 1987. This had condemned Iran and supported Iraq, and even Syria promised to try and persuade Iran to accept a ceasefire—a clear success for Saudi diplomacy. Individually, the three "neutrals" avoided pointing the finger at Iran. Oman's position was perhaps the most striking: stating his desire to maintain good relations with the Islamic Republic as these were "dictated by history and geography," Sultan Qaboos stressed that *both* sides in the war should observe the ceasefire order. When, prior to the GCC summit of late December 1987, Saddam Hussein sent Tariq Aziz and Saadoun Shakir to visit the GCC capitals, Oman was left out.[61]

Pressure from Oman and the UAE (and probably also Qatar) influenced the Summit's decisions: although the leaders noted with regret "Iran's attempt to procrastinate on the implementation" of Resolution 598, and a personal attack by King Fahd on Iran notwithstanding, the Kingdom and Kuwait acquiesced in the desire of the neutral partners to try to keep channels to Iran open and persuade it to accept Resolution 598 after all. To this end, Shaikh Zayed of the UAE was designated to lead the GCC dialogue with Tehran.[62]

Baghdad immediately made clear that such a dialogue was unacceptable except on Iraq's terms, and in January 1988 Izzat Ibrahim, vice-chairman of the Revolutionary Command Council, was sent to Kuwait and Riyadh to try and head off its development. Yet it was not only the three neutrals who were now behind the momentum for dialogue: Bahrain, too, although still wary, favored the principle. Strikingly, even in Kuwait, although the newspapers derided the proposal, the government's position became more pliable. In what was hard to see as anything but a snub to Baghdad's expressed wishes, the Kuwaiti foreign minister said on January 25 that contacts with Tehran had never ceased and that the Kuwaiti embassy in Tehran would be reopened.[63] This would appear to indicate the effects of the interplay between the existence of a pragmatic policy faction in Tehran and the functioning channels of communication maintained by the neutrals in previous months—as well as perhaps a mediating role by Syria. Baghdad's anger was expressed in the state-controlled press, with claims that the GCC governments' overtures to Iran were a flagrant violation of the Amman summit resolutions.[64] The rulers of Oman, Qatar, and the UAE, meanwhile, all made clear their opposition to an arms embargo on Iran.[65] At the same time, though, Oman also maintained its low-profile but effective cooperation with U.S. operations in the Gulf, as would later be confirmed by U.S. Secretary of State George Shultz.[66]

From Military Escalation to Ceasefire: February–August 6, 1988

The war took on a different character again with the escalation of the "War of the Cities" in February 1988. Although Baghdad had always been the more vulnerable, Tehran and Qom, well behind the Zagros mountains, were both hit. The Kuwaiti and Saudi press again supported Iraq, while the other countries were more circumspect. Yet the GCC's assistant secretary-general indicated in March that it was now up to Iran to show there was substance to its proclaimed principle of good-neighborliness.[67] The attack on Bubiyan Island by several Iranian patrol boats at the end of March and the hijacking of a Kuwaiti airliner to Mashhad on April 5 set back the tentative improvement in official relations between Kuwait and Iran—even if neither incident is likely to have been officially sanctioned by Tehran. The Kuwaiti government hoped that these hitches could be overcome, but still, together with Saudi Arabia, accused Tehran of complicity with the hijackers.[68] The visit to Baghdad by

Bahrain's Shaikh Khalifa bin Salman for "supportive" talks in April, illustrated that country's membership in the pro-Iraq camp. Iran itself continued its public relations offensive, however, sending envoys to Oman, Qatar, and the UAE to present them with evidence of Iraq's use of chemical weapons in Halabja.[69]

It was only in mid-April, however, that the gradual escalation in the war reached a decisive turning point. The intensification of the U.S. military confrontation with Iran's forces in the waters of the Gulf more or less coincided with a string of Iraqi military successes on land. In this final phase of the war, Iran experienced mainly reverses, including recapture of Faw on April 18 and the Majnoon islands on June 26. Iran accused Kuwait of having allowed Iraq to use Bubiyan in its recapture of Faw. Although the government denied this, both officialdom and the press hailed the Iraqi success. Saudi praise was equally fulsome.[70] Saudi–Iranian relations, of course, had not undergone the tentative improvement that had been evident in the case of Kuwait. If anything, the combination of Khomeini's feelings about the Al-Saud and months of recriminations over arrangements over the Hajj to Mecca had deepened the rift. In January 1988, the Iranian government had even organized a conference in London calling for the abdication of Saudi sovereignty over Mecca and Medina. The Saudi leadership remained concerned about the activities of Iranian pilgrims—worries that became more acute with fears of the numbers that might be expected. Iranian intransigence over the issue, and the refusal to accept a quota of 45,000 for the 1988 Hajj, proved the trigger for Riyadh's decision to break off diplomatic relations with Tehran on April 26. By contrast, Saddam came to perform the *'Umra* (lesser pilgrimage) on April 19, visiting King Fahd and again offering a ceasefire. The King, in his *'Id al-Fitr* message of May 16, lauded the Iraqi leadership for having successfully withstood the onslaught of "oppression and tyranny."[71]

The Kuwaiti press argued strongly for following the Kingdom's example and breaking off relations with Tehran. The government, however, never appears to have seriously considered this. Oman and the UAE, meanwhile, continued their high-level contacts with Iranian emissaries, showing that their position remained the same.[72] Nevertheless, the GCC foreign ministers' communiqué in the first week of June congratulated Iraq on its military successes, and appealed yet again to Iran to accept Resolution 598. The wording was tempered as usual by the neutrals, although Prince Saud al-Faysal's accompanying remarks were not. Bahrain's minister of defense, Shaikh Hamad bin Khalifa, rather powerfully demonstrated his country's stance by visiting the newly liberated areas of Faw and Shalamche on June 20.

It was argued earlier that perhaps the key determinant of the GCC states' attitudes toward Iran was Iran's attitude to them and to the war. Even when Iran switched to a charm offensive and tried to divide the Six, achieving a good measure of success at least with Oman, the UAE, and Qatar, its unwillingness to sue for peace on realistic terms, and the persistence of mixed messages emerging from Iran's factions, ultimately constrained what the GCC states were willing and able to do. In this sense, a crucial turning point came on June 2, when Hashemi-Rafsanjani, the pragmatic Speaker of the Majlis, was appointed acting commander-in-chief of the armed forces. He immediately stressed the need for Iran to start making friends. This was rightly perceived on the other side of the Gulf as a sign that the pragmatic element in the Iranian leadership was in the ascendant. The move toward a ceasefire was hastened the very next day, when an American warship mistakenly shot down a civilian Iranian aircraft. This incident also provided the excuse for a gradual and still tentative rapprochement with Kuwait and Saudi Arabia. Both the Kuwaiti and Saudi governments expressed their regret for the loss of life, calling at the same time for an end to the war (although the Saudi press still showed little sympathy). Kuwait also extended its condolences to the bereaved, and Iran sent its thanks in return.[73]

The combination of the military, regional, and domestic Iranian trends in evidence during this final phase in the end led to Iran's acceptance of Resolution 598 on July 18, 1988. The reaction in Kuwait, whether by officials, the press or the public at large, was jubilant. The Saudi reaction was somewhat more skeptical, while in Bahrain a cautious optimism prevailed. A message to Tehran from Shaikh Zayed of the UAE spoke of Iran's courage in taking the decision, which was described as a "turning point." Similar reactions were forthcoming from the governments and press in Oman and Qatar.[74]

The Iranian decision had indeed changed the equation, as well as the calculations of the GCC states. Essentially, all of the Six now agreed on the need to bring the war to an end, and none saw any further reason to allow Iraqi reservations to hold up a settlement. It is true that, when Iraq initially dragged its feet over the implementation of a ceasefire and even pushed into Iranian territory again, several newspapers in Kuwait and Saudi Arabia supported the Iraqi position. Yet it is safe to assume that the Saudi and Kuwaiti governments were eager for Iraq to show flexibility and for the outstanding obstacles to be removed. The Saudi denial on August 2 of reports claiming that Riyadh was indeed putting pressure on Baghdad, cannot be taken at face value. Iraq sent its own envoys around the Gulf at the beginning of August to argue its case, but that case was now much weakened. The Saudi information minister was sent to Baghdad on August 4 to argue for the acceptance of Resolution 598 as it stood, and thus an immediate ceasefire. Having decided at least as far back as 1981 that the costs of a continuing situation of war outweighed the benefits, the Saudi leadership could no longer see any convincing reason to continue to bankroll Iraqi military adventures once Iran had sued for peace. Saudi Arabia, through their ambassador in the United States, Prince Bandar, had been closely involved in the UN negotiations before, and consultations now followed between Saddam Hussein and Saud al-Faysal, among others. Saudi Arabia, in other words, played an important part in bringing about Iraq's decision on August 6 to accept the ceasefire, bringing the Iran–Iraq War effectively to an end—even if it would be another two years before Saddam, then embroiled in the invasion of Kuwait, finally agreed to accept Iran's demand of a return to the pre-war status.[75]

From the First to the Third Gulf War

Just as the patterns that characterized wartime relations between the GCC states on the one hand and Iran and Iraq on the other did not spring into being with the start of the war, but had roots going back to the Iranian revolution and the mid-1970s changes in Iraq, so the end of the war did not mean an across-the-board reversal. Some of the patterns that had developed continued after the ceasefire, although others underwent fairly swift change. In the latter case, too, however, the underlying cause was often the persistence of *other* patterns—such as the GCC states' continued wariness of Iraq and specific sources of friction such as the Iraqi–Kuwaiti border dispute.[76]

In the case of Iraq, relations initially appeared to continue their collaborative trend, with, for instance, the completion of the IPSA-2 pipeline through Saudi Arabia, and the signing of a huge water-supply deal with Kuwait. The transhipment function of Kuwait in particular remained very important. One source of friction, however, was the swift restoration or, in some cases, further build-up of the GCC states' relations with Iran: only Saudi Arabia would have to wait until some time after the death of Ayatollah Khomeini to achieve normalization of its relations with the Islamic Republic. For the three "neutrals" this continued an existing trend; but for the other three, too, it was in fact a logical outcome of what had always been an underlying pattern: that of attempting to keep open channels with Tehran, only constrained by the latter's own attitude to the war and to Saudi Arabia. When these factors changed on Iran's part, what was arguably the natural pattern could be restored. This pattern included a persistent measure of wariness of Iraq and a concern, even in the context of improved relations with Baghdad, to find a balancing factor: the Iranian revolution and the Iran–Iraq War had only suppressed this inclination, hence the end of the war and Iran's own changed attitude logically allowed it to reemerge.

The eventual dramatic reversal of relations with Iraq with the 1990–91 Kuwait War interrupted a 15-year pattern of improving relations and apparently growing Iraqi pragmatism in its relations with the region. This surprised most observers as Iraq's own development from 1975 to 1989 had seemed to give the trend a long-term character. It was caused not simply by Baghdad's irritation over the GCC states' own new attitude, but by the intimate interaction between Saddam Hussein's perception of domestic regime insecurity, with a financial crisis, and the persisting old strategic grievance of access to the Gulf: all, in fact, caused or exacerbated by the Iran–Iraq War. Saddam's virtually single-handed decision-making, of course, was also a crucial ingredient. Hence those existing patterns that inclined relations with the GCC states toward conflict would in the end outweigh the other, collaborative ones. The war had failed to restore Iraqi control over the Shatt al-Arab and had further highlighted the importance of access to the Gulf; the old friction with Kuwait over the islands and border question, which was linked to this, had never gone away; and a major financial crisis resulted from both the huge amounts of debt to Kuwait and Saudi Arabia, and the oil policies of the GCC states. Saddam's own sense of his mission, as well as of his political and material needs for survival, then led him into the ill-judged confrontation with Kuwait and, as a consequence, with all of the GCC.

The Iranian revolution, combined with Iraq's political and strategic vulnerabilities and Saddam Hussein's ambitions, had led to the Iran–Iraq War. The Iran–Iraq War, in turn, had a paradoxical effect: again combined with the same factors, it indirectly led to the Kuwait crisis—even if it had temporarily tightened the relationship with the northern Gulf states. The final outcome swept away the extensive links that had gradually been built up with the GCC states in all fields, institutional, political, and economic. Iraq would never have become a wholly trusted partner, let alone a member of the GCC, but, under different leadership, sources of friction could well have been contained, leaving the positive trends to survive. Even after the Kuwait crisis, some earlier links proved susceptible to resuscitation; indeed, Oman, true to its neutral track record, never broke off diplomatic relations with Baghdad, and Qatar subsequently argued for reintegrating Iraq into the region. As already indicated in the first section of this chapter, the GCC states—with the exception of Kuwait—remained an important source of hoped-for support for Iraq in its effort to escape its international shackles, even if such support proved in the end to be of limited effect.

The political arena aside, economic and other functional links between Iraq and the GCC states remained constrained by UN sanctions and, with regard to active membership in the regional Arab and Gulf organizations, by Kuwait's resistance. Yet it was always clear that the practical interests that interaction in the Gulf had served—whether they be in commerce and trade, transhipment, investment, environmental protection, electricity networks, oil policy, or cross-border arrangements in gas and water supplies (not to mention a range of joint functional organizations)—would retain, or regain, a constituency. The change of regime in Baghdad can only bring this closer, provided a semblance of stability is achieved there. Kuwait, whose economic and other functional links with Iraq were extensive prior to the 1990 invasion, would perhaps have the most natural potential, for the same reasons its links with Iraq had developed in the first place.[77] The potential for Kuwaiti companies' involvement in Iraq's medium- and longer-term reconstruction is significant. Even so, events since 1990 are likely to have created certain constraints: chances of reviving the preinvasion deal to supply the emirate with water from the Shatt al-Arab will probably suffer from Kuwait's reluctance to become reliant on Iraq for so vital a resource, while Iraq's role, since 1986, as supplier of much of Kuwait's non-associated gas has meanwhile been taken over by Qatar. Saudi firms, too, stand to benefit from participation in Iraq's economic regeneration, as do the financial and services hubs of Dubai and Bahrain, and the UAE's transhipment sector. In the medium to longer term, in addition to cooperation over oil policy within OPEC and OAPEC, the question of Iraq's secure oil exports may bring a return to use of the IPSA line across Saudi Arabia, and perhaps even the once and possibly future mooted strategic Gulf oil pipeline (both conceived of in the context of the Iran–Iraq War).

The key functional (and indeed political) point of friction, on the other hand, will remain that of Iraq's access to the Gulf, which almost inevitably pits the country against Kuwait—especially since the 1992–93 UN boundary demarcation had the effect of further reducing Iraq's control: on land, the return from the *de facto* to the legal border led to the loss of part of Umm Qasr, while the maritime boundary left much of the main navigation channel long maintained by Iraq in the Khawr Abdallah, in Kuwaiti hands.[78] Apart from strategic considerations, this issue is also likely to retain its nationalist resonance in Iraqi politics, regardless of the regime in power.

The GCC states, two wars later, will continue their policies of pragmatic omnibalancing, warily eyeing the two neighboring giants. They will be eager to pursue good working relationships where possible, while conscious of the persistence of the political uncertainties in both Iran and Iraq, and the geopolitical issues still affecting Iraq, that could once again bring conflict. One medium-term result of the Iran–Iraq War, then, first illustrated in the Kuwaiti reflagging operation, was the turn toward bilateral protection arrangements with Western powers. This, too, however, has now run up against domestic vulnerabilities at least in Saudi Arabia—vulnerabilities which, through the 1990–91 Gulf War that brought them (and Osama bin Ladin) to the fore, arguably are one more indirect consequence of the Iran–Iraq War.

Notes

1. This variance in policy among the six states toward the conflict receives remarkably little attention in two earlier treatments of their role and attitudes during the war: Ursula Braun, "The Gulf Cooperation Council," in *The Gulf War: Regional and International Dimensions*, ed. Hanns Maull and Otto Pick (New York: St. Martin's Press, 1989), pp. 90–102; and Barry Rubin, "The Gulf States and the Iran-Iraq War," in *The Iran-Iraq War: Impact and Implications*, ed. Efraim Karsh (London: Macmillan, 1989), pp. 121–32.

2. See Raad Alkadiri's lucid analysis, "Iraq and the Gulf since 1991: The Search for Deliverance," in *Security in the Persian Gulf: Origins, Obstacles, and the Search for Consensus*, ed. Lawrence G. Potter and Gary S. Sick (New York: Palgrave, 2002), pp. 253–73.

3. Lori Plotkin, "Kuwait, 1979–1991: Problems and Policies for Internal Security" (D.Phil. Thesis, St Antony's College, University of Oxford, 2003).

4. William Quandt, *Saudi Arabia in the 1980s* (Washington: The Brookings Institution, 1981). Over two decades later, this assessment has remained pertinent.

5. A term coined by Steven David, in "Explaining Third World Alignment," in *World Politics*, vol. 43, no. 2 (1991), pp. 233–56.

6. For a more extensive treatment of the policies of the Six toward Iran (and vice-versa), see Gerd Nonneman, "The GCC and the Islamic Republic: toward a restoration of the pattern?" in *Iran and the International Community*, ed. Anoushiravan Ehteshami (London: Routledge, 1991), pp. 102–23.

7. *Waqa'i' al-mu'tamar al-suhufi li-l-ra'is Saddam Hussain ma'a-l-suhufiyin al-Masriyin fi 20-7-85* [Documents of the Press Conference of President Saddam Hussein with the Egyptian Press on 20 July 1985] (London: Iraqi Embassy, 1985), pp. 17–18.

8. On Saddam's view of Iraq's role in the Gulf and the Arab world, see Shahram Chubin and Charles Tripp, *Iran and Iraq at War* (London: I.B. Tauris, 1988), p. 140.

9. *Al-taqrir al-markazi li-l-mu'tamar al-qutri al-tasi' haziran 1982* (Baghdad: Dar-al-'Arabiya, 1983), pp. 355–58; and Saddam Hussein, *On Social and Foreign Affairs in Iraq* (London: Croom Helm, 1979), pp. 73–87; Marion Farouk-Sluglett and Peter Sluglett, *Iraq since 1958* (London: KPI, 1988), p. 204.

10. Ahmad Yusuf Ahmad, "The Dialectics of Domestic Environment and Role Performance: The Foreign Policy of Iraq," in *The Foreign Policies of Arab States*, ed. Bahgat Korany and Ali Dessouki (Boulder: Westview, 1984), p. 159.

11. Robert Springborg, "Infitah, Agrarian Transformation, and Elite Consolidation," in *The Middle East Journal*, vol. 40 (1986), pp. 38–51; Isam al-Khafaji, "State incubation of Iraqi Capitalism," in *MERIP Report*, no. 142 (September 1986), pp. 8–9.

12. For the full text, see Anoushiravan Ehteshami and Gerd Nonneman, *War and Peace in the Gulf* (Reading: Ithaca Press, 1991), pp. 152–54.

13. See for example, the statement by Khomeini reproduced in *Foreign Broadcast Information Service*, NES-80, March 24, 1980; and by Bani-Sadr, quoted in *Al-Ra'y al-'Aamm* (Kuwait), March 15, 1980. On Iran and Saudi Arabia, see Khalid bin Ibrahim Al-Ali, "The Domestic

and Regional Determinants of Saudi Foreign Policy in the Gulf Region, 1971–1991," Ph.D. thesis, University of Exeter, 1997; and Saleh al-Mani, "The Ideological Dimensions in Saudi-Iranian Relations," in *Iran and the Gulf*, ed. Jamal al-Suwaidi (Abu Dhabi: Emirates Centre for Strategic Studies and Research, 1996), pp. 158–74.

14. Naomi Sakr, "Economic Relations between Iraq and the other Arab Gulf states," in *Iraq: The Contemporary State*, ed. Tim Niblock (London: Croom Helm, 1982), pp. 150–67.

15. *An-Nahar Arab Report & MEMO,* February 11, 1980.

16. Gerd Nonneman, *Iraq, The Gulf States and the War, 1980–1986 and Beyond* (London: Ithaca Press, 1986), p. 14; BBC *Summary of World Broadcasts*, Middle East [henceforth *SWB* ME], February 8, 1980.

17. *Middle East Economic Survey [MEES],* May 19, 1980, p. 6.

18. For a comprehensive list of exchanges and visits between Iraq and the Gulf states, see Nonneman, *Iraq,* Appendix III.

19. SWB ME, May 28, 1980; *Baghdad Observer,* May 28, 1980; *Al-Khalij,* May 31, 1980.

20. *Middle East Economic Digest [MEED],* July 4, 1980, p. 23; *SWB,* ME/6515/a/2, September 5, 1980; *Arab Times,* May 8, 1980; *Emirates News,* June 3, 1980.

21. *MEES,* August 18, 1980.

22. Nonneman, *Iraq,* pp. 22–23.

23. *Gulf News Agency* dispatch, September 20, 1980.

24. Indeed, Gary Sick reports that "Arab sources who were in contact with the Iraqi leadership in the first days of the war claimed privately that Iraq's war strategy was consciously modeled on Israel's six-day campaign in 1967." (Gary Sick, "Trial by Error: Reflections on the Iran-Iraq War," in *Middle East Journal,* vol. 43, no. 2 (spring 1989), footnote 8, p. 235.)

25. Sakr, "Economic Relations between Iraq and the other Arab Gulf states"; also Nonneman, *Iraq,* pp. 23–24.

26. Anthony Cordesman, *The Gulf and the Search for Strategic Stability* (Boulder: Westview, 1984), pp. 417, 419; Nonneman, *Iraq,* chapter II.

27. *Strategy Week,* October 20, 1980, p. 6; Cordesman, *The Gulf and the Search for Strategic Stability,* p. 397; *MEED,* November 21, 1980, p. 7; Dilip Hiro, *The Longest War* (London: Grafton, 1989, pp. 77–78). If the report about the helicopters and troops is correct, that need not mean their presence had always been for the purpose of the islands operation: some more general Iraqi military cooperation with the Sultanate had already been offered prior to the war as part of the general rapprochement between the two states in 1980. Even so, they would have been available for the purpose unless stopped by the Omani government.

28. Economist Intelligence Unit (EIU) *Quarterly Economic Report for Saudi Arabia,* 1980 no. 4, p. 4; *Time Magazine,* October 13, 1980, p. 16; Mark Heller, "The Iran-Iraq War: Implications for Third Parties," *JCSS Paper* no. 23 (Tel Aviv: Jaffee Center for Strategic Studies, January 1984); Nadav Safran, *Saudi Arabia: The Ceaseless Quest for Security* (Cambridge: Harvard University Press, 1985), p. 368.

29. *EIU Quarterly Economic Report for Saudi Arabia,* 1980, no. 4, p. 4; *Time Magazine,* October 13, 1980, p. 16; *MEED,* October 10, 1980, p. 37; October 17, p. 17; and November 21, 1980, p. 7; Cordesman, *The Gulf,* pp. 588 and 605.

30. For more detailed consideration on these financial flows see Nonneman, *Iraq,* pp. 95–96.

31. Plotkin, "Kuwait, 1979–1991."

32. *Al-Watan al-Arabi,* February 13, 1981; *Emirates News,* July 5, 1981; *Arabia,* 1981, no. 1, p. 29. See also Al-Ali, "The Domestic and Regional Determinants of Saudi Foreign Policy," pp. 143ff.

33. For details see Nonneman, *Iraq,* pp. 40–42.

34. A more detailed account can be found in ibid., chapter 4.
35. *MEES*, June 7, 1982, p. 13; Al-Ali, "The Domestic and Regional Determinants of Saudi Foreign Policy," p. 147; Frauke Heard-Bey, *Die Arabische Golfstaaten im Zeichen der islamischen Revolution*, Arbeitspapiere zur internationalen Politik, no. 25. (Bonn: Forschungsinstitut der deutschen Gesellschaft für auswärtige Politik, 1983), pp. 187–88.
36. Nonneman, *Iraq*, pp. 96–97 and 103.
37. For a more detailed treatment and sources see Nonneman, *Iraq*, chapter V and p. 103. See also *MEES*, February 13, 1989.
38. Chubin and Tripp, *Iran and Iraq at War*, p. 153.
39. See also ibid., pp. 154–55.
40. Plotkin, "Kuwait, 1979–1991," pp. 137ff, 169, 181, and 189.
41. Ibid., pp. 193–94.
42. See Al-Ali, "The Domestic and Regional Determinants of Saudi Foreign Policy," p. 150; *SWB*, ME, December 10–12, 1985, MEED, December 14, 1985; Hiro, *The Longest War*, pp. 153–54; Nonneman, *Iraq*, Chapter VI; and Chubin and Tripp, *Iran and Iraq at War*, pp. 167ff.
43. Sick, "Trial by Error," p. 237; and Hiro, *The Longest War*, pp. 153–55.
44. *SWB, ME*, July 18, 1985.
45. *Le Monde*, August 20, 1987.
46. Mordechai Abir, *Saudi Arabia: Government, Society and the Gulf Crisis* (London: Routledge, 1993), p. 131.
47. Rubin, "The Gulf States and the Iran-Iraq War," p. 127.
48. Al-Ali, "The Domestic and Regional Determinants of Saudi Foreign Policy," p. 182; Anoushiravan Ehteshami "Wheels within Wheels: Iran's Foreign Policy Towards the Arab World," in *Reconstruction and Regional Diplomacy in the Persian Gulf*, ed. Hooshang Amirahmadi and Nader Entessar (London: Routledge, 1992), pp. 155–92; and Nonneman, *Iraq*, pp. 74–76.
49. For more elaboration see Nonneman, *Iraq*, pp. 102–04.
50. Abdul-Reda Assiri, *Kuwait's Foreign Policy: City-State in World Politics* (Boulder, Colo: Westview, 1990), p. 102; Plotkin, "Kuwait, 1979–1991," p. 192; *MidEast Mirror*, July 20, 1987; Abir, *Saudi Arabia*, p. 127. For a chronology of the reflagging saga, see Mohamed Heikal, *Illusions of Triumph* (London: HarperCollins, 1993), pp. 100–03. See also Hiro, *The Longest War*, p. 224; Rubin, "The Gulf States and the Iran-Iraq War," p. 128.
51. See Chubin and Tripp, *Iran and Iraq at War*, p. 155; Hiro, *The Longest War*, p. 213. A detailed account of reactions and stances taken up to March 1986 can be found in Nonneman, *Iraq*, Chapter VII. The full text of the communiqué can be found in ibid., Appendix VII, pp. 197–98.
52. Anthony Cordesman, *The Iran-Iraq War and Western Security* (London: Jane's, 1987), p. 109; Fred Axelgard, *A New Iraq?* (New York: Praeger, 1988), p. 75; *MEED*, September 13, 1986.
53. *MEED*, November 29, 1986 and March 21, 1987; *The Guardian*, December 18, 1986; *Financial Times*, March 12, 1987; Cordesman, *The Iran-Iraq War*, p. 125.
54. *The Times*, April 14, 1987; *De Standaard* (Belgium), April 21, 1987.
55. *MidEast Mirror*, May 11, May 18, and June 1, *1987*; *MEES*, May 25, 1987; EIU, *Country Report: Bahrain, Qatar, Oman and the Yemens*, 1987 no. 3, p. 9.
56. *MidEast Mirror*, August 3, 1987.
57. See Sick, "Trial by Error," pp. 240–41.
58. *MidEast Mirror*, August 24 and 25, 1987; *Financial Times*, August 23, 26, and 28, 1987; EIU *Country Report, Bahrain*, 1987, no. 4, p. 19.

59. *Al-Thawra*, August 19, 1987; *Financial Times*, August 3 and 28, 1987; *Sunday Times*, August 30, 1987; *MidEast Mirror*, July 29 and August 21, 1987; IRNA and KUNA dispatches of August 10, 1987.

60. *MidEast Mirror*, October 15, 1987; *Kuwait Times*, October 3, 1987; EIU *Country Report: Bahrain*, 1987, no. 4, p. 19.

61. EIU *Country Report: Bahrain* . . ., 1988, no. 1, p. 18; Abir, *Saudi Arabia*, pp. 139–40.

62. Ibid., pp. 12, 18; *MidEast Mirror*, December 29, 1987; George Joffé and Keith McLachlan, *Iran and Iraq: Building on the Stalemate*, EIU Special Report No. 1164 (London: EIU, 1988), p. 15.

63. *MidEast Mirror*, January 7, 15, and 18, 1988; EIU *Country Report: Bahrain* . . ., 1988, no. 2, p. 10.

64. *Al-Jumhuriya* (Baghdad), January 19, 1988; *Baghdad Observer*, January 29, 1988.

65. Thomas McNaugher, "Walking Tightropes in the Gulf," in Karsh, *The Iran-Iraq War*, pp. 171–99, see especially p. 185.

66. EIU *Country Report: Bahrain* . . ., 1988, no. 2, p. 18.

67. *MidEast Mirror*, March 3 and 16, 1988; *Al-Sharq al-Awsat*, March 8, 1988; *Al-Musawwar* (Cairo), March 10, 1988.

68. *Riyadh Daily*, April 13, 1988; *MidEast Mirror*, April 11, 1988.

69. *MidEast Mirror*, April 13, 1988.

70. See *MidEast Mirror*, April 18–20, 1988.

71. al-Mani, "The Ideological Dimensions in Saudi-Iranian Relations," especially p. 166; *MidEast Mirror*, April 21, 1988; *Financial Times*, April 28, 1988; SPA dispatches and the Saudi Press on May 16, 1988.

72. *MidEast Mirror*, April 29, May 3 and 23, 1988; *Khaleej Times* (UAE), May 23, 1988.

73. *Al-Sharq al-Awsat*, July 5–6, 1988; *MidEast Mirror*, July 5, 1988.

74. See *MidEast Mirror*, July 19–20, 1988.

75. *Al-Qabas*, July 26, 1988; *Al-Ra'y al-'Aamm*, July 26, 1988; *Kuwait Times*, July 26, 1988; *Al-Sharq al-Awsat*, July 27, 1988; *MidEast Mirror*, August 1–4 and 8, 1988; *The Observer*, August 7, 1988. It should be noted that there is some debate over whether Saddam's letter to Rafsanjani of August 14, 1990 really was meant as a genuine acceptance of the full prewar status—even if Tehran chose to interpret it as such: see Shaul Bakhash, "Iran: War Ended, Hostility Continued," in *Iraq's Road to War*, ed. Amatzia Baram and Barry Rubin, (New York: St. Martin's Press, 1993), pp. 219–31.

76. For a detailed account of Iraq–GCC–Iran relations in the interwar period, and the lead-up to the Kuwait Crisis, see Ehteshami and Nonneman, *War and Peace in the Gulf*, pp. 57–76.

77. For a comprehensive review of Kuwaiti–Iraqi functional interests and relations since the 1970s, see my "The (Geo)Political Economy of Iraqi-Kuwaiti Relations," in *Geopolitics*, vol. 1, no. 2 (autumn 1996), pp. 178–223.

78. Richard Schofield, *Kuwait and Iraq: Historical Claims and Territorial Disputes*, 2nd ed. (London: The Royal Institute of International Affairs, 1993), pp. 150–98.

Chapter 9

The U.S. Role: Helpful or Harmful?

Rosemary Hollis

For the past 50 years, Iran and Iraq have been regarded and dealt with as elements in a wider U.S. agenda. A summary of the milestones in bilateral relations will serve to underline the ways ties with the United States influenced both parties and by extension their relations with each other. Some observations can then be made about how the United States has itself made a connection between Iraq and Iran and treated them as a pair—either by deliberately playing off one against the other, as during the Iran–Iraq War, or by lumping the two together under "dual containment" in the 1990s and on a so-called axis of evil depicted by President George W. Bush in January 2002. A year later, the U.S. intervention in Iraq was portrayed as the first step in a regional democratization strategy that would oblige Iran to change too.

Some consideration will also be given here to the existence of different schools of thought within the U.S. administration and political system. In disarray after the fall of the shah and the hostage crisis, the old Iran hands lost ascendancy in the 1980s, giving more prominence to the so-called Arabists and others who depicted Baghdad as a potential vassal in place of Iran. Conceivably, the disillusion that struck this camp after the Iraqi invasion of Kuwait opened the way for a general sense of disenchantment, or "a plague on both your houses," to prevail in the 1990s. The ascendance of the so-called neo-conservatives was then instrumental in the decision to intervene militarily in Iraq.

Certain themes have been recurrent or consistent in U.S. policy toward the Persian Gulf region since the 1950s. Access to oil and security of supplies, at prices acceptable to American consumers *and* producers, are constants among articulated U.S. interests. Concern to protect, consult, and periodically coordinate action with Israel has been a subtheme to U.S. Gulf policy. In the 1970s Iraq was perceived as an enemy of Israel and listed as a state sponsor of terrorism, principally for its support for Palestinian groups. At the time, Israeli intelligence was quietly coordinating with the Iranian secret service. In the 1980s, however, divisions within Israeli intelligence and political circles apparently mirrored those in the United States, over whether to court Baghdad or revive old links with Tehran. In any case, Israeli fears of Iraqi and Iranian nuclear ambitions predated the more recent U.S. preoccupation with the problem of nuclear proliferation.

Most notably, the idea of "regime change" has figured in U.S. dealings with both Iran and Iraq over time. In 1953, U.S. involvement in the overthrow of the government of Dr. Mohammad Mosaddeq and reinstallation of the shah set the scene for the U.S.–Iran relationship thereafter. Claims that the Central Intelligence Agency (CIA) was also behind the Iraqi coup of 1963 remain unsubstantiated, though not disproved, while the overthrow of the Iraqi regime of Saddam Hussein became an official U.S. objective in 2002, if not before. While oil interests still feature in U.S. calculations today as they did in the 1950s, the other leading determinant of U.S. policy in times past—fear of Soviet expansion—has disappeared. Instead, combating terrorism and proliferation have taken center stage, especially in the wake of the attacks on the World Trade Center and the Pentagon on September 11, 2001.

Disarming Iraq, toppling Saddam's Baathist regime and remaking the Iraqi polity then became the centerpiece of the U.S. war on terrorism, even though no direct links were proven between that regime and the Al Qaeda network responsible for 9/11. In the wake of the invasion of Iraq in 2003, relations between the United States and Iran were tense amid fears that Tehran would interfere. Yet the U.S. commitment to democracy in Iraq promises more political power for the majority Shi'i community and Iran has much at stake in the outcome.

The Cold War and Containment: From Truman to Nixon

In the decades following World War II, the Cold War provided the context in which the United States evaluated the potential threats to its interests in the Persian Gulf as elsewhere. Containment of the Soviet Union and combating the spread of communism were central objectives.

The theoretical construct or policy doctrine that underpinned U.S. thinking about both Iraq and Iran in the 1950s derived from the Truman Doctrine,[1] which established the basis for U.S. assistance to Greece and Turkey, and bolstered their governments against the potential rise of communism in southeastern Europe. By extension, Turkey, Iraq, and Iran were depicted as the bulwark or buffer between the Middle East and the Soviet Union. These Northern Tier states were therefore to be courted and assisted to deny the Soviets access to the vital energy resources and communications routes they commanded. It was President Truman who pressured the Soviet Union to withdraw its troops from Iran at the end of World War II and, as the ability of Britain to maintain its predominance in the area waned, the United States began to fill the breach.

There was little sympathy in Washington for the ambitions of the old colonial powers, Britain and France, to hold on to their dominance in the Middle East and North Africa. Indeed, both Arab and Iranian nationalists looked to the Americans for support and inspiration in their struggle to shake off the residual influence of the old imperialists. However, U.S. sympathy for nationalist aspirations was tempered by wariness of real and potential links developing between the Soviets and indigenous socialist and communist movements. Certainly these fears were a factor in U.S.

calculations about whether to intervene or not in the struggle between the shah and the Mosaddeq government in the early 1950s. Oil interests also featured in its decision to effect a reversal of Mosaddeq's nationalization of the Anglo-Iranian Oil Company (AIOC).[2]

As explained by James Bill in his seminal work on American–Iranian relations:

> Many knowledgeable analysts believe that Musaddiq was used as an American wedge to break the AIOC's monopolistic grip on Iran's oil resources. According to Mustafa Fateh, the best-informed Iranian oil economist long employed by the AIOC, there is no doubt that American and British oil interests reached an entente on this issue. In exchange for American support in overthrowing the Musaddiq government, the British grudgingly permitted U.S. companies a 40 percent interest in Iranian oil. Fateh pointed out that American companies had made several attempts to penetrate the Iranian fields but had failed until the appearance of Musaddiq.[3]

The American response to internal developments in Iraq during the 1950s demonstrated a similar concern to see communist elements and Soviet influence contained, but showed no particular regard for protecting British special interests per se. The United States was supportive of the Baghdad Pact, a defense agreement initiated between Iraq and Turkey in 1955 and joined by Iran and Pakistan later the same year. However, unlike Britain, the United States did not formally join the Pact.[4] When the British-installed monarchy of Iraq was overthrown in the coup of 1958, the Americans did not come to its rescue. Instead they limited themselves to sending troops to bolster the government in Lebanon against pan-Arab nationalist dissent, while the British performed a similar function in Jordan.

During the factional strife that characterized the tenure of Iraq's first republican prime minister, General 'Abd al-Karim Qasim, the Iraqi Communist Party (ICP) was a prominent player. Qasim took Iraq out of the Baghdad Pact and courted the Soviet Union, in the interests of obtaining arms and support, rather than out of ideological empathy. As described by historian Charles Tripp:

> The USSR had been much encouraged by the overthrow of the monarchy and the establishment of the republic. The newly tolerated activities of the ICP promised the development of a significant communist force in the politics of an important Middle East state. Equally, the withdrawal of Iraq from the Baghdad Pact was clearly a strategic gain in that it abruptly ended any possibility of the British returning to use the air bases they had handed over to Iraqi control. However, it seems improbable that the Soviet leadership had many illusions about the leanings of the new regime—unlike many in the West and in the region whose Cold War preoccupations led them to overestimate the degree of communist and Soviet influence on Qasim.[5]

His withdrawal from the Pact and rapport with Moscow put Qasim's regime on a confrontation course with the shah's Iran. They squabbled over access to the Shatt al-Arab waterway, and, in the name of a specifically Iraqi brand of Arab nationalism, Baghdad chose to rename the Persian Gulf the Arabian Gulf. It also redesignated Iran's southwestern province of Khuzistan as Arabistan, the name it was known by until changed by Reza Shah in the 1920s. One of the strategies adopted by the shah to counter Iraqi assertiveness (which included laying claim to Kuwait in 1961) was to establish links with the Iraqi Kurdish leader Mulla Mustafa Barzani.

As it turned out, Qasim was himself toppled in 1963, by a combination of Arab nationalists and Baathists (including the future president of Iraq, Saddam Hussein). Whether the CIA knew such a coup was brewing seems certain. That it had U.S. encouragement is not unlikely,[6] though according to Iraqis directly involved at the time, it would be going too far to attribute a significant role to the CIA in the toppling of Qasim.

While America's main Cold War preoccupations lay beyond the Middle East, the eruption of the Arab–Israeli war of June 1967 captured world attention and saw the superpowers ranged on opposite sides. It was from this point that the United States became the primary supplier of arms to Israel, and the quest to resolve its conflict with the Arabs became central to United States regional policy.[7] Taking a negative view of its stance, Baghdad broke off diplomatic relations with Washington.

Meanwhile, close on the heels of the 1967 war came Britain's announcement of its intention to withdraw from East of Suez. This decision, initially floated in January 1968 and actually implemented in 1971, spelled the end of Britain's role as principal guarantor of freedom of navigation (and thus access to energy supplies) in the Persian Gulf waters. In Washington there was a perception that Britain's move would create a vacuum in the region, which the Soviets might seek to fill.[8] Given U.S. commitments in Indochina and reluctance to become similarly embroiled in any other region, the Nixon administration came up with a new doctrine that called on nations around the world to assume primary responsibility for their own defense. Crucially, the shah was given *carte blanche* to acquire whatever U.S. weapons systems he wanted, short of nuclear weapons.[9]

Officially a twin pillar policy of arming both Iran and Saudi Arabia was supposed to provide a balanced approach to regional defense and security. In practice, this meant relying on the shah to act as Gulf policeman and on the Saudis to maintain the flow of oil. This was the era of nationalization of oil production across the Middle East and North Africa, and the importance and power of Gulf oil producers was underlined by the oil embargo instituted by members of the Organization of Petroleum Exporting Countries (OPEC) to support the Arab cause in the 1973 war with Israel. The blow delivered to the developed economies by the interruption in oil flows and the resulting price hike has never been forgotten.

The shah won plaudits for keeping supplies flowing during the 1973 crisis and he was apparently more than happy to assume the regional hegemon role assigned him. Increased oil revenues, thanks to higher prices, gave him the purchasing power to arm for the task. For their part the Iraqi Baathists, who displaced their nationalist rivals at the center of power in 1968, saw the British withdrawal from the Gulf as a scheme to further U.S. "imperialist" designs on the region, in league with the "reactionary" Saudis and the shah.[10] Iraq's goal, therefore, was to arm itself to carry out its "legitimate role" as principal protector of Arab interests in the area.

The outcome was a furious, expensive, and ultimately destabilizing arms race between Iran and Iraq.[11] In retrospect it is apparent that the policy of making the shah surrogate guardian of U.S. interests in the Gulf backfired badly insofar as it helped fuel the forces of revolution against the Pahlavi dynasty and identified the United States with the shah's overweening ambitions and profligate spending.

The "Second Cold War" and Intervention: Carter Doctrine and Reagan Delivery

Under President Jimmy Carter, Washington's initial preoccupations were with strategic arms talks and Arab–Israeli peace-making. No one in the administration was prepared for the unraveling of the shah's regime that overtook them in 1978.[12] Years of overreliance on the shah as regional policeman meant that Washington was also ill-equipped to counter the entry of Soviet forces into Afghanistan in December 1979. That event, on the heels of the Iranian revolution, led President Carter to articulate his doctrine of direct response to any specific threat to U.S. interests in the Persian Gulf region.[13] It was left to his successors to build the capability sufficient to fulfil his vision. Carter himself ended his presidency under the cloud of the hostage crisis in Iran.[14]

When President Ronald Reagan, the fortunate beneficiary of the eventual release of the U.S. hostages, took office in 1980,[15] he was relieved of the need to focus specifically on Iran and preferred in any case to concentrate on the strategic threat that Moscow represented in his thinking. The result was what Fred Halliday has called the Second Cold War.[16] Reagan dubbed the Soviet Union "the Evil Empire" and initiated the idea of a strategic air defense, popularly known as "Star Wars," which if realized would have undermined East–West arms control agreements and deterrence doctrine (as it has done latterly under President George W. Bush). In Latin America, the Reagan world-view translated into U.S. support for dubious regimes fighting left-wing insurgencies, or in the case of Nicaragua, aid to the Contra rebels in opposition to a left-wing government. On the Afghan front it meant arming, training, and generally encouraging the insurgency against Soviet rule mounted by the Afghan *mujahedin* along with their Muslim recruits from across the Arab world and Pakistan.

To counter the buildup of Soviet naval forces in the Indian Ocean, facilities leased from Britain in Diego Garcia were turned into a major staging post for the U.S. navy.[17] Reagan also turned Carter's putative Rapid Reaction Force into a Rapid Deployment and Joint Task Force (RDJTF) that became the U.S. Central Command (CENTCOM) responsible for the Persian Gulf region, Pakistan (and latterly Central Asia), the Arabian Peninsula, Jordan, Egypt, and the Horn of Africa. Reagan also issued a public commitment to the defense of Saudi Arabia, and pushed through the sale of AWACs (Airborne Warning and Control System) planes to the Kingdom, despite Congressional objections.

The immediate reaction of the United States to the Iran–Iraq War, launched by Baghdad in 1980, had less to do with the protagonists themselves than with anxieties about oil prices and supplies, and fears that the Soviets might be able to exploit the situation to extend their reach into the Gulf. Once it became clear that an initial oil price spike had subsided, the U.S. posture toward the war settled into one of "negligent neutrality."[18] Witnessing the success of Iran's counteroffensive in 1982, however, Washington reappraised the potential dangers. An Iranian victory was not considered desirable, not least because of fears of a radical Islamist spillover effect in Saudi Arabia. By 1983, therefore, a U.S. "tilt" toward Iraq was underway.[19]

As a prelude to the reestablishment of diplomatic relations with Baghdad in 1984, $2 billion worth of U.S. commodity credits was made available to Iraq, trade picked up, including the sale of helicopters to Baghdad, and the Arab Gulf states were encouraged to extend financial support.[20] Writing in 1984, military analyst Anthony Cordesman described the situation in terms of a "stable stalemate" between Iraq and Iran, with neither side capable of decisive victory.[21] In any case, Washington channeled intelligence information to Baghdad that helped the Iraqi war effort.[22] A formal U.S. rebuke for its use of chemical weapons against the Iranians was ameliorated by diplomatic reassurances.[23] Meanwhile, in contrast to Iran, Iraq was kept well supplied with arms, principally by France and the Soviet Union, to which Washington turned a blind eye, while maintaining its official advocacy of an embargo on arms sales to both.[24]

In effect, by 1986 Washington was more focused on the issue of regional stability than the Soviet threat writ large, although instability was seen as a potential opening for the latter. A further shift in the U.S. posture on the war came in 1987. By then the tanker war, previously tolerable, was threatening to seriously disrupt traffic in the Gulf. In addition, Kuwait petitioned Washington for protection for its tankers through reflagging or transferring them to U.S. registry. That Washington eventually conceded to the Kuwaiti request was no doubt influenced by the fact that the emirate also approached the Soviets with the same scheme and they were amenable. In March 1987 Washington informed Kuwait of its willingness to protect not only the tankers for which they had sought U.S. protection but those that the Soviets had undertaken to reflag as well.

The direct involvement of the U.S. Navy (and Air Force) in protecting tanker traffic in the Persian Gulf in the final stage of the Iran–Iraq War gave Baghdad the international intervention it had been seeking since the early 1980s. The result, as hoped for by Baghdad, was active superpower engagement to bring the war to a close on terms previously resisted by Iran. At the time, various military analysts in Washington argued that Iraq had retrieved its position on the battlefield and had come out of the conflict with its "honor" intact. In fact, as was revealed subsequently, U.S. intervention and support over time were essential to averting an Iraqi defeat.

U.S. arms supplies to Iran, under the secret "Iran-Contra" or "arms-for-hostages" scheme, which came to light in November 1986, did not fundamentally affect the course of the war.[25] (After Iran received two shipments of arms via the Israelis, American hostage James Weir was released from captivity in Lebanon.) In policy terms, also, this episode can be considered an exception or, as then-Secretary of Defense Casper Weinberger later dubbed it, an "aberration"[26] rather than a central component of U.S. strategy. However, it was illustrative of a cavalier attitude among some elements in the Reagan administration toward serious regional conflicts (whether in Lebanon, the Gulf, or Central America), with scant regard for the implications of their actions. As then-Secretary of State George Shultz says he saw it at the time:

> We have assaulted our own Middle East policy. The Arabs counted on the U.S. to play a strong and responsible role to contain and eventually bring the war to an end. Now

we are seen to be aiding the most radical forces in the region. We have acted directly counter to our own major effort to dry up the war by denying the weapons needed to continue it.[27]

Shultz himself had been kept out of the picture because he was identified with those in favor of the tilt to Iraq and opposed to a rapprochement with Iran.

The Iran-Contra affair deserves mention in two other respects. On the one hand, it left the Iranians with the impression that Washington was more than capable of double-dealing and subterfuge if it suited its purposes. On the other hand, it left the Americans with an aversion to secret talks with Iranian government officials, for whatever purposes. The net result has been to limit the use of quiet diplomacy as a way of improving bilateral relations in the post-Khomeini era.

The End of the Cold War and the Second Gulf War

The new team that took over the U.S. administration in 1989 under President George Bush was quickly overtaken by momentous events. Close on the heels of the Soviet withdrawal from Afghanistan at the beginning of 1989, which was greeted as a victory in Washington, came the knock-on effects of the policy of *glasnost* and *perestroika* not only within the Soviet Union but in Central Europe too. The collapse of pro-Soviet regimes in its former satellite states, the dismantling of the Berlin Wall and the demise of President Ceausescu of Romania brought the Cold War to an end, and once underway, it came at breathtaking speed.

Relations with Iraq or Iran were not policy priorities in Washington. At the official level, in summer 1989 the prevailing view was that Iraq was easier to deal with than Iran and Baghdad should be "constructively engaged" to bring Saddam Hussein around to supporting U.S. policy initiatives elsewhere,[28] notably on the Arab–Israeli front. In official circles in Israel in summer 1989 there were some prepared to entertain the possibility of a peace deal with Iraq. Thus, in the brief interlude between the end of the Iran–Iraq War and Iraq's invasion of Kuwait in August 1990, there was no new strategic thinking[29] and the tilt toward Iraq in U.S. policy in the Persian Gulf region basically continued. Concerns raised by some detractors about the Iraqi human rights record, weapons of mass destruction, and the ambitions of Saddam Hussein did not make an impact.

After the initial shock and near-universal international condemnation of the Iraqi invasion of Kuwait, it took some time for the Bush administration to prepare the ground for war. However, by fall 1990 Washington was already describing the crisis as the first major test of the post–Cold War era. Moscow's ability to play a significant role in dealing with the crisis was minimal. The United Nations Security Council was brought into play to impose blanket sanctions and to sanctify the use of force to oust Iraqi forces from Kuwait. Thereafter it was sidelined until ceasefire terms were needed. In retrospect it is clear that the massive military buildup of U.S. and allied forces in Saudi Arabia in preparation for war laid the ground for the transformation in U.S.–Saudi relations that was made manifest over a decade later. At the time it meant that by late 1990 there was probably no going back on the war plan.

The war did indeed take place and Iraq was fundamentally weakened as a result. The fact that President Bush decided to halt the allied advance short of either destroying the Iraqi elite forces or marching on Baghdad to confront, if not topple, Saddam Hussein, left the Iraqi president to regroup and defy U.S. hopes that he would be ousted by a coup. The idea later took hold that the war was left unfinished. At the time, however, George Bush senior pronounced the advent of "a new world order" and laid out his vision for the region.[30]

Bush foresaw a collective effort "to create shared security arrangements in the region," with primary responsibility resting with the Middle Eastern states themselves. Action would have to be taken to control the proliferation of weapons of mass destruction (WMD) and the missiles used to deliver them. Iraq, in particular, "must not have access to the instruments of war." The time had come, he believed, to put an end to the Arab–Israeli conflict, in a comprehensive peace "grounded in UN Security Council Resolutions 242 and 338 and the principle of territory for peace." In conclusion, Bush called for an effort to foster economic freedom and prosperity for all the people of the region.

From Dual Containment to the Axis of Evil

George Bush senior's vision for the Persian Gulf and Middle East region was still-born, despite the best efforts of the succeeding Clinton administration to reach a comprehensive Arab–Israeli peace deal and make the combination of sanctions and weapons inspections in Iraq deliver the intended results. In the face of the threat that Washington perceived from both Iraq and Iran to its interests in the region in the 1990s, the U.S. military ended up developing and maintaining a level of forward presence not previously envisaged. Regional economic development was patchy at best and certainly not equitable.

During the two terms of the Clinton administration no overarching, global doctrine was developed within which to position policymaking in the Gulf. Instead, U.S. policy in the region was dominated by a preoccupation with making peace between Israel and its immediate Arab neighbors, and dealings with Iraq and Iran were subordinated to this. In a speech in which the concept of dual containment was first launched publicly, then National Security Council member Martin Indyk explained that the concept derived:

> from an assessment that the current Iraqi and Iranian regimes are both hostile to American interests in the region. Accordingly, we do not accept the argument that we should continue the old balance of power game . . . we reject it because we do not need it. . . . The coalition that fought Saddam remains together. As long as we are able to maintain our military presence in the region; as long as we succeed in restricting the military ambitions of both Iraq and Iran; and as long as we can rely on our regional allies—Egypt, Israel, Saudi Arabia and the GCC, and Turkey—to preserve the balance of power in our favor in the wider Middle East region, we will have the means to counter both the Iraqi and the Iranian regimes.[31]

Under the rubric of dual containment the United States became the leading enforcer of the UN sanctions regime on Iraq, imposed after its invasion of Kuwait and sustained after its ouster pending the completion of UN weapons inspections and the elimination of Iraq's WMD. The mission of the UN Special Commission (UNSCOM) inspectors remained incomplete when they were withdrawn in December 1998, ahead of the U.S. and British bombing campaign, Operation Desert Fox. Thereafter, Baghdad resisted further inspections, until the United States threatened the war that ultimately went ahead in March 2003.

During the Clinton years sanctions were also imposed on Iran, culminating in the passage of the Iran–Libya Sanctions Act (ILSA) of 1996 which instituted a secondary boycott on U.S. allies investing in the Iranian energy sector.[32] Around that time, U.S. rhetoric suggested that Iran was considered even more of a danger than Iraq. However, the landslide election victory of Mohammad Khatami, reformist candidate for the Iranian presidency, in 1997, opened the way for a rethink in Washington's strategy. Khatami himself called for "a dialogue of civilizations" that spawned an array of academic contacts with the United States as well as some limited encounters among official figures.[33] Clinton administration efforts to produce a thaw in relations with Tehran culminated in a key speech by Secretary of State Madeleine Albright in June 1998. She called for "a road map leading to normal relations" and subsequently acknowledged U.S. involvement in the overthrow of Mossadeq and a U.S. share of responsibility for problems in the bilateral relationship.[34]

There was not to be a breakthrough, however, since both sides apparently expected more from the other before risking further initiatives. In any case, the reformists in Tehran were ill-placed to reach out to the United States, for fear of criticism from the more conservative elements. For their part, the Americans began to think that there was no appreciable difference between the factions in Tehran, in the absence of the kind of policy shifts they were hoping for from Iran. When the administration of George W. Bush took office in 2001, expectations that his connections with the oil industry would prompt a change of mood proved misplaced. On Capitol Hill, lobbyists, notably those representing Israel's interests, pressed for and won a renewal of ILSA for another five years. With respect to Iraq, meanwhile, the new administration was set on a policy of regime change.

More broadly, the new administration espoused a less multilateralist approach to international affairs than its predecessor. This thinking was partially revised after the events of September 11 obliged the Bush administration to forge a series of ad hoc coalitions to prosecute its global "war on terrorism," starting with the campaign to destroy Al Qaeda and topple the Taliban regime in Afghanistan. Pakistan's cooperation was essential to that operation and the largely unpublicized involvement of Iran behind the scenes was invaluable in forming the interim Afghan administration under President Hamid Karzai that emerged from the Bonn Conference in December 2001.

However, by then the makings of a rapprochement with Iran were faltering. Iranian assistance to its allies in northern and western Afghanistan angered Washington and Tehran was accused of enabling Al Qaeda fighters to slip away across its border. The Iranian government denied any deliberate strategy of this nature but held captive some Al Qaeda operatives apparently hoping to use them as bargaining chips. Washington's antipathy to Tehran revived with a vengeance with the apprehension of an arms shipment to the Palestinians on the vessel *Karine-A* by the Israeli navy in the Red Sea in January 2002. From the U.S. perspective this was proof that Iran was engaged in a strategy of supporting terrorist movements, and the fact that these might be Palestinians fighting Israelis rather than targeting Americans per se made no difference. After all, the U.S. war on terror had been declared against all groups and states perpetrating acts of terror on the United States and its allies and, according to President Bush: "You are either with us or with the terrorists!"

In his State of the Union address of January 2002, President Bush delivered the coup de grâce when he branded Iran and Iraq, along with North Korea, as components of an "axis of evil" that could no longer be allowed to pursue their terrorist aims. Iraq was accused of building up its WMD capabilities and was believed to be capable of teaming up with terrorist organizations to target the United States, its allies, and its interests in the future. Iran was deemed to be potentially as dangerous, if not confronted. The priority, however, was to eliminate the regime of Saddam Hussein. As was subsequently revealed, in early 2002 the CIA was instructed to set about this task by covert means, while the Pentagon was required to come up with military options including a full-scale invasion plan.

On June 1, 2002 President Bush outlined the makings of what has become known as the Bush Doctrine in a graduation address at the U.S. Military Academy at West Point. Signaling a new preparedness to act preemptively if deemed appropriate, he said:

> We must take the battle to the enemy, disrupt his plans, and confront the worst threats before they emerge. . . . In the world we have entered, the only path to safety is the path of action. And this nation will act.[35]

In the following weeks, members of the administration served notice that the ideas sketched by the president formed the basis of a new security framework to be fleshed out and formally presented in the fall.[36] Commentators depicted Iraq as the most likely first target of the new strategy. The idea that Iran might be next in line was mooted, though anything beyond a limited military strike there was thought unlikely. However, U.S. proponents of a war to topple Saddam Hussein suggested that this act by itself would serve notice to other governments in the region to "shape up" and voiced their expectation that most would likely do so for fear of the consequences of resisting the U.S. agenda.[37]

Preemptive War in Iraq

The Bush doctrine of preemption provided the rationale for the invasion of Iraq in March 2003. The administration reasoned that a decade of UN sanctions and inspections had failed to force the regime of Saddam Hussein to relinquish its WMD programs and it was only a matter of time before such weapons would fall into the hands of terrorists. According to President George W. Bush and the neo-conservatives in his administration, the democratization of Iraq would also form the centerpiece of a strategy for ending decades of autocratic rule across the region and, in the process, eliminate the root cause of Islamic fundamentalism and anti-Western terrorism.

Persuaded to seek multilateral support for military intervention by British Prime Minister Tony Blair and Secretary of State Colin Powell, Bush took his case to the United Nations in September 2002, by which time preparations for war were underway. The effort did produce UN Security Council Resolution 1441 and new UN weapons inspections, but failed to elicit more specific backing for resort to force. France took the lead in opposing UN endorsement for war before the case for it was proven.

Only Britain and Australia committed forces to the field alongside the United States when the invasion went ahead. They expected to be vindicated by the discovery of WMD stockpiles in Iraq, but when none were found all three countries had to instigate inquiries into a manifest failure of intelligence. Their expectations of a warm welcome from most Iraqis also proved unfounded. State Department contingency plans for handling the initial phases of the occupation were largely ignored, apparently because the civilians at the Pentagon and in Vice President Dick Cheney's office, advised by Iraqi exiles such as Ahmad Chalabi, were driving the policy.[38]

The toppling of the regime of Saddam Hussein was accomplished in a matter of weeks but the postwar phase presented a variety of problems that obliged the Bush administration to repeatedly change its strategy for occupation and political transition in Iraq. The United Nations was brought back into play, but U.S. forces remained in charge of security. Various allies committed troops, but not in significant numbers. Early resistance from remnants of the Baathist regime and Islamist infiltrators swelled over time to include disaffected Sunni tribal elements, notably in Falluja, homegrown Islamists and the supporters of Shi'i firebrand Moqtada al-Sadt.

The United States-installed Iraqi Governing Council (IGC) lacked credibility and popular support. Plans to hand over power to a new caretaker administration in July 2004, pending elections the following year, were complicated by U.S. reluctance to cede control of internal and border security and the absence of effective Iraqi forces following the disbanding of the Iraqi army and Chalabi's de-Baathification strategy. Meanwhile, the Shi'i community of Iraq displayed a new assertiveness and rejuvenation that put them at odds with Kurdish nationalists and alarmed some of the old Sunni elite.

Members of the Iraqi Shi'i community may be fierce nationalists but they also have links with their coreligionists elsewhere and in some cases have family connections in Iran. The latter cannot help but have a stake in the political fortunes of the Shi'i in Iraq. But Washington has accused the Iranians of backing different Iraqi Shi'i factions and repeatedly warned Tehran not to interfere. In fact, Tehran appears to have taken some satisfaction from the travails experienced by the United States in Iraq. At the very least, with its hands full in Iraq, Washington appeared unlikely to seek a new bid for regime change in Tehran.

Milestones and Metaphors in U.S.–Iran Relations

As inferred by Madeleine Albright, CIA management of the coup of 1953 that reinstalled the Pahlavi dynasty has haunted the bilateral relationship ever since. Were it not for that interference, Iran's twentieth-century history could have been very different. From the perspective of many of the revolutionaries who drove out the shah in 1979 and introduced a republic that provided for parliamentary and presidential elections, by universal suffrage, within the ascendancy of Islamic law and leadership, the shah's rule was an imposition that deprived them of their rights and aspirations.[39] To suffer this imposition at the hands of the United States was both disillusioning and sinister, given America's democratic and anti-imperialist image at the time. U.S. intervention also deprived Iran of control of its own energy resources for another couple of decades.

America's role in arming the shah and pandering to his vanity was counterproductive for the shah and the United States in the long run. No doubt the money spent on arms and Pahlavi pomp could have been better used, but U.S. officials appear to have woken up to the dangers rather late and then succeeded only in antagonizing their client. Yet the shah himself and those who gained wealth under his regime cannot be absolved of responsibility. Meanwhile, hopes for a more equitable distribution of national wealth have not been fulfilled since the revolution and U.S. sanctions cannot be solely to blame for that. In fact, accounts of the revolution would seem to suggest that U.S.–Iranian relations need not have been irreparably damaged, but the Carter administration was pulled in several directions at once by conflicting advice at home and it lacked good contacts on the revolutionary front.[40]

Carter's decision to allow the ailing shah to enter the United States for medical treatment served to confirm suspicions in Tehran that the administration was opposed to the revolution. The embassy hostage crisis, lasting as it did until the very end of the Carter administration, and covered as it was on national television news for the duration, left a scar on the U.S. side that was almost as durable as the CIA coup plot had been for the Iranians.

The U.S. tilt toward Iraq in the 1980s war was clear cause for resentment in Iran. The fact that the Iraqis had launched the war on Iran was glossed over and Washington's formal condemnations of Iraqi use of chemical weapons were token and ineffectual. Washington even managed to blame Iran more than Iraq for the latter's mistaken attack on the USS Stark in May 1987. It was at that time that President Reagan called Iran "this barbaric country."[41] A particularly bruising episode for Iran occurred when U.S. forces in the Gulf mistakenly targeted and shot down an Iran Air civilian airliner, killing the 290 people on board. Subsequent payment of compensation for this tragedy did not assuage the hurt or remove the sense of injustice. By most accounts, U.S. assistance to Iraq could well have deprived Iran of a military victory in the field, though no one can say if Iran could then have proceeded to topple Saddam Hussein, as was its stated objective. In any case, U.S. intervention in the tanker war was instrumental in bringing the conflict to an end on terms that were apparently available to Iran much earlier in the war, thereby calling into question the Iranian leadership's justifications for persisting as long as it did, with all the costs that that entailed.

The Iran-Contra affair did nothing to improve U.S.–Iranian relations, even if Tehran made some limited material and propaganda gains from it. After the episode became public, a commission of inquiry in the United States enabled the Iranians to learn more about U.S. intentions at the time. It did not soothe Tehran's feelings to learn from the testimony of Colonel Oliver North to the Tower Commission that he had made a practice of lying to the Iranians.

The conclusion of the eight year Iran–Iraq War and the advent of a new Iranian leadership, under Ali-Akbar Hashemi-Rafsanjani, following the death of Ayatollah Khomeini, seemed to provide a new window of opportunity for improved relations. Iran's neutrality during the war to end the Iraqi occupation of Kuwait was beneficial to the U.S. coalition. However, in the aftermath of Iraq's battlefield defeat, Iran was accused of assisting the Shi'i rebellion against Saddam Hussein's regime and Tehran could not escape suspicions of harboring ambitions in this direction.

A series of executive orders passed by the Clinton administration banned all trade with and investment in Iran by Americans in the mid-1990s, under the rubric of dual containment.[42] There was talk in Washington of forcing a regime change, and at a minimum the alleged intention was to deprive Iran of funds for building WMD. The passage of ILSA in 1996 represented an attempt to stop foreigners doing what Americans were already forbidden to do, and make Iran's isolation complete. One positive outcome of this U.S. policy for Iran was to fuel a determination in Tehran to build better regional and international relations in defiance of Washington.

Notwithstanding some tentative moves toward rapprochement after President Khatami's call for a dialogue of civilizations, seemingly the two sides were looking for different types of engagement, and each needed more from the other side to overcome their distrust and domestic constraints. By the end of the Clinton administration the idea was gaining ground in Washington that U.S. expectations of the reformist elements in Tehran were overblown. The renewal of ILSA under Bush signaled a retrenchment and cooperation in Afghanistan did not survive the *Karine-A* episode.

Some say that Bush's depiction of Iran's unelected leadership in his State of the Union address of 2002 triggered a healthy debate in Iran. In the event, Iran provided tacit cooperation in the U.S. invasion of Iraq and was subsequently disappointed that this did not lead quickly to better ties with the United States. Washington was apparently deterred from reaching a rapprochement with Tehran by detractors who argued that this would reward and bolster the conservative clerics who trounced the reformists in the 2004 Majlis elections.

Ups and Downs in U.S.–Iraqi Relations

In the decades preceding the 2003 occupation of Iraq, U.S.–Iraqi relations never attained the level of political intimacy, economic cooperation, and military support that characterized the U.S.–Iranian relationship under the shah. It took the collapse of the U.S. relationship with Iran to trigger a rapport with Baghdad, but the impetus remained more negative than positive.[43] Even with the restoration of full diplomatic relations in 1984, the capacity of the Americans to exercise a benign influence was limited. The U.S. embassy more resembled a fortress than a base for extensive social interaction. In 1986 Ambassador David Newton described the population as "terrified" and powerless in the face of a pervasive security apparatus.[44]

In retrospect, Washington's tolerance of Iraq's military adventurism, use of chemical weapons, militarization of society, record of torture and other forms of human rights abuse, culminating in the gassing of members of its own population, must have left Saddam Hussein with the impression that the Americans could be managed to suit his interests.

The U.S. pursuit of rapprochement prevailed over the abhorrence of civil rights campaigners and some politicians at news of Iraq's *Anfal* campaign against the Kurds in 1988.[45] When April Glaspie was appointed ambassador to Iraq in early 1989 she went with a brief to develop the bilateral relationship. In any case, when she had her fateful meeting with Saddam Hussein, and the matter of the Iraq–Kuwait border was raised, he apparently gained the impression that America would not presume to interfere in his dealings with the emirate. That the Iraqi president was deliberately misled into thinking he could get away with a full-scale invasion is not substantiated in the record. Glaspie apparently did not discern what he had in mind, and so did not think to respond with the kind of warning signal that presumably she would have given, had she really understood what was at stake.

The American reaction to the invasion of August 2, 1990 was surprise. The disillusion and anger among Iraq's apologists in Washington was profound. The failure of judgment of which they then stood accused was difficult for them to live down and may account for the visceral animosity subsequently directed toward Saddam Hussein. The history of the U.S.–Iraq relationship in the 1990s was unrelievedly confrontational. The way the Bush administration responded to the popular uprisings that erupted in Iraq in the wake of the 1991 war has fed various conspiracy theories and certainly left the impression that Washington preferred military rule to chaos in Iraq. The Iraqi regime was not prevented from using both land forces and helicopters to suppress the revolt in the south. Subsequently, it became clear that the intention was to allow the Iraqi armed forces to maintain overall control, while the officer corps was somehow expected to remove Saddam Hussein from the presidency.

After that, the Iraqi regime managed to derail various U.S.-backed plots to instigate a coup and build up opposition forces inside Iraqi Kurdistan. Washington meanwhile insisted on the strictest enforcement of the sanctions regime through the United Nations, notwithstanding growing disenchantment in the wider international community with the overall effects on the population. After the weapons inspectors left in 1998, it turned out that Iraqi accusations that Washington had indeed used these as a vehicle for spying were correct.

The net result of U.S. enforcement of its official containment policy on Iraq in the 1990s was failure, if indeed the goal was regime change or full disarmament. For a time it was possible to argue that the policy worked insofar as Iraq was prevented and deterred from attacking any of its neighbors again. However, the regime actually managed to tighten its grip on power inside Iraq and gradually the sanctions became more and more porous, as neighboring countries assisted in smuggling operations. The regime also made money out of illicit surcharges on oil sales. After the arrival of George W. Bush in the White House, and especially after 9/11, the official and central U.S. goal of regime change was finally implemented. Yet the ambivalence and suspicion with which the Iraqis, and especially the Shi'is, greeted their American liberators in 2003 was no doubt fed by the sense of betrayal engendered by U.S. passivity during the 1991 uprising and subsequent repression.

Iran and Iraq as a Duo

In the 1950s, Iraq and Iran were grouped together as part of the Northern Tier of the wider Middle East region. That put these states in the front line, along with Turkey, of the confrontation with the Soviet Union. They were to be courted and assisted as a buffer between the Soviets and the oil-rich Persian Gulf, Arabian Sea, and Indian Ocean. During the Cold War the view prevailed in the West that it was Moscow's ambition to obtain access to "warm water" ports for its navy. This fear was revived with the Soviet entry into Afghanistan in December 1979.

Conscious of Britain's privileged position in the Iraqi and Iranian oil sectors in the 1950s, it was also an ambition of the American oil industry to gain access to these riches. In this sense, Iraq and Iran represented opportunities for U.S. business and their identities as individual polities were somewhat subsumed within the geostrategic depiction of the Gulf region as the world's most abundant source of energy reserves.

After the development of America's cozy relationship with the shah, it seems that Iraq's potential was neglected by default. The focus was on Iran and Washington's dealings with Iraq reflected Iranian interests. U.S. connivance in Iran's machinations in Iraqi Kurdistan, when this was Tehran's chosen way to undermine its neighbor, serves as an example of this orientation. When U.S. attention switched to Baghdad, it was driven in large part by the perceived need to contain the Iranian revolution. The fact that Syria, to the west of Iraq and on the Israeli front line, decided to side with Iran in the 1980s war, against its Baathist rival, provided further reason to court Baghdad. An Iraqi defeat at the hands of Iran, enabling Iran and possibly Syria to preside over the spoils was too threatening to contemplate. Iraq had to be bolstered. To this day, the vision of an axis of unfriendly and radical states from the Mediterranean to Afghanistan informs Washington as well as Israeli thinking about the Northern Tier.

In the absence of relations with Tehran, and after Washington fell out with Baghdad over the invasion of Kuwait, disenchantment determined that Iraq and Iran should be branded together as enemies, and dealt with as one under the rubric of dual containment. As Martin Indyk said at the time, Washington was no longer going to play the balance of power game.[46] Instead, the two were depicted as part of the "outer rim" of states potentially threatening to Israel, which had to be contained while the Israelis tried to make peace with the inner circle of their immediate neighbors. The Arab–Israeli peace process of the 1990s took Syria into the peace camp and thereby countered the possibility of the Northern Tier states joining forces. In fact, the United States may have done Iraq and Iran a favor during this period. Their shared pariah status did give them the impetus or cover to begin to tackle residual issues of contention between them, such as prisoners of war, and safe passage for Iranian pilgrims wishing to visit Shi'i shrines in Iraq. They also cooperated on smuggling Iraqi oil. Most importantly, the boundary on the Shatt al-Arab was supposedly settled and there was no resumption of direct hostilities between them. However, U.S. antipathy to both could not bind Iran and Iraq together. The Iranian opposition movement, the Mojahedin-e Khalq Organization (MKO), continued to operate out of Iraq and the Iraqi Shi'i opposition, the Supreme Council for the Islamic Resistance in Iraq (SCIRI) continued to find safe haven in Iran.

During the period of dual containment Washington vacillated in its allocation of "worst villain" status. From the invasion of Kuwait to the end of the first Bush administration, Saddam Hussein was villain number one in the region if not the world. In the early Clinton years the Iranian leadership was for a time depicted as America's greatest enemy. Following the election of President Khatami, Iran was given a reprieve, and dual containment was redubbed "containment plus and containment minus," with Iraq the object of greatest hostility. The theory was that while the only option for Iraq was a complete change of regime, for Iran reform was deemed possible. This more nuanced approach to Iran survived even the renewal of ILSA in the new Bush administration. In any case, Saddam Hussein was viewed as unfinished business and a singular target.

Against this background and given Iranian cooperation in the war in Afghanistan, it came as all the more of a shock among many in the Washington circuit as well as in the region, when President George W. Bush branded Iran and Iraq together in an axis of evil. If anything, this heavy-handed terminology, with religious undertones and alarming in intent, could have served to boost Saddam Hussein's sense of his own importance. It may have enhanced his waning status on the Arab "street" as the champion of anti-Americanism. For Iran there could be no cause for satisfaction in Bush's insult. For the Iranian leadership, to be depicted in this way, alongside Iraq of all countries, was taken as demonstration of a dangerous ignorance and arrogance at the head of the most powerful country in the world. After the Bush administration decided to take on Iraq and turn it into a beacon of democracy, Iran inevitably became the singular villain, though Syria's pariah status was also enhanced by default. Assuming a new political system in Iraq accords the Shi'i more power, it will be interesting to see whether this will distance Iraq from the rest of the Arab world and bring it closer to Iran or not, and how Washington will judge the outcome.

Drawing Conclusions for the Iran–Iraq Relationship

The principal argument developed here is that the United States has generally dealt with Iran and Iraq as part players in a larger strategic drama. They were subordinates in the confrontation with the Soviet Union during the Cold War. They were also valued as oil rich prizes for U.S. business and components in U.S. planning for its own energy security. They were depicted variously as both allies and enemies in the quest for Middle East peace and regional security. They both attained the status of rogue states for their pursuit of WMD and support to terrorist groups.

Both countries, at different times, have been favored with a special relationship, Iran under the shah more than Iraq at any point until 2003. When Iran was America's most favored ally in the region, the relationship was warm and pursued with enthusiasm, at least at the elite level. Even among the young firebrands of the revolution in Iran, many were the beneficiaries of an American education and many of these have retained the capacity to admire certain American attributes and achievements. Among Iran's clerical scholars there are those who have studied and appreciated Western philosophy and ideas, and President Khatami was clearly sincere when he called for a dialogue of civilizations. For those Iranians who found a home in the United States after the revolution, the relationship has been an altogether positive one. Among the younger generation in Iran itself, who form the majority of the population, none share the experiences of their parents under the shah or in the revolution, since they were all born and grew up later. For youngsters American consumer goods, music, and dress have an undeniable appeal. The potential for a U.S.–Iranian rapprochement is there, but for the intransigence of elements on both sides who focus on the negative and fuel each other's propaganda. Most importantly, perhaps, a special relationship endures in the sense that both U.S. and Iranian policymakers are somehow fascinated by each other and use their relations, even when antagonistic, as a measure of their respective strengths and status domestically.

In their relationship with each other, Iran and Iraq have both derived some benefit from U.S. hostility to the other at certain times. The United States took Iran's side in the 1960s and 1970s, in its dealings with Iraq. Subsequently, Iraq avoided defeat by Iran thanks to American help in their eight-year war. America's reversal of the invasion of Kuwait and containment of Iraq thereafter served to protect Iran from a potentially rampant Iraq. The two countries managed to achieve a reasonably stable modus vivendi during the 1990s, though neither lost its distrust of the other. Perhaps more to the point here, neither lost its distrust of the United States, even though both are the beneficiaries of U.S. action to topple Saddam Hussein.

On balance, it cannot be said that the U.S. role in Iran–Iraq relations has been helpful, but perversely it may not have been unremittingly harmful either. For decades America's strategic agenda led it to deal with Iraq and Iran as elements in that agenda, rather than as complex societies with their own domestic and regional preoccupations, problems, aspirations and potential. Since taking on the task of remaking Iraq, however, the effectiveness of U.S. policy in the region will depend on U.S. capacity to work with these complexities without being overwhelmed by them.

Notes

1. Bruce Robellet Kuniholm, *The Origins of the Cold War in the Near East: Great Power Conflict and Diplomacy in Iran, Turkey, and Greece* (Princeton: Princeton University Press, 1980), pp. 410–31.
2. See James A. Bill, *The Eagle and the Lion: The Tragedy of American-Iranian Relations* (New Haven: Yale University Press, 1988), p. 79 where he cites four reasons for the U.S. decision to intervene, namely preoccupation with the Soviet threat, oil interests, the success of British persuasion, and Mosaddeq's negotiating techniques that eventually backfired.
3. Ibid., p. 80.
4. Charles Tripp, *A History of Iraq* (Cambridge: Cambridge University Press, 2000), pp. 140–42.
5. Ibid., p. 164.
6. Former U.S. diplomat James E. Akins asserted CIA involvement in a BBC Radio Four program entitled "The Making of Saddam, the Iraqi Dictator," which aired on January 27, 2003.

7. Steven L. Spiegel, *The Other Arab-Israeli Conflict: Making America's Middle East Policy, from Truman to Reagan* (Chicago: University of Chicago Press, 1985), pp. 119–64.

8. For discussion of the deliberations in Washington see: Hussein Sirriyeh, *U.S. Policy in the Gulf 1968–1977: Aftermath of the British Withdrawal* (London: Ithaca Press, 1984), chapter 2.

9. Gary Sick, *All Fall Down: America's Tragic Encounter with Iran* (New York: Random House, 1985), pp. 13–21.

10. Sirriyeh, *U.S. Policy in the Gulf 1968–1977*, p. 22.

11. Anthony H. Cordesman, *The Gulf and the Search for Strategic Stability: Saudi Arabia, the Military Balance in the Gulf, and Trends in the Arab-Israeli Military Balance* (Boulder, Colo.: Westview Press, 1984), p. 160.

12. Sick, *All Fall Down*, chapters 4 and 5.

13. State of the Union Address, January 23, 1980.

14. Sick, *All Fall Down* and Barry Rubin, *Paved with Good Intentions: The American Experience and Iran* (London: Penguin Books, 1981).

15. Apparently by connivance rather than just good fortune, as recounted by Gary Sick in *October Surprise: America's Hostages in Iran and the Election of Ronald Reagan* (New York: Random House, 1991), especially pp. 145–46.

16. Fred Halliday, *The Making of the Second Cold War* (Norfolk, UK: Thetford Press, 1986).

17. For a discussion of the Soviet naval presence in the Indian Ocean and U.S. countermeasures see Alvin J. Cottrell and Michael L. Moodie, *The United States and the Persian Gulf: Past Mistakes, Present Needs,* Agenda Paper No. 13 (Washington, D.C.: National Strategy Information Center, 1984).

18. William B. Quandt, "The Gulf War: Policy Options and Regional Implications," in *American-Arab Affairs*, no. 9 (Summer 1984), p. 3.

19. Bill, *The Eagle and the Lion*, p. 306.

20. Bruce W. Jentleson, *With Friends Like These: Reagan, Bush and Saddam* (New York: W.W. Norton, 1994), pp. 42–48.

21. Anthony H. Cordesman, "The Gulf Crisis and Strategic Interests: a Military Analysis," in *American-Arab Affairs*, no. 9 (Summer 1984), p. 8.

22. Bill, *The Eagle and the Lion*, p. 306; Jentleson, *With Friends Like These*, p. 46; and Alan Friedman, *Spider's Web: Bush, Saddam, Thatcher and the Decade of Deceit* (London: Faber and Faber, 1993), p. 27.

23. See chapter 7 in this volume by Joost Hiltermann. See also documents compiled by the National Security Archive in December 2003, which illustrate U.S. concern to sooth Iraqi ire at public criticism of its use of chemical weapons. See especially documents 5, 6, and 7, located at www.gwu.edu/~nsarchiv/NSAEBB/NSAEBB107/index.htm.

24. Statement of Assistant Secretary Richard W. Murphy before the Subcommittee on Europe and the Middle East of the House Foreign Affairs Committee, August 14, 1986.

25. This was the scheme by which some members of the White House staff, including John Poindexter, Robert McFarlane, and Colonel Oliver North, together with head of the CIA William Casey and other intelligence analysts, secretly supplied arms to Iran as a way to secure the release of U.S. hostages being held by Shi'i Islamist groups in Lebanon. The proceeds of the sales to Iran were destined, according to Oliver North (in testimony to the Tower Commission which later investigated the affair) for the Contra rebels in Nicaragua.

26. Caspar Weinberger, *Security Arrangements in the Gulf,* Gulf Cooperation Council Reports Series, no. 3, 1988, p. 6.

27. George P. Shultz, *Turmoil and Triumph: My Years as Secretary of State* (Macmillan: New York, 1983), p. 790.

28. Zachary Karabell, "Backfire: US Policy Toward Iraq, 1988-2 August 1990," in *Middle East Journal*, vol. 49, no. 1 (Winter 1995), p. 33.

29. According to National Security Directive 26, "U.S. Policy Toward the Persian Gulf," of October 2, 1989: "Access to Persian Gulf oil and the security of key friendly states in the area are vital to U.S. national security. The United States remains committed to defending its vital interests in the region, if necessary and appropriate, through the use of U.S. military force, against the Soviet Union or any other regional power with interests inimical to our own" (see Friedman, *Spider's Web*, Appendix B, pp. 321–22).

30. President Bush, "The World After the Persian Gulf War," address before a joint session of Congress, March 6, 1991, in *U.S. Department of State Dispatch*, March 11, 1991, pp. 161–63.

31. Martin Indyk's address to the Washington Institute for Near East Policy, May 18, 1993, quoted here from a partial transcript published in *Middle East International*, no. 452, June 11, 1993, pp. 3–4.

32. For an assessment see Hossein Alikhani, *Sanctioning Iran: Anatomy of a Failed Policy* (London: I.B.Tauris, 2000).

33. Gary Sick, "US policy in the Gulf: objectives and prospects," in *Managing New Developments in the Gulf*, ed. Rosemary Hollis (London: RIIA, 2000), p. 44.

34. Secretary of State Madeleine Albright, "Remarks at 1998 Asia Society Dinner," June 17, 1998, as released by the Office of the Spokesman, U.S. Department of State, June 18, 1998.

35. Mike Allen and Karen DeYoung, "Bush Charts First-Strike Policy on Terror Cells," *International Herald Tribune*, June 3, 2002.

36. *The National Security Strategy of the United States 2002*. See "Full Text: Bush's National Security Strategy," *The New York Times*, September 20, 2002.

37. Richard Perle, "Why the West must Strike First Against Saddam Hussein," *Daily Telegraph*, August 9, 2002 and Brian Knowlton, "War talk by Cheney is tougher," *International Herald Tribune*, August 27, 2002.

38. For analysis of the internal politics behind U.S. decision-making see Bob Woodward, *Plan of Attack* (New York: Simon and Schuster, 2004) and Richard A. Clarke, *Against All Enemies: Inside America's War on Terror* (New York: Free Press, 2004).

39. Ali M. Ansari, *Iran, Islam and Democracy: The Politics of Managing Change* (London: Royal Institute of International Affairs, 2000), chapter 3.

40. Bill, *The Eagle and the Lion*, chapters 8 and 11 and Sick, *All Fall Down*, chapter 4.

41. Bill, *The Eagle and the Lion*, p. 307.

42. Alikhani, *Sanctioning Iran*, chapter 10.

43. Robert D. Kaplan, *The Arabists: The Romance of an American Elite* (New York: The Free Press, 1993), p. 263 and Jentleson, *With Friends Like These*, p. 33.

44. Kaplan, *The Arabists*, p. 271.

45. See Jentleson, *With Friends Like These*, chapter 2.

46. As noted previously and referenced at note 31.

Contributors

LAWRENCE G. POTTER has been Deputy Director of Gulf/2000 since 1994 and has taught at Columbia University since 1996, where he is Adjunct Associate Professor of International Affairs. A graduate of Tufts College, he received an M.A. in Middle Eastern Studies from the School of Oriental and African Studies, University of London, and a Ph.D. in History (1992) from Columbia University. He taught in Iran for four years before the revolution. From 1984 to 1992 he was Senior Editor at the Foreign Policy Association, a national, nonpartisan organization devoted to world affairs education for the general public, and currently serves on the FPA's Editorial Advisory Committee. He specializes in Iranian history and U.S. policy toward the Middle East. He coedited (with Gary Sick) *The Persian Gulf at the Millennium: Essays in Politics, Economy, Security, and Religion* (St. Martin's Press, 1997) and *Security in the Persian Gulf: Origins, Obstacles, and the Search for Consensus* (New York: Palgrave, 2002). He published "The Persian Gulf in Transition" in the Foreign Policy Association's *Headline Series* (January 1998). His most recent article is "The Evolution of the Iran-Iraq Boundary," in *The Creation of Iraq, 1914–1921*, ed. Reeva Spector Simon and Eleanor H. Tejirian (New York: Columbia University Press, 2004).

GARY G. SICK is the Executive Director of Gulf/2000 and former Director of the Middle East Institute at Columbia University. Dr. Sick served on the U.S. National Security Council staff under Presidents Ford, Carter and Reagan, where he was the principal White House aide for Persian Gulf affairs from 1976 to 1981. He is the author of two books on U.S.–Iranian relations and many other articles and publications on Middle East issues. He coedited (with Lawrence Potter) *The Persian Gulf at the Millennium: Essays in Politics, Economy, Security and Religion* (1997) and *Security in the Persian Gulf: Origins, Obstacles, and the Search for Consensus* (2002). Dr. Sick is a captain (ret.) in the U.S. Navy, with service in the Persian Gulf, North Africa, and the Mediterranean. He was the Deputy Director for International Affairs at the Ford Foundation from 1982 to 1987. Dr. Sick holds a Ph.D. in political science from Columbia University, where he is Senior Research Scholar and adjunct professor of international affairs. He is a member of the board of Human Rights Watch in New York and chairman of the advisory committee of Human Rights Watch/Middle East.

SHAUL BAKHASH is Clarence Robinson Professor of History at George Mason University. Until 1978, he worked as a journalist in Iran, where he was a correspondent and editor for *Kayhan* newspapers and reported on Iranian political, economic, and oil affairs for such publications as the *Times*, *The Financial Times*, and *The Economist*. After returning to the United States in 1980, he taught at Princeton University before joining the faculty at George Mason University. He is the author of *Reign of the Ayatollahs: Iran and the Islamic Revolution, Iran: Monarchy, Bureaucracy and Reform under the Qajars, 1848–1896*, and other works. His articles on nineteenth and twentieth-century Iranian and Middle East history have been published in various scholarly journals and books, and his articles and Op-Ed pieces on current Iranian politics have appeared in a number of publications. Dr. Bakhash has held fellowships at the U.S. Institute of Peace, the Woodrow Wilson International Center for Scholars in Washington, D.C., and the Institute for Advanced Study at Princeton. He is a member of the Advisory Committee of Human Rights Watch/Middle East and the Editorial Board of *The Middle East Journal* and the *Journal of Democracy*.

FARIDEH FARHI, an independent scholar and Affiliate Graduate Faculty at the University of Hawai'i at Manoa, is the author of *States and Urban-Based Revolutions in Iran and Nicaragua* (University of Illinois Press, 1990) and a number of articles and book chapters on the comparative analysis of revolutions and Iranian politics and foreign policy. She has taught comparative politics at the University of Colorado, Boulder, the University of Hawai'i at Manoa, the University of Tehran, and Shahid Beheshti University (Tehran). She was also a research associate at the Institute for Political and International Studies (Tehran) between 1993 and 1998. She is currently working on a project focused on the reconfiguration of the public sphere in Iran funded by the United States Institute of Peace.

JOOST HILTERMANN is the Middle East Project Director for the International Crisis Group, heading the ICG's regional office in Amman, Jordan. From 1994 to 2002 he was the Executive Director of the Arms Division of Human Rights Watch. Dr. Hiltermann holds a Ph.D. in Sociology from the University of California, Santa Cruz, and taught as an Adjunct Professor at Georgetown University from 1990–2002 and as a Professorial Lecturer at the Johns Hopkins School for Advanced International Studies in 2001. He is the author of *Behind the Intifada: Labor and Women's Movements in the Israeli-Occupied Territories* (Princeton University Press, 1991). In 1992–94 he was the principal researcher for Human Rights Watch on the Iraqi genocide of rural Kurds, conducting a field investigation of several months in northern Iraq and directing a two-year project of archival research of captured Iraqi government documents in Washington, D.C. This research culminated in *Iraq's Crime of Genocide: The Anfal Campaign Against the Kurds* (Yale University Press, 1995), written by George Black. Dr. Hiltermann is currently working on a book on U.S. support of Iraq during the Iran–Iraq War with support from the MacArthur Foundation and the Open Society Institute.

ROSEMARY HOLLIS is Head of the Middle East Programme at the Royal Institute of International Affairs (Chatham House) in London. She has been at Chatham House since 1995, and is responsible for formulating and directing research projects and analysis on political, economic, and security issues in the Middle East and North Africa. From 1990 to 1995, Dr. Hollis headed the Middle East Programme at the Royal United Services Institute for Defence Studies. Earlier she was a lecturer in Political Science and International Affairs at George Washington University in Washington, D.C., where she earned a Ph.D. in Political Science. The focus of her research and writing is on foreign policy and security issues in the Middle East—particularly in the Gulf and Arab–Israeli sectors—and relations between the Western powers and the region. Among her most recent publications are "Iran and the United States: Terrorism, Peace in the Middle East and Iraq," in *Iran and Its Neighbours*, eds. Johannes Reissner and Eugene Whitlock, vol. 2 (Berlin: SWP, March 2004); contributing editor, "Iraq: The Regional Fallout," in *RIIA Briefing Paper* (February 2003); "Getting Out of the Iraq Trap," in *International Affairs*, vol. 79, no.1 (January 2003); "Iran: External Relations and Possible Regional Role," in *Al Mustaqbal al Arabi*, no. 258 (August 2000); and "The End of Historical Attachments: Britain's Changing Policy Towards the Middle East," in *Globalization and the Middle East: Islam, Economy, Society and Politics*, ed. Toby Dodge and Richard Higgott (London: RIIA, 2002).

M.R. IZADY has been teaching simultaneously at the Department of History, Fordham University, New York, and at the Joint Special Operations University, United States Air Force, Florida, since 1997. He received his Ph.D. from the Department of Middle Eastern Languages and Cultures at Columbia University in 1992, following a B.A. from Kansas University (1976) and an M.A. from Syracuse University in 1979. From 1991 to 1995 he was a full-time lecturer in Persian and Kurdish at Harvard University. Dr. Izady is the author of *The Kurds: A Concise Handbook* (second edition, 2000), and a multivolume annotated translation of *The Sharafnama* (forthcoming from Mazda Publishers), a key work on Kurdish history. He has written numerous articles on Kurdish and other socio-ethnic topics and edited *The International Journal of Kurdish Studies* from 1992 to 1998.

FALEH A. JABAR is a Senior Fellow at the United States Institute of Peace in Washington, D.C. He previously taught at the Department of Governance and International Relations, London Metropolitan University and was a Research Fellow at the School of Politics and Sociology, Birkbeck College, University of London. He has lectured at many universities on the topics of Iraq, religion and the Middle East. He holds a Ph.D. in sociology from Birkbeck College and has written extensively about Iraq and the Middle East. His areas of research include social organization, cultural systems, and religion and state. He has published a number of works in Arabic and English, including three edited volumes, *Post-Marxism and the Middle East*, *Tribes and Power: Nationalism and Ethnicity in the Middle East*, and *Ayatollahs, Sufis and Ideologues: State, Religion and Social Movements in Iraq* (2002), all published in London by Saqi Books. His most recent book is *The Shi'ite Movement in Iraq* (Saqi Books, 2003).

LAITH KUBBA, a native of Baghdad, is the Senior Program Officer for the Middle East at the National Endowment for Democracy, in Washington, D.C. He has a

Bachelors degree from the University of Baghdad (1976) and a Ph.D. from the University of Wales in the United Kingdom (1982). Dr. Kubba has been an active participant in a number of Iraqi organizations. He served on the Iraqi Joint Action Committee, the first broad alliance of the Iraqi opposition. He coordinated the INC meeting in Vienna and was a spokesman for the organization in 1992. Following the Iraqi invasion of Kuwait, Dr. Kubba took a high public profile and participated in numerous debates and media programs on Iraq. Also, he was a columnist for two Arabic weekly magazines and served on the boards of regional institutions including the Iraq Foundation, the Arab Organization for Human Rights, and the International Forum for Islamic Dialogue. From 1993 to 1998, he worked for the Al Khoei Foundation in London as their Director of International Relations.

GERD NONNEMAN is Reader in International Relations and Middle East Politics at Lancaster University (United Kingdom), and a former Executive Director of the British Society for Middle Eastern Studies (BRISMES). Born in Flanders and educated at Ghent University (Belgium), in Oriental Philology (Arabic) and Development Studies, he worked in Iraq for a number of years during the 1980s, before taking a Ph.D. in Middle East politics at Exeter University. He has taught Middle East politics and political economy at Manchester and Exeter Universities. After a spell as Visiting Professor at the International University of Japan, he joined the faculty at Lancaster in 1993. He has acted as a consultant to a range of national and international government bodies, organizations and companies. Among his books are *Development, Aid and Administration in the Middle East* (Routledge, 1988); *War and Peace in the Gulf* (Ithaca Press, 1991); *The Middle East and Europe: The Search for Stability and Integration* (Federal Trust, 1993); *Political and Economic Liberalization: Dynamics and Linkages in Comparative Perspective* (Lynne Rienner, 1996); *Muslim Communities in the New Europe* (Ithaca Press, 1997); and *Analysing Middle Eastern Foreign Policies* (Routledgecurzon, 2004). Recent articles include: "The Middle East between Globalisation, Human 'Agency' and Europe," in *International Affairs* (vol. 77, no. 1, January 2001); "Saudi-European Relations 1902–2001: A Pragmatic Search for Relative Autonomy," in *International Affairs* (vol. 77, no. 3, July 2001); and "Constants and Variations in British-Gulf Relations," in *Iran, Iraq, and the Arab Gulf States*, ed. J. Kechichian (New York: Palgrave, 2001).

RICHARD SCHOFIELD is a Lecturer in Boundary Studies in the Department of Geography at King's College, University of London, where he directs the Masters program in International Boundary Studies (which he founded in 1997 at SOAS). Schofield is the author of *The Evolution of the Shatt al-Arab Boundary Dispute* (Menas Press, 1996), *Kuwait and Iraq: Historical Claims and Territorial Disputes* (Royal Institute of International Affairs, 1991; second ed., 1993), and *Unfinished Business: Iran, the UAE, Abu Musa, and the Tunbs* (forthcoming). He is the editor of *The Iran-Iraq Border, 1840–1958* (Archive Editions, 1989) and *Territorial Foundations of the Gulf States* (UCL Press/St. Martin's Press, 1994). He is also the founding editor of the journal *Geopolitics* (Frank Cass, 1996–) and has penned numerous articles on territorial issues in the Arabian peninsula/Persian Gulf region. He is currently engaged in researching the symbolic and cyclical nature of boundary and territorial disputes.

Index